# JUDAISM

## A WAY OF LIFE

# JUDAISM

## A WAY OF LIFE

### BY SAMUEL S. COHON

THE UNION OF AMERICAN HEBREW

CONGREGATIONS · *Cincinnati* · 1948

דרש בר קפרא איזוהי פרשה קטנה
שכל גופי תורה תלוין בה? בכל דרכיך
דעהו והוא יישר ארחתיך (משלי ג, ו).

–ברכות סג, א

# EDITOR'S INTRODUCTION

F OR a long time the need has been felt for a book that would describe Judaism in its varied aspects of religious living, as ethical experience, as social justice, as prayer, as love of learning, as worship, as self-discipline, repentance, and atonement. *Judaism—A Way of Life*, by Samuel S. Cohon, Professor of Jewish Theology at the Hebrew Union College, presents such an authoritative description of Judaism as a way of life from a modern, liberal point of view. Though written from the Reform point of view, Jewish tradition is not overlooked and the major ideas underlying the Jewish way of life are carefully presented by the author. The volume will therefore serve two primary purposes. It will meet the needs of Jews who are in search of an account of Judaism that goes beyond the ordinary brief descriptions now available in the English language. It will serve also the needs of non-Jewish ministers and laymen who would like to read a popular account of Judaism written from a Jewish point of view, rooted in tradition, yet modern in its approach and presentation. The book will be especially helpful to Christian ministers and teachers of religion who, in these days when all values are being challenged, would wish to see an account of Judaism, the mother religion of Christianity, which seeks to grapple with the problems of men in the twentieth century, yet does not depart from basic traditional theological doctrine. In their contact with Jews in their own communities, they have often sought to find such information.

The themes of Religion in Life, the Life of Faith, the Ethical Life, and the Threefold Way of Religious Practice will be of greatest interest to Jews and Christians alike. Practical questions which are often asked by laymen in synagogues and in churches, such as, What about the problem of evil? What can religion contribute to mental adjustment or to health? What does religion teach about social justice? are treated by Dr. Cohon in a scholarly yet popular manner. Furthermore he has appended a valuable bibliography, a glossary, and questions for study and discussion. The book may therefore be used for general reading by the layman, or adult and youth study, especially in academic discussion circles, as well as for more detailed study by other select groups interested in the problem of religion in general and of Judaism in particular.

The author and publisher will be grateful to readers for any suggestions which they may have growing out of their experience with the use of this book with groups of Jews or non-Jews of various ages.

EMANUEL GAMORAN

# PREFACE

SEVERAL books have been devoted in recent decades to the discussion of the nature of Judaism and its doctrines. Among them are my own *What Is Judaism?* in *Christianity and Judaism Compare Notes* (with H. F. Rall), and *What We Jews Believe*. Little if any attention has been paid to defining and charting the religious life from the standpoint of modern Judaism. The present work undertakes to supply this long-felt need. The Jewish religious life consists of a complex of intimacies and associations, of personal devotion to God, of identification with the Jewish people, of participation in its spiritual, cultural, and philanthropic endeavors, and of sharing in the tasks and obligations of one's country and the world. This volume probes Judaism as a personal dynamic, as a body of ethical teaching, both individual and social, and as a concrete program of practice. It concerns itself with the general direction of the Jewish way of life rather than with specific ceremonies and observances. It seeks not so much to analyze the actualities of present day Jewish practice as to chart the ideal forms which it should assume in the light of its inherent character.

The work is written from the viewpoint of Reform or Liberal Judaism, conceiving of Judaism not as a final deposit of faith, revealed at Sinai and transmitted unchanged through the ages, but as a growing religion, ever striving for fuller and clearer vision of God and of duty. In the course of its development it has under-

gone many changes in response to the needs of the
Jewish people and in accord with advancing knowledge. Despite these changes, it continues unbroken its
prophetic tradition, struggling to overcome the forces
of evil, and endeavoring to endow human life with
sanctity and worth.

To show the significance of Judaism for our day,
we shall trace its ideas and practices to their roots in
the past before appraising them in the light of contemporary thought and experience. It is not our
purpose to produce a detached work on religious
psychology or philosophy, but to elucidate the historical faith of Judaism. We shall repeatedly turn to
its time honored beliefs and observances to help us
find our way to modern Jewish religious expression.
Thus we shall strive to provide a bridge between past
and present and to maintain the essential unity of our
faith despite its diverse manifestations. Endeavoring
to chart its way of life, we shall search not for colorful
and odd archeological specimens with which to stock
a museum of antiquities, but for the vital elements that
may keep alive the spirit of Judaism for men and
women today.

Because of the close kinship of Judaism and Christianity, illustrations occasionally will be drawn from
Christian experience by way of comparison and contrast with the Jewish way of life. The results may be
instructive for liberals of both camps.

In dealing with interrelated phases of the religious
life, a certain amount of repetition is unavoidable.
The lines that separate the different parts of the book,

too, cannot be sharply drawn. Ideas treated under the Life of Faith or the Ethical Life might well be included in the Threefold Way of Religious Practice.

This work is the fruitage of years of teaching at the Hebrew Union College. It was originally prepared for use by students in the department of Jewish Theology. It has been completely revised so as to meet the needs of the lay reader who may seek to understand the deeper levels of Judaism as a personal and social experience. All technical details have been removed to the notes. However, it was thought advisable to document the problems under discussion with ample illustrations from authentic Jewish sources.

May the portrayal of the ways in which Judaism enriches and hallows human life stimulate the will of some of our people to translate them more literally into practice.

SAMUEL S. COHON

*Hebrew Union College*
*Cincinnati, Ohio*
*January, 1948*

# ACKNOWLEDGMENTS

My THANKS are extended to the committee of readers, Drs. Barnett Brickner, S. B. Freehof and Louis L. Mann and to Dr. Emanuel Gamoran, editor of the publications of the Union of American Hebrew Congregations for his interest in the issuance of the book and for a number of useful suggestions; to Mr. M. Myer Singer for lending his high craftsmanship to the technical side of the work; to Miss Sylvia Schiff for her conscientious attention to the correction of the typescript and the proofs; also to Rabbi Stanley Dreifus for reading the first proofs and a number of helpful suggestions, and to Mr. Robert Marx for assisting in the preparation of the Index.

It is with further pleasure that I express my appreciation to the following publishers for granting their kind permission to quote from their books:

Central Conference of American Rabbis, from *Yearbook*, Vol. xxxvii (paper by Dr. Bernard Glueck) and *Union Prayerbook*

The Clarendon Press, Oxford, from L. R. Farnell, *Attributes of God*, and R. H. Charles, *Apocrypha and Pseudepigrapha*

E. P. Dutton & Co., from *The Life of the Spirit and the Life of Today* by Evelyn Underhill

Funk & Wagnalls, from *English Synonyms, Antonyms and Prepositions* by James Fernald

Harvard University Press, from Colson and Whitaker's translation of *Philo*, H. St. J. Thackeray's *Josephus*, G. F. Moore's *Judaism*, and E. Brightman's *Immortality and Post Kantian-Idealism*

Henry Holt and Co., from *Psychology* by William James

Houghton Mifflin Co., from *Accepting the Universe* by John Burroughs

The Macmillan Co., from *The Religious Consciousness* by James Bisset Pratt, copyright, 1920, and *Reality in Worship* by Willard Sperry, copyright 1925

Oxford University Press, from *Prayer* by Friedrich Heiler

Paul R. Reynolds and Son, from *Varieties of Religious Experience* by William James, copyright 1902

Charles Scribner's Sons, from *The Life of Prayer in a World of Science* by W. A. Brown, *The Idea of Immortality* by G. Galloway, and Hastings' *Encyclopedia of Religions and Ethics*

Student Christian Movement Press Ltd., from *Prophet and Priest in Ancient Israel* by Adam C. Welch

The University of Chicago Press, from *The Moral Life of the Hebrews* by J. M. P. Smith

Yale University Press, from *Human Nature and Its Remaking* by W. E. Hocking

I am also grateful to the Universal Jewish Encyclopedia, Inc., for permission to utilize a number of paragraphs from my articles "Atonement" and "Brotherhood."

S. S. C.

# ABBREVIATIONS

| | | | |
|---|---|---|---|
| A.P.E. | Apocrypha and Pseudepigrapha | Erub. | Erubin |
| | | Ex. | Exodus |
| Ab. | Abot | Ex. R. | Exodus Rabba |
| Ab.R.N. | Abot of Rabbi Nathan | Ezek. | Ezekiel |
| | | Gal. | Galatians |
| Ab.Z. | Abodah Zarah | Gen. | Genesis |
| Am. | Amos | Gen. R. | Genesis Rabba |
| Ant. | Antiquities | Git. | Gittin |
| art. | Article | Guide | Guide of the Per-plexed |
| B.B. | Baba Batra | | |
| B.D.B. | Brown, Driver and Briggs, *A Hebrew and English Lexicon of the Old Testament* | H., Hil. | Hilchot |
| | | H.E.R.E. | Hastings' *Encyclopedia of Religion and Ethics* |
| | | H.U.C.A. | *Hebrew Union College Annual* |
| B.K. | Baba Kamma | | |
| B. Metz. | Baba Metzia | Hab. | Habakkuk |
| Ber. | Berachot | Hag. | Haggai |
| C.C.A.R. | Central Conference of American Rabbis | Heb. | Hebrews |
| | | Hor. | Horayot |
| Chr. | | Hos. | Hosea |
| Chron. | Chronicles | Is. | Isaiah |
| Com. | Commentary | J.E., Jew. Enc. | *Jewish Encyclopedia* |
| Deut. | | | |
| Dt. | Deuteronomy | J.Q.R. | *Jewish Quarterly Review* |
| Deut. R. | Deuteronomy Rabba | | |
| | | Jer. | Jeremiah |
| Eccl. | Ecclesiastes | Jer. | Jerushalmi |
| Eccl. R. | Ecclesiastes Rabba | Jos., Josh. | Joshua |

| | | | |
|---|---|---|---|
| Ket. | Ketubot | Prov. | Proverbs |
| Kid. | Kiddushin | Ps. | Psalm |
| Lam. | Lamentations | Rel. | Religious Educa- |
| Lam. R. | Lamentations Rabba | Educ. | tion |
| | | Rom. | Romans |
| Lev. | Leviticus | Sab. | Sabbath |
| Lev. R. | Leviticus Rabba | Sam. | Samuel |
| Lk. | Luke | Sanh. | Sanhedrin |
| LXX. | The Septuagint | Spec. | De Specialibus |
| Macc. | Maccabees | Leg. | Legibus |
| Mal. | Malachi | Suk. | Sukkah |
| Mat., Mt. | Matthew | T., Test. | Testament |
| Meg. | Megillah | T. Ben. | Testament of Ben- |
| Mek. | Mekilta | | jamin |
| Men. | Menahot | T. Jos. | Testament of |
| Men. Ham. | Menorat Hamaor | | Joseph |
| Midr. | Midrash | T. Zeb. | Testament of Zebulun |
| N.S. | New Series | Taan. | Ta'anit |
| Naz. | Nazir | Tanh. | Tanhuma |
| Ned. Nedar. | Nedarim | Tos. | Tosephta |
| Num. | Numbers | Un.J.E. | Universal Jewish Encyclopedia |
| Num. R. | Numbers Rabba | | |
| O.S. | Old Series | Yeb. | Yebamot |
| Pes. | Pesahim | Zech. | Zechariah |

The transliteration of Hebrew follows the general scientific usage, with the exception that the letter *Tzadi* is written *tz* instead of the usual *z*. Biblical names are given in the form in which they appear in the translation of the Jewish Publication Society.

Quotations from the Bible follow, with occasional deviations, the translation of the Jewish Publication Society, Philadelphia, 1917. New Testament passages are from James Moffat's translation or from the Revised Version.

Passages from Plato are taken from B. Jowett's translation.

The citations from rabbinic literature, unless otherwise indicated in the notes, were prepared by the author.

# CONTENTS

# RELIGION IN LIFE

# I. THE ART OF LIFE

Among the chief characteristics which distinguish man from other living creatures is his ability, while forming part of the order of nature and subject to its laws, to rise above nature and to set up laws for himself. As a thinking being, he reflects upon his own nature and formulates ideals and purposes for his conduct. Thus he develops his philosophies and sciences, his arts, religions, and ethical systems.

Religion and art grow out of different roots in the human soul. One stems from the consciousness of the holy, the other from the sense of the aesthetic. Religion seeks to endow life with sanctity; art strives to enrich it with beauty. One draws its vitality from belief, the other from make-believe. One builds upon conviction, the other upon creative imagination. Nonetheless a common measure unites the two. Both direct themselves to man, endeavoring to invest his life with meaning and significance.

It is the persistent effort of Judaism, as of every advanced religion, to fashion human character and behavior. It strives to raise man above the dull round of animal existence and the satisfaction of physical wants, and to endow him with worth and dignity. It seeks to lift him from the realm of biology to that of spiritual and moral values, to awaken the child of earth to the consciousness of his Divine heritage.

Thus considered, Judaism functions as an art of life. Falling behind the ancient Egyptians and Greeks in the plastic arts, and in the cultivation of physical beauty, the Jews, under the inspiration of religion, excelled them in the art of life.* Sacred Jewish literature was not addressed to the intellectuals alone, as was the case in Greece and in Rome, nor to the priests alone, but to the masses at large. The Torah constituted the heritage of the entire congregation of Jacob. Its loftiest ideals were cast into forms simple enough for the humblest of men to follow. Free from abstract discussions, the Torah presented definite norms or rules tending to enrich and to ennoble life. Its ultimate purpose is the sanctification and perfection of humanity. The Torah indeed serves as "pedagogue" for the training of man in the laws of God and of true humanity.[1] The popular character of Judaism partly accounts for its sober tone. It is free from the extremes to which speculation, bent upon logical consistency, on the one hand, or the extremism and austerity of ascetics, on the other, often lead, and teaches a robust doctrine in harmony with the best in human nature and conducive to general human welfare. It is not world denying but world transforming. Though not worldly, it is an ethic of this world, an art of noble living for the individual and for society.

---

* Josephus characteristically paraphrases God's words to Samuel (1 Sam. 16:7): "I make not of the kingdom a prize for comeliness of body, but for virtue of soul, and I seek one who in full measure is distinguished by this, one adorned with piety, justice, fortitude, and obedience, qualities whereof beauty of soul consists" (*Antiquities* VI, 8, 60, tr. Thackeray). The contrast between the Greek and the Jewish ideal could not be more sharply drawn.

Art, as distinguished from mere skill, technique and virtuosity, is an expression of a flaming ideal. A great poem, a masterly symphony, a superb painting or statue derives its inner unity and harmony from some central emotion, thought, or conviction. A life, too, grows beautiful when it expresses a worthy purpose. Unlike a picture or a piece of sculpture, its beauty is not confined to externals but permeates heart and soul, and molds the disposition and character as well as the conduct of man. The perfect blending of inner spirituality and truth with outward action represents the supreme manifestation of the art of life.

Whereas the plastic and the pictorial arts form the sphere of the skilled few, the art of life is the province of all. We receive life as a gift, but it is not complete until we have fashioned it in accordance with some ideal or pattern. As a goldsmith shapes a lump of gold into the vessel of his desire, and as a sculptor chisels a shapeless block of marble into the image of his vision, so every human being is called upon to carve out his own character, to remove his rough edges, to tame his passions and desires, and to train himself for definite ends. The result depends not only upon the ability of the worker, nor even upon the nature of the material at his command, but also upon his aims, motives, and life pattern. Religion urges man to fashion his being after the pattern shown him in the height of vision. It admonishes him further that his life is bound up with the life of his fellow men, and that his self-perfection and well-being are conditioned by the standards and forces that control his people and society at large.

Hence the full view of the art of life includes the vision of national and international morality. The religious technique of ritual and observance affect man's inward and outward life and mold it into the pattern of the Divine.

# II. SPIRIT AND FORM IN RELIGION

Religion is not so much knowledge of God as godly living. What distinguishes a religion from a system of science or philosophy is its concern with man's behavior. Theories of reality are vital to it only to the degree to which they help transform the lives of men and to affect their conduct. The inner response to the Divine, which forms the root of all religion, crystallizes itself into concepts of the holy, into ideas of God and of the human soul and its destiny, and into convictions regarding personal and social duty. Emerging from the realm of vague feeling into definite thoughts and beliefs, it permeates the mind and the will. By serving as an extra dimension of their souls, inspiring, uplifting, and disciplining them, religion transforms the lives of men. The sacred, though as sharply distinguished from the secular as sunlit mountain air is distinguished from the air of the valley, does not remain isolated from it. The sacred strives to irradiate the secular, to purify and to ennoble it, and to endow it with its own transcendent values. In this regard the sacred resembles the beautiful, which while forming the special province of art, seeks to affect all experience. It translates itself into a quality of living and finds expression in thought and in action.

Of the precepts of the Torah it was stated that man was to observe them in order that he may live by them (Lev. 18:5; Ezek. 20:11, 13, 21). *Halachah* or rule of conduct is the key-word of the Written and of

7

the Oral Torah. Even those who exalted the study of the Torah as the highest good did so on the ground that study leads to practice. Priests, prophets, and rabbis alike demanded not only that men sustain a right attitude to the Holy One but that above all they embody their attitude to Him into conduct. In their dealings with their fellow men as by their acts of adoration they were to sanctify the name of God, and thus enthrone Him in the hearts of men. The paths which have led the countless generations of Jews to the realization of the religious ideal have been concrete and practical.

It is this practical phase of religion that is most frequently on the firing line. Not only avowed enemies of religion, but also some of its friends, aim their shafts in this direction. A misguided liberalism prompts them to attack every form of religion as "formalism" and as a potential stumbling block to the higher life. They prize religion as a pleasant atmosphere of the soul, as an emotional, poetic, and mystic state of mind, as an inspiration and an aspiration, and as a feeling of relationship to the universe and to its Divine Author. They separate the religious spirit from religion as an actual experience and as a social institution. Translate the spirit into definite observances, bring it out of its cloudiness and vagueness, sinew it with action, and enrich it with appropriate forms and symbols and the cry goes up from its platonic friends that its pure essence has been tarnished and that its vital spirit has been impaired.

The Jew with a historical perspective of his religion

dissents from these views which threaten to dissolve religion as a vital factor in human life.* If in the excessive stress upon forms he finds a fertile root of idolatry, he sees in the total disregard of all forms the no less serious danger of the etherealization of religion and of its consequent evaporation. He knows that though men are said to be incurably religious, they can be serious in their religion only under certain conditions and forms. Some expressions stimulate the religious consciousness, while others paralyze it. Religion cannot be grasped as pure disembodied spirit. Even as matter cannot be conceived without form, so religion cannot be imagined apart from certain forms, emotional associations, reasoned convictions and actual practices and deeds. As beauty becomes real when expressed in definite objects, pictures or statues, and as music comes to life only when articulated into particular melodies, so religion grows vital only when rendered tangible to the mind and to the heart through the avenue of the senses.

At its root religion is an awareness of the sacred, an inner illumination and an enthusiastic espousal of the Divine ideal. It comes as an inspiration. Suddenly the

* Adam C. Welch writes: "Religion consists in what men do because of what they believe, and their acts are as vital as their creeds . . . These acts of faith, which a man would never have performed except at the bidding of his faith, are no mere formalities or insignificant accretions which gather round the sublimated essence of his faith and may be ignored. They constitute an active religion, and without them the religion of a community or nation cannot exist." *Prophet and Priest in Old Israel,* pp. 30–31.

heart of reality is bared to us and we feel ourselves standing on holy ground. Like Jacob we may grow conscious of a ladder which links earth and sky, and we seem to behold God Himself above it. But inspirations are evanescent. When gone, not even the man of genius may be able to recall them. The very dream which fired Jacob's heart might have faded forever out of his consciousness, with incalculable loss to the spiritual life of mankind, had not the means been found for its preservation. With the aid of memory and of the art of writing it was recorded for all time, so that it may serve as an inspiration to all.

It is so with the artist. A vision appears to him as in a flash. He sees a figure or scene of exquisite beauty. And with the suddenness with which it comes to him, it may vanish and completely fade out of his consciousness. To capture the fleeting gleam, he strains every nerve and devotes all his powers and skill through a long period of time. At last he may succeed in turning his personal inspiration into an enduring joy for others as well. So it is with the poet, with the scientist and with the social idealist. Though truth fires their minds, it remains dead unless it is caught and preserved through proper formulation. Enthusiasms flare up and die out. To keep them alive is no less important than to envision them.

It may be true that the glow of religious emotion once kindled will never completely disappear. Like the prophetic spell which took possession of Saul, it transforms men into new beings. One whose eye has beheld the glory of the Lord may never wholly forget the vision. However, emotions when not transmuted into action generally fade and vanish. Inspirations grow into power when transformed into discipline and habit. Idealism grows into reality when it guides and controls human behavior.

The living stream of Jewish religious creativeness has produced not only Prophecy, Psalms, Wisdom, and *Haggadah*, but also priestly Torah and Halachah. The essence of Judaism is revealed not only in its creedal affirmations and rational conceptions but also in the ethical and ceremonial law. Six hundred thirteen commandments, say the rabbis, were given unto Moses at Sinai: two hundred forty-eight mandatory, corresponding to the number of parts in the human body, and three hundred sixty-five prohibitory, corresponding to the days of the year.[2] The whole body of Halachah is derived from the Heaven-revealed Torah, and is coextensive with life. It represents the means whereby men express their faith.

While Judaism is not a mere *nomism*, as stigmatized by its Paulinian critics, neither is it a religion without law, as some Jewish antinomians would have it. Halachah or rule of conduct is pivotal in Judaism. In the scheme of Jewish spirituality external commands and prohibitions are vitalized and sustained by living faith in the Holy One. What S. R. Driver said with regard to the Mosaic law applies to historical Judaism as a whole. In all its stages it "held before the eyes of Israel an ideal of duty to be observed, of laws to be obeyed, of principles to be maintained; it taught them that human nature needed to be restrained; it impressed upon them the necessity of discipline, and in an age when disintegrating influences might have operated disastrously upon the nation, the institutions of the law bound together the majority of its members in a religious society, strong enough to resist the forces which threatened to dissolve it." [8]

If Reform Judaism has broken away from the construction of the Torah as pure nomism, it is not on the Pauline ground that Law forms the root of sin and hence is incompatible with faith (Rom. 5:13). True to its Jewish character, Reform conceives of religion not as a profession of faith conducive to other-worldly salvation, but as a faith which dictates norms for this-worldly existence. Unless religion affects human life and conduct it is of small worth. Reform has set out to correct the difficulties involved in Orthodoxy. The very virtue of traditional Judaism proved to be its chief defect. In its endeavor to direct the lives of men, it multiplied rules and prescriptions to the straining point. By becoming burdensome it grew ineffective under the Western conditions. Its claim to absoluteness and its inflexibility impaired its usefulness in a rapidly changing world. In the light of the historical sciences, Reform Judaism recognized the Halachah as relative rather than absolute. Law, both Pentateuchal and Rabbinic, represents a gradual growth in response to the needs of men of different times. The experience of the past has its bearing upon the present and future. If Judaism is to function as a vital force, it must not fail to direct the thought and action of Jews today. Its essential truths must be tested anew by the acid test of experience and applied to the new perplexities that have arisen in our industrial and mechanical age. Reform faces the consequences of this crucial test. Some time-honored ideas and forms stand unshaken by modern winds, while others have been blown away like chaff. In the process of adaptation to present circumstances, Reform has set itself not only to a theoretical revaluation of Judaism but also to a practical reshaping of its forms in accord with the tastes and standards of men and women of today.

For Reform no less than for Orthodoxy, religion cannot be a mere talking point or a mere ideal to be *yearned for*. Aspiration must be consummated by practice both in the realm of ethics and of ritual. Forms and symbols are potent instruments in fostering the life of the spirit. Through them inner states of consciousness come to power and effectiveness. However, while forms and symbols aid us to express our emotional reactions, they only confuse us when applied to the Heart of Reality. The Divine is imageless. Through the cloud and thick darkness that envelop the undying fire of Divinity we perceive no likeness but only the voice which reechoes in our consciences. In relation to God, the paradox holds that the more we invest Him with concrete forms the farther He is removed from us, and the more we refrain from giving Him sensual presentations and seek Him in His purposes, the closer His presence may be to us. The abstract nature of Jewish monotheism is compensated by the wealth of ceremonial observances which serve to make its message tangible. Through fixity of form

religion, like art, music and poetry, grows into a
steady light and power for humanity.

Accordingly all religions have developed their own
technique for self-expression. Their leaders have felt
that the religious sense, like any other, if left to itself,
runs the danger of wasting away or of turning to seed
and of developing along irrational and anti-social lines,
examples of which abound in history. They have,
therefore, sought to direct it into channels that are
socially as well as personally useful. They have cast
it into forms that are aesthetically satisfying and
morally stimulating. Out of the experience of the
group, nation or community, they have selected elements that may serve as behavior patterns and have
set them up as signs and symbols of the sacred. These
forms and ceremonies express the spiritual strivings
and the moral ideals of the religious community. They
serve as effective means in the religious education of
the people and in holding them together as a united
body. Though often practiced blindly, they tend to
evoke something of the spirit which called them forth.
The Midrash calls attention to the sequence of the
verbs in Numbers 15:39—"Ye shall *look* upon it (the
fringe), and *remember* all the commands of the Lord,
and *do* them"—and remarks that "seeing leads to remembering, and remembering to doing." [4]

Friedrich Paulsen observes: "The doctrines of the
philosophers, the theories of the savants, the systems
of the theologians, pass away like the clouds that come
and go from night to morn, but the great symbols remain like stars in heaven, even though the passing mists

momentarily hide them." [5] The symbols and ceremonies, the forms and observances of religion are not
of secondary character. The practical needs of humanity raise them to first rate significance. Though they
be considered means to an end, it must be remembered
that the end is vitally conditioned by the means that
lead to it. A living religion guards not only its emotional springs, its beliefs and moral ideals, but also its
organized forms and techniques of worship. The external forms which religion assumes constitute the
protective garments of its essential nature as well as
the instruments of its self-preservation. Growing out
of personal needs, they grow into social institutions
and forms upon which the religious order rests.

A mistaken view of human psychology has
prompted some Jewish as well as Christian liberals to
think it prophetic to denounce every form, sign and
symbol, to belittle ceremony and ritual, to discount
the synagogue and school, to slight the value of history
and tradition and to depreciate Hebrew prayer and
Jewish song as potent factors in cultivating the religious consciousness. They forget that in the atmosphere of present day secularism in which the noise of
the market-place and clatter of machinery drown the
still small voice of faith, if organized religion fails,
disorganized religion has still less chance of succeed-
ing. The remedy of the ills of religion is more religion.
What is required is a resurgence of the spirit that shall
burst through the dried up organizational forms of
religion and rekindle the sacrificial fires of devotion
upon the altars of the public sanctuaries. With it must

come the recognition that for the religious life to be fruitful its inner spirit and external expression must continually nourish and stimulate each other. A sound balance of the religious life must be effected that shall keep its personal and institutional aspects within their proper spheres, that shall ever hold out the search after God as *the goal* and employ rites, forms and institutions that have been found spiritually stimulating as *means* to its attainment, and that shall truly make of religion a *kiddush hahayyim*—a way of consecrated living.

## III. THE RELIGIOUS LIFE

Duality of religion. The recognition of the dual character of religion as both an inner state of heart and mind and a body of outward acts is of fundamental importance to our understanding of the spiritual life. Their unity sometimes dissolves under the overstress of one phase at the expense of the other. Thus the priests of ancient Israel identified piety with scrupulous regard for the requirements of the national cult. The way to securing God's favor was through the punctilious fulfillment of the prescriptions of ritual in minutest detail. The prophets, on the other hand, with their deeper sense of the holiness of God, repudiated the sacrificial cult as well as the stated festivities as the all-effective means of gaining God's favor, and called for a piety that expresses itself in the self-consecration of the individual and the nation to God, in untarnished personal purity and integrity and in social righteousness. For the sages piety consisted in the knowledge of God which made for moral probity.

Rabbinic Judaism, too, while based upon the indissoluble unity of spirit and form, occasionally lapses into identifying piety with the one or the other. Meticulous regard for traditional practice was recommended as the way of complying with the will of God. Statutes and ordinances, which are rationally inexplicable, are presented as divinely instituted; they are heavenly decrees and must be obeyed without question.[6] On the other hand, the view is voiced that

17

the aim of the Commandments of the Torah is the moral perfection of man.[7] The statement that the fulfillment of the commandments is not conditioned by the inner motive is matched by the other that "the Holy One demands the heart." [8] By the side of a piety which contents itself with external acts, we have a piety which demands complete self-consecration to God. Bahia ibn Pakkudah differentiated between the "duties of the limbs of the body" and "the duties of the heart" [9] in the full program of Judaism.

More recently Hasidism raised a protest against the mechanical observance of the rabbinic law, and called for an intensification of the religion of the spirit. It has emphasized a piety which consists of filial and loving relationship to the Heavenly Father, of spiritual exaltation and of a life motivated by faith in and love for God and man. Reform Judaism, too, has protested against a piety of formal obedience of the rules of the Shulhan Aruch. On the positive side it placed the weight of its emphasis upon morality more than upon personal religion. Under the influence of Deistic and Kantian thought, the pioneers of Reform virtually identified religion with morality. The purest essence of religion they beheld in conscience, in the ethical nature of the human spirit. To follow the dictates of the categorical imperative constituted for them the whole of the Torah and the prophets. Dropping ceremony and ritual and a return to the prophetic ideals of social righteousness and peace recommended themselves to them as the supreme ends of the religious regeneration or reformation of Judaism.

Newer insights into the nature of religion have prompted some modern thinkers to distinguish religion from both morality and reason. Though in its highest stages religion grows inseparable from them, it represents at its root a unique element, which may best be characterized as the consciousness of the sacred. Where the sense for the transcendent or the holy is wanting there may still be morality but not religion. While in Judaism religion is unthinkable without morality, a difference is recognized between a religious being and a moral being. Consequently a program of religious living must include something beyond ethical culture, something that may nourish the roots of the specifically religious element and bear the richest fruitage in the life of man, such as appropriate symbols and ceremonies and definite acts of worship and observance.

MEANING OF THE RELIGIOUS LIFE. The consideration of the dual manifestation of religion prepares us for the question: What is meant by the religious life? Those who overstress the external observances of religion tend to place the religious life on a par with the vocational life. As one's occupation or profession demands of him a definite part of each day, so religion requires set hours for devotion daily, weekly, and annually. Having discharged his obligations to God, one may surrender himself with an easy conscience to the ways of the world, and devote himself to pursuits free from further religious concern or scruple. The sacred is thus divorced from the secular. The Kingdom of Heaven retains no relations with the realm of the mundane. Accordingly, in some instances, ritual punctiliousness exerts little effect upon lives miserably sordid.

This fractional view of religion, while not uncommon in every communion, has few defenders among true exponents of the spiritual life. It need only to be stated to be recognized as a travesty. The religious life claims the whole man. While the formal exercises of religion require set hours, its spirit cannot be limited to them. It grows into reality when it pervades the whole life. The sacred must interpenetrate and transform the secular as the light of the sun illumines and vivifies the earth. Like the moral and cultural so the religious life either controls the whole personality or it is hopelessly inadequate. It must be not a fraction but a mode of life, a way and a quality of living. The religious life is human life lived in the sunlight of religious idealism. It is a mode of living dominated by the four C's of religion. It represents a joyous participation in the religious *Community*, its problems and tasks, and a sharing in its *Creed*, *Code* of conduct, and *Cult* or forms of worship.

For those who would experience its true nature, religion must not be a pastime, but a life dedicated to the Holy One. It does not enter into competition with other interests, with social, economic, political, cultural, and scientific activities, but rather manifests itself through them, stimulates and refines them by endowing them with added significance and worth. Its controlling motive of doing all things for God's sake (*vechol ma'asecha yihyu leshem shamayim*) is to lift all human efforts into a unity of purpose, to render the lowest task a mean to the attainment of life's highest purposes. Plotinus observed that members of a chorus do their best not by concerning themselves exclusively with their individual parts in the song, but rather by following their leader. By centering their thoughts upon God, religious men have attained to the noblest harmony of life, irrespective of their daily pursuits and occupations.

PIETY AND SPIRITUALITY. The mental temper produced by religion is generally known as piety or spirituality. A difference in meaning may be detected in these two words. The *New Standard Dictionary* distinguishes piety or godliness from "formal or from utilitarian religion." James C. Fernald writes: "Piety is primarily filial duty, as of children to parents, and hence, in its highest sense, a loving obedience and service to God as the Heavenly Father." [10] Piety generally stands for personal or subjective religion and expresses itself in acts of ritual with corresponding earnestness of heart or devotion. It represents the intensification of religious experience, of self-dedication and consecration. Spirituality, which is the opposite of materialism, applies to a character free from worldliness, or a "holy elevation of mind." *

* See article "Spirituality," Hastings' *Encyclopedia of Religion and Ethics;* C. P. Tiele writes: "Religion is, in truth, that pure and reverential disposition or frame of mind which we call piety." *Elements of the Science of Religion,* II, pp. 197–198.

Present day usage has robbed both of these terms of their former prestige. To some people piety denotes a state of artificial or counterfeit religiosity. Spirituality, too, is variously associated in many minds with refinement of taste in any of its modes as contrasted with coarseness, with an air of other-worldliness which shuns all contact with earthly realities, or with freakish eccentricities of effeminized ascetics and pseudo-saints, signally lacking in practical sense. It is supposedly detected in the soft and hushed tones and unctuous phrases of the sanctimonious, who speak with eyes lowered and hands folded. The overdose makes virtue odious. To the cynically minded both piety and spirituality appear as affected and pretentious ways of walking smugly with God.

Despite their abuse and depreciation, both of them are words to conjure with. Spirituality best expresses the nature of religion as a personal possession, as a state of mind, which, unbefogged by the so-called realities of sense perception, pierces the surface of matter and beholds the abiding reality of the spirit. It expresses faith in religious values and a joyful surrender to them. Jewish spirituality consists in consciously living under the inspiration and guidance of Jewish ideals, and in translating into daily conduct the values and convictions of Judaism. It represents the acceptance of the "yoke of the divine kingdom," and gaining in consequence a new freedom. The spiritual man embodies within himself the orderliness which he finds in the universe around him, and reflects the Divinity which pervades and sustains the universe.

His life becomes a testimony to God, a *Kiddush Hashem*. The antithesis of worldliness, spirituality is not necessarily other-worldly. Far from fleeing life, it brings to life increased zest and power. It is a quality of living distinguished by aspiration and self-consecration to the Holy One.

Over the entrance to the shrine of Aesculapius at Epidaurus an inscription read: "Piety consisteth in holy thoughts." To this Judaism would add, "and in holy deeds." Piety for the Jew has meant not only a feeling of filial relationship to God but also a life motivated by it, in which emotion, thought, and action blend into a harmonious unity, in which holy sentiments are translated into corresponding deeds, and faith makes men faithful.

# IV. PIETY—OLD AND NEW

TRADITIONAL VIEW. Traditional Judaism uses three terms for the designation of a man of piety: *Tzaddik*, *Hasid*, and *Kadosh*. The prophet states that the tzaddik lives by his faith,[11] His way is that of *tzedakah*, of righteousness and of charity. The hasid derives his name from his pursuit of the rule of *hesed*, of loving-kindness and of grace.[12] Hasid is the Hebrew equivalent of saint, and is used in the sense of devout, reverent, godly. The kadosh lives a life of holiness, as a witness to the Holy One and a willing martyr to his faith. It is reserved for men of extraordinary religious attainments, though occasionally it is interchangeable with hasid. The latter term has even figured as a party name.

The characteristic of a pious man, in the traditional Jewish sense, is that he does more than the law requires. He aims at complete spiritual self-realization. Stressing the spiritual, he is not necessarily antinomian. He is no rebel against either the law of God or of man. He rather finds his spiritual freedom through law, through discipline, and through voluntary obedience to authority. He lives in an atmosphere of devotion and rejoices in every opportunity to express his love of God in concrete acts. Going beyond the formalism of mere custom, habit or external law, he sets his mind upon their underlying spirit. He fulfills his simplest duties with joy and with enthusiasm as a service of God. He scrupulously applies the rules of his faith to the affairs of the world. In the opinion of the rabbis, "he who wishes to be a hasid should observe the requirements of *Nezikin* (i.e., the application of the principles of religion to his business affairs); Raba says, he should carry out the teachings of Abot (i.e., ethics); and others say, the prescriptions of Berachot (Benedictions)." [13] Piety, according to rabbinic teaching, shows itself in scrupulous regard for business ethics as well as for worship and right belief.

The qualities of the truly spiritual person are frequently dwelt upon by the rabbis. They are conveniently summarized in Rabbi Meir's statement concerning the person who studies Torah for its own sake (*Lishmah*). He is "a lover of the All-present, and a lover of mankind; it clothes him in meekness and reverence; it fits him to become just, pious, upright, and faithful; it keeps him far from sin, and brings him near to virtue; . . . . He becomes modest, long suffering and forgiving insults." [14]

Mountain peaks may not be reached by single leaps. Religious heights, likewise, are scaled gradually. Rabbi Pinhas b. Yair enumerates the steps in the direction of spirituality: "Care leads to cleanness; cleanness to purity; purity to (asceticism; asceticism to) holiness; holiness to fear of sin; fear of sin to piety; and piety to the holy spirit." [15] As a religion of Torah, Judaism bases piety upon knowledge. "The ignorant person cannot be truly pious." [16] The fine distinctions of religious idealism pass him by.

M. H. Luzzatto, who made the saying of Pinhas b. Yair the text of his Mesilat Yesharim, comments that the path of piety, while leading to the same goal, takes on different forms in the lives of different men. "The way of piety of one whose profession is the study of Torah is not the way of piety for one who hires himself to work for another; neither is it the fit way for a man who engages in business." [17] Each person must embody his faith in the work which he is doing and in the particular life which he is leading.

The ways of piety naturally vary with different people as their ways of life vary. Some may seem trivial, while others shine with resplendent beauty, but they all have their worth. From the standpoint of subjective enrichment, the efforts of the lowly may be no less valuable than the imposing endeavors of the great. As the rabbis said concerning sacrifices: "It is all one whether a person offers much or little as long as he directs his thought to God." [18]

This does not imply that Judaism sets up different standards of religiosity for common folk and for scholars or for sinners and saints. Judaism knows of no double standards of either morals or religion. Distinctions between the beliefs and practices of the initiates and the common folk are foreign to its spirit. Rabbis and laymen share the same responsibilities and obligations of faith. In the view of Judaism the religious way has but one direction for all, viz., the sanctification of life, although its pursuit takes on diverse forms in accordance with the differences of character, intelligence, interest, and occupation. While all men must aspire after the highest, the noblest, and holiest, their attainments vary with their endowments.

Spirituality is realizable in every life no matter how humble. Instead of being confined to transcendent visions of ideal worlds, it is brought into close contact with earth. Holiness need not be something distant. It may be experienced in the common round of daily life. The thirty-six righteous ones who, according to legend, sustain the world,[19] pass for ordinary men. The fulfillment of the most menial duty, according to the rabbis, has sanctifying force. While fixing our minds upon religion, we must not overlook our particular religion nor discount its simple demands and rites. The way to the ultimate is through the near at hand. Thinking of the Infinite we must not blind ourselves to the fact that as finite beings we attain our best through careful regard to the immediate needs of the hour. The measure of our highest spirituality often consists in humble and unassuming loyalty to the simple precepts and observances of our religion.

THE NEW PIETY. As in olden times so today there are two conceptions of piety. The popular conception generally identifies it with pursuing the religious ways of former generations. The other conception refuses to limit the vision of the ever-living God to the past and strives to find Him in the new world view and in the tasks of the present. The ideas of religion we entertain, the forms we follow, the institution we cherish, and the prayers we offer must be grounded in present knowledge and experience. We must learn to love God with our own hearts and minds rather than with those of our forefathers.

Orthodoxy ventured to prescribe all the minute details of man's religious life. There were evident advantages as well as disadvantages in that procedure. The average man derived from it authoritative guidance in the complex relations of life. But its standardization of practice amounted to stereotype, often devoid of spirit. Its logical basis was the belief in the Divine origin of the Written and the Oral Law. As the will of God, it was to be obeyed unquestioningly. With the scientific reinterpretation of the Torah as the product of human striving after God rather than as the word of God mechanically delivered to man, the old basis of obedience has been removed. Hence Reform cannot uphold the heritage of ancient custom and ceremonial as binding for all times and circumstances. While recognizing antiquity as a possible testimony to the enduring worth of an idea, practice or institution, and to its service to man in the course of past centuries, Reform refuses to regard its continuance as part of religious duty unless, in addition to age, it possesses other qualities which make it socially, morally, and spiritually significant.

Tradition, from this standpoint, is not an end in itself but a means. It is the vital process whereby the life forces and social usages, the moral and religious convictions and aspirations of bygone times are preserved and rendered operative in the living present. Tradition thus conceived represents an instrument of progress. Without retaining what he has won in the course of his experience, man can make little advance. Indeed, part of his distinction from the animal consists in his ability to accumulate traditions of former endeavors to aid him in new situations. However, tradition may also become an obstacle to progress. Whether in social, political and economic spheres, or in science, ethics and religion, tradition must not be permitted to turn so rigid and inflexible as to exclude necessary change and improvement. To be creative, tradition must not serve as an embalming fluid for the preservation of dead remains. It must rather be a living stream that makes glad the city of God. In touch with the lifesprings, it must help man to greater freedom and growth. This is the function of tradition in art, in literature and in science, and cannot be less in religion.

Taking a historical and pragmatic view of tradition, Reform Judaism cannot treat it as the sole basis of authority. Reason must function by its side to determine the path of duty. Instead of prescribing the norms of religion as absolutely binding, Reform can only recommend values, standards, and institutions on the ground that they have proved themselves spiritually efficacious in the life of the Jewish people. Unlike Orthodoxy it cannot appeal to supernatural sanctions for its claims, but only to the collective experience of the Jewish people and to the mind and conscience of the individual. From the standpoint of the masses, this is obviously a defect; for it cannot exert as powerful a hold upon their minds as did Orthodoxy. However, from the standpoint of the spiritual integrity, this is undoubtedly a great asset. As it builds upon solid foundations, it may look forward to a future of usefulness.

Jewish piety, whether old or new, expresses itself in voluntary enlistment in the service of the Kingdom of God. And this kingdom is not merely within the heart of the individual person but in the trials and experiences of groups of men as well. The spiritual is in large measure conditioned by the social and comes to full fruition within it. Self-dedication to God means to carry religion into the home, the market-place, the factory, the shop, the city hall, the courthouse, the studio, the classroom, and the laboratory. The Kingdom of God is as wide as civilization and as broad as the spiritual efforts and aspirations of men. While religion is conceptually distinguishable from other human interests, it must never be isolated from them. They must be stamped and permeated with its spirit and purpose. It must furnish the sanctions and ideal patterns if not the fabric and constituent elements of civilization.

What has ever distinguished Jewish piety is its concern with the affairs and needs of men. In line with the teachings of the prophets as well as with the priestly law and rabbinic Halachah, Reform Judaism has emphasized that piety must be of this world. With the minimization of other-worldly rewards as incentives to right conduct, it seeks to affect the life of the individual in the here, and to religionize the present order, by applying the principles of religion to our social and economic relations, to our industry and commerce, and to our national and international politics. The social programs, which modern religions are advancing, aim at the elimination of human misery and suffering, of exploitation, ill will and warfare. They seek to direct the hearts of men to the promotion of harmonious and brotherly relations between the struggling classes and peoples and to the creation of conditions that shall render the flowering of the spiritual life possible. Part of the new as of the old piety is the striving toward the establishment of the world in righteousness.

Spirituality as the flower of personal religion may appear as a gift of grace, but in reality it is the outgrowth of earnest cultivation of the consciousness of the Divine presence. As the Psalmist expresses himself, "I have set the Lord always before me" (16:8). The rabbis hold that "everything is within the power of Heaven save the fear of Heaven."[20] Man himself must acquire the faith by which he is to live. At the same time the rabbis maintained that Heaven helps him who pursues the religious path. "The subject of holiness," M. H. Luzzatto teaches, "is double; at one end is work and at the other reward; it begins with effort and ends as a gift." [21] It does not come to a person as something complete and perfect, but rather as a potentiality, as a seed of character, which, if properly cared for, will grow and flourish. While some are more disposed to spirituality than others, no one is wholly unresponsive to it. In all persons it appears as a consequence of continuous upreaching and striving, of questing after the Divine.

# THE
# LIFE OF FAITH

# V. FUNCTION OF RELIGION

INTEGRATION OF PERSONALITY. How does Judaism as a life of faith affect personal well-being? The answer to this question is bound up with the dual nature of man. He is neither all matter nor all spirit, but a combination of the two. While rejecting the notion that the body is evil and the seat of corruption, Judaism recognizes that, like all material things, the body is subject to the laws of matter, of growth and change, of disease and death. The flower delights us with its loveliness and fragrance, but we must reconcile ourselves to its fragility and evanescence. The vigor and health of the body, too, pass, and sickness and decay set in. There are health and sickness of the spirit as well as of the body. While the spirit is the Divine element within us, it does not come into being fully complete and perfect. It appears as a potency which may grow into the beauty of holiness or into an abhorrence. In the school of experience, it may become a thing of glory or be stifled in ugliness.

In psychic life we have been taught to distinguish between the conscious and the sub- or un-conscious parts. The conscious awakened only yesterday. The unconscious has been slumbering since the beginnings of the race. Normally the two function together harmoniously. At times, however, they clash and produce the crises of life. The conscious consists of the basic functions of sensation, thinking, feeling and intuition. Within it are stored representations, ideas,

35

emotions, and perceptions. It strives to hold them to-gether and to give them direction and purpose. But from the depths of the unconscious surge up hidden and uncanny forces inherited from the distant biologi-cal past, which are either forgotten or suppressed by the awakened conscious, instinctual urges and appe-tites, morbid cravings, irrational fantasies, perilous il-lusions, and strivings. They burst through the rational controls of the conscious and take on forms that em-barrass and shock our own selves. These shadowy sides of our beings black out our reason, and seem strange to our normal selves. Outbursts of uncontrollable rage, hatred, pugnacity, lust, and greed overwhelm us so that we fail to recognize ourselves. Under animistic forms of thought they were accounted for as the work of the *evil* inclination, the *yetzer hara*, the "strange god" within us, or the devil. In extreme cases of schizophrenia, the personality seems to be completely divided into a "Dr. Jekyll and Mr. Hyde." The bestial and the angelic, the destructive and the creative, the good and the atrocious mingle within the same being. These invasions from the unconscious create physical as well as moral disorders. A sick spirit does not leave the body unaffected any more than a broken body preserves the spirit wholly undamaged. To these must be added the conscious perversions of the mind and will, calculated egotism, cruelty, and malice. The indi-vidual who is at war with himself does not contribute to the peace of society. The social ills, crime, vice, im-morality, strife, war, and the like stem from malad-justed and unintegrated individuals.

"If a unitary personality is to be achieved," William McDougal writes, "the various sentiments must be brought into one system within which their impulses shall be harmonized, each duly subordinated to the higher integration of which it becomes a member. This higher integration is what we call 'character'; it is achieved by the development of a master sentiment which dominates the whole system of sentiments, subordinating their impulses to its own."

Religion supplies this master sentiment. It is born of the inner need of unity, and comes as a response to the prayers: "Unite our hearts," "Purify and sanctify us," and "Teach us Thy ways." The sense of the holy, which underlies the rituals, symbols, institutions, codes, and beliefs of religion, integrates us with the cosmic source of our being, and binds our discordant selves into unified persons. To some men it comes as a sudden burst of light, flooding their souls and transforming them into new beings. In most men it emerges slowly as the result of careful nurture and training. All religion may be viewed as a way of integrating personality. Belief, knowledge, worship, consciousness of sin, and striving for atonement aim at binding man together as a spiritual unity.

By means of its technique of worship and instruction, religion helps to control man's whole psychic life, the conscious as well as the unconscious, to master his perceptions, his feelings and his will, and to direct them into useful channels. Wherever religion functions properly, it helps to overcome the conflicts of personality, to remove the inner tensions, to bind to-

gether the loose ends of character, and to recenter the
conscious mind upon the ideas and ideals, the ways
and values that make life worth while. From an ego-
centric existence, religion raises man to a conscious
relationship with his fellow men and with the universal source of all being, with God.

ENRICHMENT OF LIFE. The restoring and invigorating
effects of religion produce a special type of reaction
to experience. We do not deal with things as they are
in their naked selves, but with the way they appear to
us. This always depends upon our own mental and
physical condition. The color of the lens through
which we look upon the world tints our view. There
are times when the sunlight itself offends and when
darkness offers no rest. On occasion the world seems
to be a mere vale of tears, and existence an intolerable
burden. With the change of mood or circumstances
it reappears as the joyous scene of festive beauty and
radiant glory. The suffering Job curses the day upon
which he was born. The whole universe was shrouded
for him with the drabbest gray. The Psalmist sings
paeans of praise for life and light. The mourner,
weighted down by grief, bewails the weary round of
existence. The lover thrills to the rhythm of the dance
of life. The universe largely reechoes our calls and
responds to our moods. As our emotions change so do
the hues of the chameleon-like external world.

Reality, as far as we are concerned, consists not
merely of physical facts but also of the emotional
values which we attach to them. It is the product of

both perception and apperception, i.e., of perception modified by intellect, imagination and memory. Our valuation and appreciation, whether of life or of things, depend upon our inner states of consciousness. Fear, despair, hatred, envy, jealousy, generosity, love, trust, faith, joy, hope, adoration, etc.—transform the world for us. Without an inner sense of beauty the glories of art possess no significance. Without music in one's soul the noblest melodic creations of genius are mere noise.

Religion strikingly affects our apperceptions. William James observed that in its highest flights, religion, like love, wrath, hope, etc., is an infinite passion, which endows life with an enchantment which cannot be derived from anything else. It comes as a gift rather than as the fruit of effort. It brings an absolute addition to man's range of life. When all grows dark and the outward struggle seems lost, religious feeling revives the dried up springs of the inner life.

To be meaningful, he writes, religion must be regarded as "this added dimension of emotion, this enthusiastic temper of espousal, in regions where morality strictly so called can at best but bow its head and acquiesce. . . .

"This sort of happiness in the absolute and everlasting is what we find nowhere but in religion. It is parted off from all mere animal happiness, all mere enjoyment of the present" by an element of solemnity.[22]

J. B. Pratt similarly testifies to the enrichment of spirit which comes with faith. The deeply religious person, as compared with the best and bravest of those who are not religious, possesses something which the others lack. He may not be superior morally, nor more appreciative of beauty and love nor any braver. But he has a confidence in the ultimate outcome of things which the other does not have. He may not be more at home in this world than the other, but he seems more at home in the universe as a whole, and feels himself in touch with a larger environment. "He either has a more cosmic sense or his attitude toward the cosmos is one of larger hope and confidence. Beside this, or as a result of this, he has an inner source of joy and strength which does not seem dependent on outer circumstances, and which in fact seems greatest at times when outer sources of strength and promise fail. He is, therefore, able to shed a kind of peace around him which no argument and no mere animal spirits and no mere courage can produce." [23]

By enriching the emotional content, religion makes a most significant contribution to man's welfare. It reaches out into his subconscious self, and as with fairy fingers draws him toward the sunny side of existence. By removing the inner discords, generating enthusiasm for life and enhancing its value through its connection with the Divine, religion strengthens man's grip upon reality, and thereby aids him in most positive manner in his struggle for existence. Religion thus connects man with the tendency in things toward normalcy and soundness, with the will to live and to carry on. It invests life with meaning and purpose. It offers men goals toward which to strive, and imbues them with faith in their value and with hope in their achievement. Evelyn Underhill observes, "A compelling power exists in the world—little understood, even by those who are inspired by it—which presses men to transcend their material limitations and mental conflicts and live a new creative life of harmony, freedom and joy." [24] Religion seizes upon this power and employs it for the exaltation of life. In the words of the Psalmist: "God gives strength unto His people; God blesses His people with peace" (29:11).

LIBERATION FROM FEAR. The faith state of the mind vivifies and refreshes man's inner life which otherwise would be an arid and empty waste. While affecting his subconscious life, it also enriches his mental outlook and strengthens his will. By centering his ideas around the belief in a righteous and loving God, religion liberates man from the bondage of fear, which holds the lower animals in fetters and which clings to him as part of his biological heritage.

Under the sheltered conditions of modern civilization, it is possible, at least during peace times, for many people to go through life without being exposed to the shock of fear. In consequence the boast is sometimes made that with the further progress of science, fear will be completely banished. To be sure, science has freed the mind of many harassing fears, but it has also produced hosts of new ones. While opening new horizons, it has disclosed new threats to human well-being, new fears of hitherto unknown perils, diseases and accidents.

As an ever-present factor in human life, this emotion must have served some purpose in man's struggle for existence. It appears to have functioned as an aid to man in his adjustment to the hostile forces of his environment. "It is the cry of alarm raised by the senses which act as the guardians of the body; and at the signal, in virtue of the nervous automatism, the organism is put in a position of defense." [25] As an emotional reaction to the strange and the unknown and as an anticipation of painful experience, fear is a healthy and natural form of resistance to danger, helping to maintain and to prolong life. Soldiers in the battlefield who ignore the danger signal of fear until they are overwhelmed by the enemy are lost. Responding to it in time, discovering the exact nature and magnitude of the peril which confronts them, and preparing manfully to meet it may give them the courage to fight victoriously. "Making up their own minds" brings them greater self-assurance in action. If, in addition, they are convinced of the rightness of their cause, they increase the invincibility of their armor. [26]

In his *Study of Fears*, Stanley Hall concludes: "There is no one without fear, and those few who so emphatically disclaim all fear, and the psychologists who tabulate the percentage of fearless people, are thinking of shock or panic or acute fright, or special physical dread, but not of the subtler forms, like the fear of God, of dishonor, failure of their highest purposes, for themselves or others. Not only does every one fear, but all should fear. The pedagogic problem is not to eliminate fear, but to gauge it to the power of proper reaction. Fear that paralyzes some may be good for others. In some form and degree all need it always." [27]

The author of the Wisdom of Solomon connects fear with cowardice and unreason. "Fear," he writes, "is naught but a surrender of the succors which reason offereth" (17:11–12). He could not have thought of the fear of cowardice itself, of unreason, or of wickedness in all its tempting and bewitching forms. The more refined the ethical and spiritual nature of a person becomes, the more keenly he feels the danger of slipping from the moral heights to which he has attained. Hence the hesitancy on the part of the rabbis to call a person righteous until the day of his death. There is always the fear of his falling from grace.

However, there are fears which do not seem to serve any useful purpose, and only threaten man's welfare. They persist through normal childhood, adolescence, and adult life. As long as we enjoy good health, our normal fears require no particular attention from us. With the exhaustion of our nervous energy and the depletion of our mental and physical resources, our fears take on disquieting forms, such as fear of day and fear of night, fear of the known and fear of the unknown, fear of men and fear of animals, fear of open spaces and fear of closed spaces, fear of life and fear of death, fear of sickness and fear of poverty, etc. They attach themselves to almost any object, situation or idea. Their victims grow apprehensive of the imminence of danger, hypersensitive, irritable, restless and unhappy. Fearing themselves, their own feelings and actions, they become incapable of enjoying the normal processes of life. Their fears grow into obsessive phobias, producing illnesses and developing symptoms of illnesses which do not exist. Worry is an acute form of fear which affects healthy minds with disastrous effects. An eminent neurologist speaks of worry as "the one shortener of life under civilization." [28]

We must either conquer fear or be conquered by it. Pathological fears properly belong to the sphere of scientific medicine and of psychiatry. Inasmuch, however, as fear affects the emotions and the mind as well as the body, religious faith may prove of inestimable help. The antidote and corrective of many a fear and worry is a religious life, expressing itself in heroic submission to the will of God and in high moral purposes. [29]

Religion sublimates fear by diverting it from all temporal things and confining it to God alone. The fear of God, which may have represented at first a depressing state of consciousness, in course of time developed into solemn awe and reverence. The Hebrew word *yireah* covers both meanings. *Yireat hakabod*, "fear of the Glory," appears as an aspect of *kedushah*, holiness.* It ministers to the higher life and produces a sense of confidence within the human soul. The heart is taught to sing: "The Lord is my light and my salvation, whom shall I fear?" Amid direst distress

* The fear of God shades off into awe and reverence, the characteristic aspects of the sense of creaturehood, inspired by the numinous, the mysterious object of religious apprehension. See, for example, Gen. 28:17; Ex. 3:6; 15:11; 19; 20:18–21; 34:30; Jer. 10:7; Hab. 3:2; Ps. 111:9.

the religious spirit feels confident. "The Lord is my shepherd. I shall not want. . . . Yea, though I walk in the valley of the shadow of death, I shall fear no evil, for Thou art with me" (Pss. 27:1; 23:1, 4). The surging floods and ravages of time do not terrify the soul that is steadfast in its faith. "He shall not be afraid of evil tidings; His heart is steadfast, trusting in the Lord" (Ps. 112:7). Though caught in the waves of whirling circumstance, it experiences a sense of permanence and security.

> God is our refuge and strength,
> A very present help in trouble.
> Therefore will we not fear, though the
>     earth do change,
> And though the mountains be moved in the
>     heart of the seas,
> Though the waters thereof roar and foam,
> Though the mountains shake at the swelling
>     thereof.
> —Ps. 46:2ff.; see also Ps. 102:26–29.

The conquest of fear represents at the same time the triumph of faith. Living in the conscious presence of God makes for inner peace. By awakening confidence in the ultimate rightness of the Divine order of nature, it produces an abiding sense of tranquillity and safety. With somber temperaments the temper of tranquil-mindedness partakes of resignation and is purely passive; with those of cheerful cast of mind it is joyous consent, and takes on an active character, a defiance of danger, of temptation and of evil, and an enthusiastic espousal of the true, the good, the beautiful and the holy. It awakens a feeling of patience, fortitude, and good will. James writes: "The transition from tenseness, self-responsibility, and worry, to equanimity, receptivity and peace, is the most wonderful of all those shiftings of inner equilibrium, those changes of the personal center of energy; and the chief wonder of it is that it so often comes about, not by doing, but by simply relaxing and throwing the burden down. This abandonment of self-responsibility seems to be the fundamental act in specifically religious, as distinguished from moral practice. It antedates theologies and is independent of philosophies." [30] The message of religion is: "Cast thy burden upon the Lord, and He will sustain thee" (Ps. 55:23; also Ps. 37:7).

Religious people of all times unite in their testimony that the practice of the Divine presence brings not only peace to the heart and mind but also renewed strength. Fear often issues from weakness and lack of self-confidence. Faith is a measure of energy and of self-assurance in the face of peril. Confident that God is on their side, the weakest of men have felt as mighty hosts. Like Elisha's servant, they see the forces of Heaven ever on their side (II Kings 6:15ff.). Experiencing an inrushing of power, they readily go forth to battle in behalf of righteous causes. "They that wait for the Lord renew their strength; they mount up with wings as eagles" (Is. 40:29-31). The history of the Jews and the record of religious martyrs everywhere bear eloquent proof of the genuineness of this conviction. Often combating the pressure of public opinion and the intellectual and moral standards of the whole world, these stiff-necked people displayed a fortitude unknown to the rest of men. The faith which they held so intensely enabled them to see through the inmost nature of things, and to vision the highest goals. "In the mountain of the Lord it is seen" (Gen. 22:14). The darkness is lifted, and where chaos and bewildering confusion reigned, the eye of the soul beholds the creative forces of God shaping worlds of harmony. The disordered fragments of existence begin to fit into patterns of meaning and of purpose. Religion reveals things both *sub specie temporis* and *sub specie aeternitatis*. It makes us see life steadily and see it whole.

"Yea, though I dwell in darkness," Micah announces, "God is my light" (7:8). The fear-ridden, narrow and cabined existence is flooded with light from distant stars. New paths of action, sometimes of heroic character, are disclosed. We learn to regard not only the step immediately ahead, but also the events of the distant future, and take heart in our struggles for a saner and better world. We come to recognize that ideals are not stripped of their value because of their temporary depreciation. They have a future as well as a past and a present.

The religious life embodies two contradictory elements: passivity, on the one hand, and activity on the other. If it involves absolute dependence upon the all-sustaining power of God, a sense of creaturehood and submission, it also involves personal freedom, responsibility, initiative and creativeness. "Man's security is ultimately within himself." The very resignation to the will of God nerves man with power to fight all that is ungodly and threatening. The whole of religious life oscillates between these two extremes. One finds its embodiment in mysticism, the other in ethical idealism. Judaism has striven to prevent the two from falling apart, and has endeavored so to integrate them as to make the one the instrument of the other. In its system the moral and the spiritual have formed a harmonious whole.

# VI. DELIVERANCE FROM EVIL

RELIGION makes its greatest contribution to human well-being by lifting the crushing burden of evil from the hearts and minds of men. Indeed the existence of evil grows into a world problem only in a theistic system of thought. A materialistic conception of nature and of human life leaves no ground for complaints against the order of things, its lack of value or its incoherence, even though it may find fault with this or that hindrance, pest or nuisance. Assuming no rationality in the world, it does not have to account for the irrational. Only as we conceive of the world within a teleological setting as an ordered universe, created and governed by God in accordance with His wisdom, justice, and purpose, does evil appear as a challenge to both faith and reason. Religion and idealistic philosophy face the baffling question: "if God is good and omnipotent, and if the universe is an expression of His goodness, whence comes evil?"

Philosophy by its very nature concerns itself with the explanation and justification of this anomaly in the scheme of things. Religion, on the other hand, is primarily concerned with the conquest of evil. Religions of salvation, like Buddhism and, to a lesser degree, Christianity, derive their very being from the human need of deliverance from evil. Judaism, too, while essentially a religion of law and moral discipline, directs much of its attention to the question how to face evil. In its struggle with evil, religion sometimes resorts to the philosophic way of dealing with the problem, because an analysis of the nature of evil, of its origin and of its operations tends to remove much of its poignancy if not its reality.

SHADOWS AND LIGHT. At the outset we must bear in mind that our appraisals of existence as either good or bad depend in part upon our temperaments, personal experience and preference. What may be desirable for one may seem dreadful for another. What recommends the world as beneficent to one person may form the ground for another to condemn it as baneful. Such appraisals represent judgments of value, which admit of no objective standard.

This consideration notwithstanding, unless our minds are narcotized by Pollyanna optimism we are all too aware of the murky shadows that hover over us. So much ruthlessness and brutality terrify us, so much indiscriminateness, recklessness and waste shock our moral sense, and so much hideous suffering baffles our intelligence that our vision is often darkened. If astronomy discloses the process of wrecking of worlds, biology shows nature as a scene of unending struggle and carnage. "Kill to live" has been suggested as a fit description of the animate order. Modern naturalism discloses the universe in a new way, as groaning in travail and pain. Nature does not readily appear as a merciful nurse, solicitous for human welfare. It follows its own mysterious ways, disregardful of our needs and hopes. Like a Juggernaut it often moves over us, crushing us in the process. From the external conditions of the world and from the blind play of its physical forces, the moral and spiritual order is hardly derivable.

Furthermore, the basic conditions of human life subject us to hardship, to pain, to sickness, to decay, and to death. Neither are our social relationships brighter. Moral wrong and wickedness, exploitation, deceit, hatred and strife add to the bitterness of our lot, rendering life repugnant and unbearable. The strain upon our mentality produced by personal and social misery renders many of us world-weary and melancholy. An elegiac note steals into most reflections upon human life and destiny. Despite the healthy-mindedness, robust faith and hopefulness of the prophets of Israel, they too reecho the universal complaint against the transience, folly and misery of the human lot. Job curses the day upon which he was born, and Ecclesiastes bewails all things as vanity of vanities.

While keeping an open eye upon the apparently irrational, wretched and brutal, we cannot overlook the light which pierces the clouds, the rudiments of order, well-being and intelligence, which even a Schopenhauer and a Hartman were forced to recognize as conditions of cosmic continuance and coherence. Though perplexed by much that goes on in the world, we have ground for the belief that if the world was not constructed exclusively for our happiness, neither was it organized to plague us. As F. R. Tennant remarks, "If there is enough disorder to embarrass the theist, there is surely too much order in the world to allow the materialist to feel at home there." [31] If nature is "red in tooth and claw," it also displays signs of care for others. The will to live, the sex instinct, mother love, and mutual aid, even in the animal realm, point to the operation of a creative by the side of the destructive force. The struggle for self-preservation through the destruction of others is but one phase of nature's story; the incessant struggle for the preservation of others is a no less significant phase.*

Furthermore, though man is part of the kingdom of animate life, he enjoys a place of distinction among its citizens. Matthew Arnold declared:

* "I see the Nature Providence going its impartial way. I see drought and flood, heat and cold, war and pestilence, defeat and death, besetting man at all times, in all lands. I see hostile germs in the air he breathes, in the waters he drinks, in the soil he tills. I see the elemental forces as indifferent toward him as toward ants and fleas. I see pain and disease and defeat and failure dogging his footsteps. I see the righteous defeated and the ungodly triumphant—this and much more I see; and yet I behold through the immense biological vista behind us the race of man slowly, oh, so slowly! emerging from its brute or semi-human ancestry into the full estate of man, from blind instinct and savage passion into the light of reason and moral consciousness. I behold the great scheme and evolution unfolding despite all the delays and waste and failures, and the higher forms appearing on the scene. I see on an immense scale, and as clearly as in a demonstration in a laboratory, that good comes out of evil; that the impartiality of the Nature Providence is best; that we are made strong by what we overcome; that man is man because he is as free to do evil as to do good . . . that power awaits upon him who earns it; that disease, wars, the unloosened, devastating elemental forces have each and all played their part in developing and hardening man and giving him the heroic fiber."
—John Burroughs, *Accepting the Universe*, pp. 12, 13.

Know, man hath all which Nature hath but more,
And in that *more* lie all his hopes of good.[32]

The physical world is but the external scene of human
existence. Our life, itself, is lived inwardly. Within
this inner realm of consciousness, or spirit, are the real
issues of life, of happiness and of misery, of good and
of evil. The eye of faith is, therefore, able to look
upon life, even amid tears, pain and despair, and discern signs of benevolence, loveliness and beauty.*

JEWISH OPTIMISM. As God's gift life is a manifestation
of His beneficence. In their reverence for life, the
masters of Judaism, unlike the Hindu thinkers, could
not renounce all existence as inherently evil and condemn the desire for life as the root of all evil, from
which men must seek deliverance. The opening chapters of the Bible recognize evil without defining its
nature. It is accepted as a tragic element in existence,
which is essentially good. Evil is regarded as disciplinary in character. It may be overcome by wise choice
between good and evil. This very power of free
choice accounts for the ills of life, for man is often
enticed by evil, and yielding to it, becomes a victim of
sorrow and grief. According to the prophets, the

---

* The aged Schopenhauer could pen these lines at the close
of his career:

> Aweary stand I at my journey's goal,
> My tired brow can scarce its laurels bear,
> And yet my life brings gladness to my soul;
> Tho' others mocked I have been steadfast e'er.

> —Werke, Vol. V., p. 696; tr. by Brightman,
> *Immortality in Post Kantian Idealism*, p. 35.

physical disorders themselves are due to evil doing. Their moral and religious conceptions centered in the doctrine of retribution, in the light of which suffering is the fruit of sin and of folly, and happiness the reward of obedience and of goodness.

This simple creed of the Biblical authors was shaken by the suffering of the righteous and the prosperity of the wicked. Prophets, psalmists, and sages alike complained against the topsy-turvydom of the moral order.[32] Job rejected the orthodox belief, championed by his friends, of an equation between evil and suffering, and left the matter veiled in impenetrable mystery. The Parsis had solved the problem in a wholly different way. They envisaged the world as governed by two conflicting powers, one good and the other evil. Deutero-Isaiah, rejecting the dualistic conception of the world, reaffirmed the doctrine of ethical monotheism: "I am the Lord, and there is none else; I form light, and create darkness; I make peace, and create evil. I am the Lord that doeth all these things" (Is. 45:6–7).* This manifesto of monotheism, while ruling out dualism from the range of Jewish belief, left the ethical problem where it was. How can a good God create evil? Does not evil cast a reflection upon His character? Deutero-Isaiah resorts to two novel conceptions to supplement the old doctrine of retribution. With Deuteronomy 8:5 he interprets suffering as dis-

---

* Cf. Sanh. 39a. Lam. 3:38 lends itself to two opposite constructions. Taken as a question, it supports the belief of Deutero-Isaiah. As a direct statement it asserts that evil and good proceed not from God, but that they are man-made.

ciplinary in character, as the rabbis subsequently termed it, "chastisements of love." * Chapter 53 of Isaiah advances the belief that suffering is vicarious. The righteous does not suffer merely in expiation of his own sins. By his suffering, he bears and expiates the guilt of his wicked fellow men.

The author of the prologue of Job suggests a compromise between the dualistic and monotheistic views of suffering. The patriarch's affliction came not from God but from Satan. However, Satan, unlike Angra Mainyu in Parsism, is not a rival of God, eternally opposing and thwarting the good. He is one of God's ministering angels and acts as the district attorney of heaven, testing man's probity. This conception figured prominently in post-Biblical thought. In the latest strata of the Bible, the final judgment and punishment of evil is postponed to the hereafter. Rabbinical teaching raised this idea to the position of a fundamental dogma.

In the main the sages of the Bible and the rabbis approach the problem of evil not from the standpoint of metaphysics but of practice, viz., how shall man conduct himself in a world so full of pitfalls, of misery, of wickedness and of folly? They did not speculate in the manner of a Leibnitz or a Schopenhauer, whether this is the best or the worst of all possible worlds. The schools of Shammai and of Hillel did engage in a pro-

---

* Isaiah 63:9 goes so far as to assume that God Himself shares in the affliction of Israel. However, in the light of the Septuagint the verse reads: *lo tzir*—"neither messenger nor angel but He Himself saved them."

tracted discussion of three and a half years concerning the value of human life. The Shammaites maintained that it would have been better for man had he not been created and the Hillelites argued that it is better that he was created. They finally agreed that while it might have been better for man had he never come into existence, since he exists he must make the best of life through moral perfection.[34]

The essential optimism of both Biblical and rabbinic Judaism stems from the belief in the Divine government of the world and in man's moral freedom. Though the wicked temporarily prosper and the righteous suffer, the scales of Justice will not be permanently perverted. "Yet a little while, and the wicked is no more; yea, thou shalt look well at his place, and he is not. But the humble shall inherit the land, and delight themselves in the abundance of peace" (Ps. 37:10–11; cf. Sirach 39:20–46). Falsehood and injustice may hold the throne for the present, but the dominion of the future belongs to truth and right. The present prosperity of the wicked spells their ultimate doom.[35] It is the long rather than the short view of history that reveals the workings of God. Through suffering and judgment man moves toward the Messianic goal of triumphant righteousness and perfect felicity. The rabbis, as we have indicated above, found further comfort in the belief that the injustices of this life will be righted in the next. The doctrine of otherworldy compensation in a heaven and hell is largely derived from the human craving for a final balance. Accordingly Rabbi Simeon ben Lakish interpreted the

Divine approbation of creation in the words "behold, it is very good" (Gen. 1:31) as applying to this world, and the additional conjunction "and" which precedes these words ("*and* behold, it is very good") as referring to the hereafter. God beheld both worlds at one glance. The present order is completed by the next. In the words of Robert Browning: "Here, a broken arc, there a perfect whole." R. Meir interpreted the same text, "and behold, it is very good" as applying to death. Other masters applied it to the evil inclination, to suffering, to Gehenna and to retribution.[36] Seemingly evil, they all serve useful purposes in the Divine order. "No evil comes from above."[37] Nahum of Gimzo's motto, "This too is for the best"—*gam zu letobah*,[38] expresses the optimistic note in Judaism. R. Akiba teaches similarly, "Whatever God does is for the best."[39] It forms part of the Divine law of compensation. "There is no death without sin, and no suffering without iniquity."[40] While coming as punishments, both have atoning power. The pious prized suffering because it purges man of sin. The afflictions of the righteous are but blessings in disguise. They are the chastisements of love, visiting man in this life that he may be purified of the effects of evil and prepared for the bliss of the hereafter.[41] The evil inclination or passion was prized because it stimulates love of life and of activity, and thus ministers ultimately to the good.[42] The words " 'Evil shall not sojourn with Thee' (Ps. 5:5) were taken to mean: Thou dost not abide with evil, nor does evil abide with Thee."[43] As the source of good, God does not come into contact with evil. In the words of R. Elazar b. Pedat, which are related to Philo's teaching, "God never associates His name with evil but only with the good." [44]

PHILOSOPHIC APPRAISAL OF EVIL. Under Greek philosophic influence, the problem of evil became the subject of serious consideration on the part of Jewish thinkers. Philo, who followed Plato in identifying God with goodness, followed him also in absolving God of evil. The process of creation represents the revelation of God's goodness. Out of existent primordial matter, unordered, propertyless, lifeless, chaotic and disharmonious, God by means of the Logos (Wisdom) and the Divine powers fashioned the universe. However, He imparted of His beneficence not in accordance with His endless mercy, but rather in accord with the measure of the capacities of the recipient, for the ability of the creature to endure the good does not correspond to God's power to bestow it. Whatever of outer harmony and rationality there is in the world must be ascribed to God, whereas the imperfections and evils are due to matter.[45] Creation inheres in God's nature. As it is the property of fire to burn and of snow to cause cold, so it is God's way to create. The Hebrew prayer, Yotzer, expresses the kindred thought: "In His goodness He renews daily, continually, the work of creation." Creation means bringing order out of chaos, subduing matter and overcoming obstacles. The world is, therefore, the scene of an incessant struggle in which the goodness of God triumphs over evil, without, however, completely annihilating it.

Evil is both positive and final. It, too, serves a purpose. Without it the creative process would cease. "For the manifestation of the better there was necessary the creation of the worse, but both are due alike to the power of the same goodness, namely, to God." [46]

Man, consisting of body and spirit, combines both evil and good. His body is the seat of corruption. Considering the senses as evil, sin appears innate in man. As in rabbinic teaching, suffering coming as punishment of sin is good despite its seeming badness, for it disciplines and sobers sinners and their associates.[47] In the verse, "The thornbush is not consumed" (Ex. 3:20), Yedaiah Hapenini takes the word "thornbush" as a symbol of evil.[48] Like the thorn on the rose bush, evil is a permanent element in the world, whose goal is goodness.

Matter as the positive principle of evil reappears in the philosophy of Ibn Gabirol and in the Cabbalah. The idea that evil is a necessary contrast to good figures frequently in Jewish mysticism. Israel Baal Shem Tov, for example, teaches that "the evil of the world is but the lowest degree of the absolute good. When man does good, the evil is transformed into absolute good; but when he sins, the evil turns into a real evil." "Evil is the throne of the good." "The source and root, which vitalizes all worlds," says R. Shneor Zalman of Liadi, "is good." [49]

Maimonides introduced a new and enlightening note into the discussion of this subject by calling attention to the fact that the whole problem of evil grows out of the anthropocentric view of the world.

"An ignorant man believes that the whole universe exists only for him; as if nothing else required any consideration. If, therefore, anything happens to him contrary to his expectation, he at once concludes that the whole universe is evil. If, however, he should take into consideration the whole universe, form an idea of it, and comprehend what a small portion he is in the universe, he will find the truth. . . . It is of great advantage that man should know his station, and not erroneously imagine that the whole universe exists only for him." [50] Contrary to popular religious belief, the chief purpose of creation is not man but rather the unfoldment of all of its potentialities. Taking a larger cosmic view of things and abandoning the notion that man is the final measure of existence, the ground for our complaining against what seems to us evil is in large measure removed. What is injurious to man may be useful to other parts of nature or to the universe at large. In identifying God with goodness and in regarding all things proceeding from Him as good, we must guard against gauging the good by human standards. As the prophet warned: "My thoughts are not your thoughts, neither are your ways My ways, saith the Lord" (Is. 55:8). God transcends our human distinctions of good and evil.

The problem of evil, therefore, must be treated not from the cosmic but from the human standpoint. From this consideration, Maimonides—following Abraham ibn David [51]—regards evil as a negative rather than a positive principle. "All evils are privations." They are the proverbial hole in the doughnut. Death is an evil, because it represents man's non-existence. Similarly illness, poverty and ignorance are evils because they represent lack of health, riches and knowledge. From this proposition Maimonides deduces that God cannot be considered the creator of evil either directly or intentionally. "He only produces existence, and all existence is good; whilst evils are of a negative character and cannot be acted upon." It can only be said of God that He created evil indirectly, by virtue of creating the corporeal element, which is "always connected with negatives, and is on that account the source of all destruction and all evil." However, the corporeal element itself, though constituting the source of death and of all suffering, is not wholly evil, for it serves the good purpose of insuring the permanence of the universe and the continuation of the order of things.

The evils that grow out of the physical nature of man, his deformities, his suffering and death, cannot be held as absolute evils from the cosmic viewpoint. "We have already shown," Maimonides writes, "that, in accordance with the divine wisdom, genesis can only take place through destruction, and without destruction of individual members, the species themselves would not exist permanently." "If a man were never subject to change there could be no generation; there would be one single being, but no individuals forming a species." Whoever thinks that he can have a material body and escape the accidents of matter seeks to combine two opposites. Evil is, therefore, not absolute but relative and inheres as a negative principle in matter.

Corruption, decay, destruction, and defect are accidents of matter rather than of spirit. In the same way man's moral shortcomings are due to his bodily limitations, to his cravings and passions. To overcome these limitations man has been endowed with mind, whereby he may rule his body and inclinations.

It is from the inadequate control of mind over body that the social and personal evils result. The injuries which men cause one another, because of conflicting desires, ideas or religious beliefs, are likewise due to privation; "they originate in ignorance which is absence of wisdom." No more than evils resulting from the physical order can these social evils be averted by the sufferer himself. It is different with evils growing out of personal faults. We suffer from them because of our own acts. By our own volition we inflict them upon ourselves and then blame them upon God. In the words of the sage: "The foolishness of man perverteth his way, and the heart fretteth against the Lord" (Prov. 19:3). "The chief evils," Maimonides insists, "which befall man are due to his own actions. They originate in man's vices, such as excessive desire for eating, drinking and love, indulgence in these things in undue measure, or in improper manner, or in partaking of bad food. This brings disease and afflictions upon body and soul alike." The soul is affected by the conditions of the body, and becomes a victim of insatiable desire for superfluities.[52]

Evil is not part of the texture of the universe. However, while eliminating evil as a condition of reality, Maimonides recognizes its outward manifestations and considers its conquest the chief aim of the moral and spiritual life.

A MODERN VIEW OF EVIL. The Jewish philosophical ideas of evil require restatement in the light of evolutionary doctrine. Rabbi Abahu spoke of God as having created many worlds and destroyed them before He created the present world order.[53] Philo and the author of the Yotzer conceived of the process of creation as continuous and eternal. From the standpoint of evolution the universe is not static but dynamic. Our world has not, and possibly never will reach the Sabbath state of completion and perfection. It is an ongoing process, ever in the making, ever growing and developing. Imperfection or evil is thus the inevitable concomitant of cosmic experimentation. The processes of natural selection and adjustment of parts to the whole proceed apace. Organs, functions, bodies, nations, races, and worlds are worn out and discarded and replaced by new ones, more fit to serve the cosmic ends. Viewed from the finite, temporal end, this wreckage and decay represents evil, but "taken in their eternal context as aspects of the whole" they serve as "the way to and condition of the good."

Human life, too, offers ground for the belief that there is a soul of goodness in things evil. The sufferer of "an ill due to external natural agencies," Royce believes, endures "a part of the burden of the world's struggle with temporal finitude, or with sin and with its consequences." Endurance under these circumstances becomes "no mere self-centered Stoicism," intended only to show one's own powers, but a willingness to cooperate, whenever possible, "in the Divine task of giving meaning even to the seeming chaos of our present temporal existence." [54]

Perfection, both personal and social, is not something ready for us to be found, but something to be attained and acquired. Man is a portion of the unfolding world. Its ends are partly realized through his cooperation. By virtue of his mental endowment he plays not a wholly passive but, at least to a degree, an active role in the world drama. He feels himself called upon to shape his environment, to extirpate its thorns and thistles, and to render it a fit home for his body and spirit. Man is a co-worker with God—a *Shutaph l'hakkadosh baruch hu.* Life and good as well as death and evil are set before him, and he is called upon to make his choice.

As a laborer in the garden of life, man is naturally exposed to hardships and to dangers. His toil often entails pain and suffering, and he eats his bread in the sweat of his brow. Nonetheless, his very misery is a mark of his dignity. He suffers more than the brutes because he feels more keenly than they, and he thinks. He is partly the builder of his own life and character. His very reason and moral freedom involve possibilities of error, of stumbling and of choosing evil as well as good. Yet without these possibilities he could hardly achieve his triumphs in the spheres of science, morals and religion.

What invests man's moral, spiritual and intellectual striving with true significance is the solidarity of the human race. Closely related to one another, the acts, achievements and failures of one individual affect all the rest. If we benefit from the labors of our forebears and contemporaries, we are also compelled to expiate their misdeeds as well as our own. Though free to choose our measures of good or evil, we are not exempt from suffering in consequence of evil not of our own making. Indeed, the greater part of our woes grows out of the oneness of the race, and is in nowise wholly due to the personal acts of the sufferers. We bear the burdens of wars, though we individually have no responsibility for their occurrence. We feel the strain of the social order, of its periodic crises, of unemployment, of racial discord, class divisions and bigotry, in the creation of which we had no share. There is no isolation in the moral order. We are part of one another, in the manifold sense of the word. It follows, as Royce pointed out, "that, in our moral world, the righteous can suffer without individually deserving their suffering, just because their lives have no independent Being, but are linked with all life." [55] Indeed, the more one grows in saintliness and in moral refinement, the more sensitive he becomes toward the pain, the misery, the sin, and the sordidness which burden the lives of others. Vicarious suffering is one of the awesome realities in the life of every spiritual personality. However, as long as the laughter of children will fill the air with mirth and the hearts of men and women will beat with love, and as long as human hands and minds will be set to creative tasks, to increase truth, beauty, and goodness, life's cup of joy will overflow and the song of praise will rise to the Giver of all good.

OVERCOMING EVIL. The recognition that our world is still in the making and that as moral agents we must share in its betterment gives a new direction to life. We are obliged to posit the belief, upon which all science and philosophy rest, that nature is intelligible, that despite all appearances to the contrary, it partly responds to our thought. The investigator may not be able to prove the uniformity of nature or the causal connection between events. Nonetheless upon the acceptance of these hypotheses depends his success.[56] Our moral and religious life depends upon a similar faith that above the *tohu vabohu*, the disorder and chaos, is a Power, Principle or Being, making for order, that a wisdom and a purpose shape and direct things to their destined end. God brings good out of evil and harmony out of discord. To revere and to align oneself with the order-making tendency in his life, i.e., of righteousness and love, is man's highest good and supreme wisdom. Where God's power does not seem to be in accord with His goodness, it is still proper to trust in Him. He whose infinite energy and inscrutable purposes uphold the vast creation can be relied on to sustain our little lives. All doubts about life's value terminate as did the scepticism of Ecclesiastes in the sober recognition that: "The end of the matter, all having been heard: fear God, and keep His commandments, for this is the whole of man" (12:13).

The religious consciousness does not lull one into

blissful oblivion to pain and suffering. As we have observed, the more sensitive man becomes to the holy, the more he grows in refinement of spirit and conscience, and the more his soul craves for righteousness and love, the more poignantly he feels the desecrating influences, the defacement of the Divine, the wrongs and the brutality that turn life into a hell, the brazenness and cynicism that mock at character, virtue and piety. The evil and misery that frustrate human hopes and aspirations pass through his soul. Like the suffering servant of Deutero-Isaiah's vision, he bears the burden of human shame and selfishness. Opposition to the world thus becomes a characteristic mood of the religious spirit, an opposition to things as they are in the interest of things as they ought to be. From the currents and cross-currents of the external world, the religious man turns to the depths of his own spirit to strengthen his consciousness of the Divine. His inner nature expands, and he grows not only critical, but morally creative. Turning away from the world's evils, he enlists as a fighter in the Kingdom of God. His object is not happiness in the sense of creature comforts, complete satisfaction of natural impulses, and rest from struggle, but rather the quest after the larger human good, which consists in the full freedom of personal growth in harmony with social welfare and in a life lived in the light of God. To be on the side of the forces that make for an increase of good over evil, of justice over wrong, and of brotherhood over strife is its own reward. Despite all obstacles, life may flower forth into ethical and spiritual perfection.

# VII. RELIGIOUS AID TO ADJUSTMENT

RELIGION makes man captain of his soul. It dispels the shadows that darken his horizon and frees him from the bondage of fear and evil. Out of his stony griefs he is taught to build his *Beth El*. If he may not master the external conditions of his environment, he can control his reactions to them. Despite the dangers which threaten him, he is heartened to face circumstances with renewed courage and hope. In the light of faith he finds that the world affords him the necessary opportunity to realize his ideals. The very stumbling blocks in his way may be used as stepping stones to achievement. He is taught to recognize that he no longer lives in a paradise, as pictured in the Bible legend, but in a stern world which demands labor and struggle as the price of life. The fact that he is a bearer of burdens may crush him, but it also exercises him and builds his inner strength. Without loads to carry, without conflicts and dangers to overcome, without physical, moral and religious problems to solve, without work to do, life, indeed, would be irredeemable. Men generally quarrel with their circumstances and complain against their hardships. What they often fail to recognize is that their difficulties serve as the conditioning stimuli of their development.

The struggle against circumstances begins at the cradle and ends at the grave. It is fought by every human being not only in the physical but also in the social realm. The trophies of victory go to those who master the secret of adjustment. Passing over the period of infancy, which is not guided by conscious volition, we find the child forming associations with other playmates, which involve constant clashes of will. From its self-centeredness the child enters into social and cooperative existence, of continuous give-and-take, in which personal advantage has to be forgone for the sake of others. In adolescence the problem of adjustment grows particularly acute. Blind instincts and passions roar for satisfaction, deafening the voice of reason and of conscience. The young person appears to be their plaything. Is he to master or to be mastered by them? Upon this question depends his future as a useful or parasitic member of society. At college, at the office or at the factory, a thousand and one problems harass him. Habits of childhood and of adolescence demand correction. A cold, hard, irresponsive, and occasionally hostile physical and social order tax the young person's powers of endurance. Marriage, because of the most intimate character of its relationships, intensifies the difficulties of adjustment. Not all men and women are either temperamentally or physically capable of sharing their lives with others, of sacrificing self-interest and creature comforts for the sake of others; hence the frequent shipwrecks on the matrimonial seas. Social and commercial relations likewise present endless pitfalls to most men and women. Yielding to their instinctual cravings or to their predatory impulses, they become the present day Ishmaels whose hand is against all, and all hands are against them. Victims of social maladjust-

ments, they swell the population of the prisons, hospitals, and insane asylums. The infirmities of the body
further harass all men and torment their minds. Anxiety, fear, disease, worry, frustration form perpetual
threats. Added to these private plagues are wars, tyranny, famine, pestilence and other afflictions which
sweep over communities, nations, and the whole of
humanity. They press hard upon man and demand his
utmost energies.

The problem of adjustment to his environment becomes steadily more bewildering for the modern man
by virtue of the ceaseless changes in the realms of industry, politics and science. No sooner is an equilibrium established between his nervous system and the
normal demands made upon it than new factors arise,
causing a complete shift in the world around him. Our
environment is not only changing but growing ever
more complicated. New inventions steadily alter our
modes of life and of activity. The tools which we have
forged to do our bidding become our masters. We
have grown hopelessly dependent upon steam and
electricity, upon steamship, railroad, automobile, and
airplane transportation, upon the telegraph, telephone
and radio. They have become the arteries of our civilization. When they stop, life itself is at a standstill.
Furthermore, with the advancement of civilization
human needs have multiplied. What were formerly
considered luxuries have become necessities without
which existence seems intolerable. These various devices have made life more attractive and beautiful, but,
by accustoming us to ease and to comfort, they have

taken much of the iron out of our blood. Consequently our amazing triumphs over nature and the increase of our wealth and power have confronted us with new dangers. As was rightly said: "We must wrestle against effeminating luxury, against corrupting materialism, against our own debilitated nervous system, against the vastest doubts which have ever dismayed the minds of men, against the very richness and complexity of the life we have inherited." [57]

Life threatens to become too manifold, too strenuous, "too exacting in its demands, for our weak organisms." The hustle and bustle, the haste and unrest, which mark our existence, assume the nature of a disease. The strain of our Niagara civilization, the feverish rush which attends our activities, the worries and anxieties growing out of the uncertainties and fluctuations of our businesses and professions, of periodic unemployment and social crises bear down heavily upon our physical and mental health. The mounting of nervous disorders, insanity and suicides is symptomatic of the malady which gnaws at the vitals of our high-powered civilization.

It is growing ever more evident that progress in science and technology alone cannot insure the welfare of the individual and of society. What is needed in addition is the growth of the ethical and religious spirit and of increased faith in life's ideal values. Religion appears as a truly redeeming power in human life, an *elixir vitae*, as a biological as well as a social necessity. As an extra dimension of emotion and as a sobering and sanctifying force, it helps man effect a proper adjustment to circumstances, to escape frustration and defeat amid all the turning points and crises of his life, and to crown himself with victory. Amid the noise and confusion of the modern scene, religion concentrates upon the sanctity and worth of personal life and upon the inviolability of the eternal laws of righteousness, goodness and truth.

By enriching his emotions and by purifying his vision, religion endows him with strength to meet the waves of adversity and of failure and to hold his head erect in a manner befitting man. It stimulates him to control his passions, feelings and thoughts by directing them from the lower to the higher plane, from moral defeat to success, and from parasitism to social idealism. By stressing his moral freedom, religion rouses man to war on the tyranny of heredity and environment. It further guards him against the pitfalls that all too often follow success and victory, by ever emphasizing his moral and spiritual endowments and by holding to his attention the added responsibility to society, which power and affluence entail.

FAITH-CULTS. To religion men and women have turned not only for strength in their struggle for existence but also for deliverance from sickness and for increase of health and of life. Out of every form of distress, they have called unto God. In modern times a number of religious movements have been organized for the express purpose of healing the sick, the despondent and the forlorn. Most prominent among these are New Thought and Christian Science—both of which stem from the New England mind-curist, Phineas Parkhurst Quimby [58]—and the Unity School of Christianity, based partly on the teachings of the other two and organized in the form of a correspondence school. The Jewish variety of the movement represents an adaptation of its workings to Judaism and is known as "Jewish Science." Their all-absorbing object is therapeutic, to the exclusion of philanthropy and social betterment. Since its founding, New Thought has shifted its emphasis somewhat from health to wealth, promising the disabled and the disinherited power, prosperity and harmony.[59]

Though their theologies vary considerably from one another, a measure of agreement is detectable in their teachings. They all operate with the beliefs in (1) the efficacy of prayer, in (2) the effect of the spiritual state of mind upon the body, in (3) physical health following upon religious exercises, and in (4) the cure of all ailments through faith and—as in the case of Christian Science—without medical or surgical treatment. They are predicated upon metaphysical theories of being, ranging from absolute Idealism to materialistic Pantheism.

Christian Science, for example, combines Berkeleyan Idealism, which denies the reality of matter, with Emersonian Transcendentalism, which exalts the spiritual above the physical, and stresses the self-sufficiency of the individual. The combination is flavored with Hindu teaching regarding the illusory character of sense perception, and with the doctrine, which we noted above, of evil as negative. The whole is based upon a mystical Christology.

Its creed is summed up in the following syllogism:

> God is all-in-all.
> God is good. Good is mind.
> God, Spirit, being all, nothing is matter.
> Life, God, omnipotent good, deny death,
>    evil, sin, disease.
> Disease, sin, death, deny God, omnipotent
>    good, Life.[60]

Being good, God cannot be responsible for the shadowy side of existence.

Cloaked in different metaphysical terms, the principle of Christian Science is expressed in a formula which runs in a circle:

"There is no life, truth, intelligence or substance in matter. All is infinite mind and its infinite manifestations, for God is all-in-all. Spirit is immortal truth; matter is mortal error. Spirit is real and eternal; matter is unreal and temporal. Spirit is God and man His image and likeness. Therefore man is not material; he is spiritual." [61] He belongs to an order which is free from pain, sin, sorrow, and death. Disease has power to kill only as mortal mind thinks it has. Thought that is not subordinated to the Christian Science principle can be extremely dangerous. It is mortal error. In this system ideas take the place of germs and bacilli as causes of sickness and of death. In her Preface to *Science and Health*, Mrs. Eddy writes: "The physical healing of Christian Science results now, as in Jesus' time, from the operation of divine Principle, before which sin disease lose their reality in human consciousness and disappear as naturally and as necessarily as darkness gives place to light, and sin to reformation." Being a mental error, disease disappears with the introduction of spiritual truth into the thought of the person. Deny it and it ceases to exist.

A spokesman of New Thought writes similarly: "The many inflammatory diseases that come from poor circulation and poisoned blood are simply the expression of inflamed mental conditions." [62] He distinguishes between the philosophies of healing of New Thought and Christian Science. Both agree "that all life is one; that God is all-in-all; that all intelligence is one. And they disagree on the following points: Christian Science says the visible world is mortal mind; the New Thought declares the universe to be an expression of God's work. Christian Science asserts sin, sickness and death have no existence. The New Thought affirms that they have an existence; but that their existence is only limited and their destruction comes through right thinking and hence right living." [63]

These "buoyant philosophies," it will be noted, derive much of their strength from the American ideal of "getting on" and from the popular confidence in applied psychology. Indeed the strongest ingredient in the recipes of the faith-cures is what James called "healthy-mindedness" as exhibited in the "belief in *the all-saving power of healthy-minded attitudes as such*, in the conquering efficacy of courage, hope, and trust, and a correlative contempt for doubt, fear, worry, and all nervously precautionary states of mind." [64] A morbid thought or emotion is depressing, whereas a cheerful idea or feeling increases vitality. "Every psychical event," we are informed, "is attended by a corresponding nervous event. Joy, happiness, a sense of well-being, are invariably healthful and health-bringing. Grief, pain, anger, and anxiety have also their concomitants in the brain and nervous system and these are injurious or destructive in character." [65] (In passing we may note that Epictetus taught likewise that things do not hurt us, but only our opinion of them. Our false ideas represent the root of our suffering. Hence we must repudiate feeling.)

The faith-cults have been attacked by both rationalists and religionists. They have been ridiculed for their abstruse Bible exegesis, for their theological and philosophical vagaries and for their backwardness in their methods of therapy. Christian Science has been assailed as a misnomer, being neither Christian nor scientific. These criticisms notwithstanding, the faith-cults have continued to spread. They make a strong appeal to large numbers of men and women. Despite the incongruities, inconsistencies and absurdities of their teachings and practice, they have answered a deep-felt need which neither the existing religions nor medical systems have known how to supply. They offer a type of salvation that appeals to suffering men and responds to the will to be well.

Indeed, the faith or mind-cults have been explained as a reaction against the "religion of chronic anxiety," which characterized the evangelical confessions of England and America in the early part of the nine-teenth century, as well as against the materialistic school of medicine, which persistently refused to rec-ognize any facts other than those of measurable and visible matter. Sigmund Freud's psychoanalysis repre-sents a similar protest against the refusal on the part of the regnant schools of medicine to recognize psy-chic causes of disease. As a medical practitioner, he found further "that not only actual shocking experi-ence which had been repressed, but fantasies also, could cause mental illness." The faith-cults further owe their existence and remarkable spread to the in-stinctive fear of the surgeon's knife and medical thera-peutics in general, as well as to the quackery that gnaws at the roots of the medical as of other profes-sions. In the case of Christian Science, its rapid spread is in no small measure traceable to a remarkable sense of organization, to the enlistment of women among its healers, and to the resolute effort to translate religion into a personal dynamic of faith and love. The rise of the Jewish brand is due partly to the same fear of medicine and partly to mimicry of or as antidote to Christian Science. In part at least, it came as a protest against the rationalism that prevails in Jewish pulpits and congregations, and which reduces religion to group loyalty, good-fellowship, civic idealism and social service. Its declared aim is "to intensify the spiritual consciousness of the Jew and reveal to him the resources for health and serenity and peace of mind that are found within his own faith." [66]

These cults have doubtless relieved the minds of sufferers from ailments both imaginary and real. Dr. H. H. Goddard testifies that faith-cures take place, but that they are in no respect different from those which are now recognized in medicine as cures by suggestion. On the basis of his investigation, Dr. Goddard concludes that "the proper reform in mental attitude would relieve many a sufferer of ills which the ordinary physician cannot touch; would even delay the approach of death to many a victim beyond the power of absolute cure, and the faithful adherence to a truer philosophy of life will keep many a man well, and give the doctor time to devote to alleviating ills that are unpreventable." He further declares that "Religion has in it all there is in mental therapeutics, and has it in the best form. Living up to [our religious] ideas will do anything for us that can be done." [67]

NOTE ON PSYCHOTHERAPY. Faith-cures are in no sense the exclusive property of a particular cult nor are they something new. Judging by the close connection, which has existed in the human mind between magic, medicine and religion, psychotherapy may be considered not only as the earliest form of the healing art but also as the most persistent. The priests of early religions acted as physicians. Almost every religion boasts of shrines, relics or saints who cured the sick. The cults of Aesculapius in Greece, of Isis in Egypt, of Christianity during the first fifteen centuries of its existence as well as the renascent faith-cults of today testify to the therapeutic claims of religion.[68] "The spirit of man sustains his infirmity" (Prov. 18:14).

They illustrate that in therapy the faith of the sufferers and those around them forms a contributing factor. Sometimes it acts directly without the mediacy of any medicaments whatever. Frequently medicines are employed but they are merely means of psychotherapy. W. H. R. Rivers points to the continuing process in the history of pharmacology in which medicaments owe their reputation for efficacy to nothing but faith and suggestion.[69] The wonderful results sometimes secured through *aqua distillata* and bread-pills are apparently due to faith in their efficacy and to the confidence in the physician who prescribes them. He claims further that, contrary to the general impression, psychotherapy is useful not only in cases of hysteria and kindred diseases but in every other type of ailment as well, whether functional or organic. In his opinion the scope of psychotherapy is as wide as medicine itself, though it is especially applicable in neuroses.

Psychotherapy is based upon the faith in (1) super-human powers or the Supreme Being, as healing the sick either directly or through natural means, and upon faith in (2) human agents, whether medicine men, physicians, or priests; and it operates through the power of suggestion. The term "suggestion" through the commercialization of applied psychology has been reduced, in the popular mind, to the level of quackery or to a magician's formula, which works on susceptible minds. What we understand by the much-abused term is the influence exerted by the mind upon feeling, thought and behavior. This influence may be stimulated from the outside or may be generated from within as autosuggestion. (Hypnotism is but suggestion in its strongest form.) Its operations are continual within the region of the subconscious, storing up impulses to act, inhibitions to conduct and obsessive notions. Thus quite unconsciously the suggestive influence of religion may manifest itself within us and create a sense of confidence and security which is essential to the victorious life and to physical welfare.

Faith and suggestion, though frequently identified, are poles apart psychologically. Whereas in suggestion the essential feature is passive receptiveness, faith denotes a process of active striving. However, they are often combined, faith producing its effects through suggestion. They are generally helpful where the mind of the patient is intact and where the mental disorder shows itself by some physical manifestation. When the mind itself is injured, the tension and anxiety, grief or other disturbed emotional state can be relieved by resorting to the additional agency of *catharsis*, whether in the form of religious confession or of a medical procedure. Even when the sufferer has nothing with which to reproach himself, his communication with others produces a sense of relief.

An important element in confession and in the revival of past memories is the patient's coming to know himself better. Much suffering results from mistaken notions of one's state of health in general and of mental stress in particular. *Autognosis* or self-knowledge thus becomes a therapeutic agency of the first order. It occasionally helps to remove misapprehensions of neurasthenics and melancholiacs regarding their moral and spiritual condition and thereby lifts a crushing burden of sin whether real or imaginary. The sufferer is helped by being shown the way the disorders developed. The natural history of the case tends to remove the exaggerated fears in his mind. Psychoanalysis seeks to discover the complex, or body of forgotten experience, which is believed to underlie the abnormal state. The endeavor is, therefore, made to recall to memory past experiences which may have completely faded out of consciousness.

Rivers writes: "Of the agencies common to the work of physician, priest and teacher, none is more important than that to which the name *sublimation* has been given. The process of autognosis often shows the presence of some faulty trend of thought and action which is capable of being turned into a more healthy channel. Many nervous and mental disorders depend, at any rate in part, on tendencies which are altogether

anti-social, or, while suitable to one kind of civilization, are out of place in the society into which the
sufferer has been born. In such a case sublimation furnishes an alternative to satisfaction or repression."

In the process of sublimation religion may render
great service. The sentiments and emotions, which
form the psychological basis of religion, often can be
substituted for those associated with morbid energies
and anti-social trends. By virtue of its union with
morality, religion may satisfy practical as well as emotional needs.

The agency of reason seems to be limited in psychotherapy. It is often useless to argue with sufferers from
mental disorders. Reasoning may be helpful when used
to reinforce processes of other kinds, which operate
through emotional and instinctive channels. It also
forms an important element in autognosis. "Once the
true emotional cause of a morbid state has been discovered and explained to the patient, the exercise of
his own reason comes to form an essential element in
his amendment or recovery." [70]

The effectiveness of moral and religious teachings
in the restoration of health depends upon the firmness
with which they are held. The cures, which are often
reported by the adherents of Catholicism, Christian
Science and other therapeutic cults, are based upon the
faith state of the mind. Where men are prevented by
training or temperament from giving the necessary
mental assent to the claims and suggestions of the
faith, no cures follow. The ordinary practice of the
religious life, by strengthening man's hope and cour-

age, exerts a healthful effect upon his physical and mental condition. The more intense religious forms of sacrifice, devout worship, confession, atonement, etc., by placing the worshipper in a receptive relation to God, possess great psychotherapeutic value. They remove the tension produced by the sense of guilt and bring the penitent relief. Elwood Worcester writes: "I have never ceased to be surprised at witnessing marked physical improvements which have followed the release of the soul from anxiety, fear, a sense of inferiority and condemnation, or as the result of a new and more serene spiritual life." [71]

Dr. Bernard Glueck, discussing "The Clinical Significance of Religion," refers to a statement by an eminent psychiatrist "that of all the people that he sees in his office consulting him about all sorts of troubles of the mind and soul and spirit, the ones who are conspicuous by their absence are those who have somehow achieved a practical Christianity."

To this he adds: "My practice, while not exclusively a Jewish practice, gives me occasion to see many Jews in difficulties, and I could say the same thing, that I seldom see a patient coming into my office who has achieved that unity with himself and with his fellow men and with the world about him, which somehow I conceive to be a characteristic of the religious state. And as a psychiatrist, with considerable experience in various phases of human maladjustment from the most profound to the slightest, as we see them just beginning in children, I am frequently impressed with a feeling that somehow these patients have missed in their lives something that religion might have given them, and something which might have worked very consistently in preventing the maladjustment." [72]

DANGER OF FAITH-CURES. Though psychotherapy renders immense service to health, it turns into a source of danger when set up as the exclusive mode of treating all ailments whether organic or functional. In the metaphysical foundations of the faith-cults, notably in Christian Science, there lurks a fatal sophism, which forms the root of the practical danger to health. It consists in the confusion of *phenomena* with *the thing in itself*, or of experience with its transcendent ground. In excessive subjectivism, states of consciousness are substituted for objective reality. Maintaining the mystic position, Christian Science, as we have pointed out, teaches that an experience of evil is an experience of unreality, and, therefore, an illusion, a dream, a deceit. Such a comment upon life is itself deceptive. As Josiah Royce remarks: "If evil is merely called finite error, this finite error remains, nonetheless, as a fact of human experience. One has only changed the name. The reality remains what it was." [73] Within limits it is true, as the proverb states, that "as a man thinketh in his heart so is he" (Prov. 23:7). It does not follow that as a man thinks so is the world around him. Experience gives no warrant for such belief. In knowledge itself, as distinguished from illusion and imagination, we must reckon with perception as well as with apperception. The denial of the data of perception, because we disapprove of them, does not improve the state of things. The refusal to trade with the enemy or to recognize his existence solves neither political nor physical difficulties.

The method of curing disease by refusing to recognize its existence is strikingly illustrated by the story which Lord Macaulay tells of his experience with a Buddhist priest: An English commission of physicians and scientists came to study the cholera germs which infested Buddha's sacred river, the Ganges, and which were spread by the pilgrims that came to bathe in and to drink the fetid water, east toward China and west toward Europe. To convince the priest, the scientists put a drop of water under a microscope and showed him the death germs. Lifting his eyes from the instrument, the proud priest said to Macaulay: "I can destroy the disease," and demonstrated his claim by smashing the microscope on the marble floor. The faith-cults assume similarly that by destroying the knowledge of evil they annihilate its dread effects.

Viewing disease as purely imaginary and as a mere error of the mortal mind, the practitioners of the various faith-cults disregard the physical and mental examination of the sufferer which often results in grave consequences. Dr. Coriat observes that what surgery was in the hands of the barbers of the Middle Ages, psychotherapy is today in the hands of the mind-curists. "Their errors fill our hospitals and clinics and add to the number of obituary notices. We only hear of the few successes; of their many mistakes they preserve a wise silence." [74] Life is sacrificed to a dogmatic formula.

James, after extolling the genuineness of the faith-cures, analyzes the "sick soul" and the "grisly blood-freezing heart-palsying sensation" of evil, and warns that "the method of averting one's attention from evil, and living simply in the light of good . . . breaks down impotently as soon as melancholy comes; and even though one be quite free from melancholy one's self, there is no doubt that healthy-mindedness is inadequate as a philosophical doctrine, because the evil facts which it refuses positively to account for are a genuine portion of reality; and they may after all be the best key to life's significance, and possibly the only openers of our eyes to the deepest levels of truth.

"The normal process of life contains moments as bad as any of those which insane melancholy is filled with, moments in which radical evil gets its innings and takes its solid turn. The lunatic's visions of horror are all drawn from the material of daily fact. Our civilization is founded on the shambles, and every individual existence goes out in a lonely spasm of helpless agony. If you protest, my friend, wait till you arrive there yourself!" [75]

The power of faith and suggestion has its limits. Not all emotions are voluntary, and hence cannot be effectively checked by one's own thinking. Some of them are "symptoms of a more general disease in which body and soul suffer together." [76] Not all sicknesses are due to faulty states of mind. Many of them definitely come from physical disorders, whether internal or external, over which the mind has little if any control. Accordingly while recognizing the value of healthy mental states, we must not expect the mind to accomplish things which seem more properly within the province of physical instrumentalities. In this realm scientific medicine and surgery are rendering great service and can be ignored only at one's own peril.

The faith-cults not only endanger health but religion as well. The wisdom of overemphasizing therapy and making it their primary concern is open to question. Physical welfare is thus made the supreme test of religion, thereby narrowing its interests to the pathological and the neurotic. The value of religion comes to be measured in terms of cures and well-being. And conversely its worth sinks with the failure of securing physical relief. Tyler records the case of a Chinese who had paid the idol-priest to cure his daughter, but she died. Thereupon the swindled worshipper brought suit against the god, and succeeded in banishing him for fraud.[77] As decay and mortality are the portion of all men, religions which ignore these facts and undertake to secure for their followers unimpaired health are destined to abject failure. Furthermore, as William Brown points out, they appeal to superficial emotion and to primitive credulity, and tend to intensify that hysterical or infantile condition of mind from which many of the neurotic patients are already suffering. In some cases there may be a disappearance of hysterical symptoms and apparent cure, but only at the expense of replacement by another symptom—namely, reliance upon quasi-miraculous possibility, the expectation of getting something for nothing, as it were, of getting direct gifts without full appreciation of corresponding

demands upon personality. Mass-suggestion may produce startling results of a temporary and superficial
kind, but individual treatment is more likely to produce deep and lasting benefit.[78]

JUDAISM AND MEDICINE. Concluding our discussion of
faith-cures, let us consider the relation of Judaism to
medicine. We noted that Judaism derives its optimistic
view not from shutting its eyes to evil in all its forms
but rather from the conviction that it can be overcome. As a colaborer with God in the creative task of
bringing order out of chaos and of endowing existence
with meaning and with value, it is man's object to
exterminate the weeds from the garden of life, to
harness his intelligence, skill and adventuresome spirit
to the removal of the obstacles that block the road to
his physical and mental health and to his full self-
realization as a moral and spiritual being. To recognize
evil as a tragic fact is essential to the effort to alleviate
it. Not to ignore disease or to dismiss it as mortal error,
but to mobilize all the resources of human knowledge
in order to resist its ravages, is the religious duty of
man. Human welfare can best be promoted by advancing the science of medicine, by improving the instruments, the methods and the institutions of healing, and
by increasing the knowledge and the general conditions of hygiene. To further the material as well as the
spiritual means for the improvement and enrichment
of life ever constituted the goal of Judaism.

At no time in its history has Judaism demanded that
the art of healing be limited to a procedure that may

be described as faith-cure. Neither did it concentrate the healing art exclusively in the hands of the priests, who inspected skin diseases and kindred disorders; * other healers are referred to in the pages of the Bible. Elijah and Elisha engaged in healing the sick through the agency of the miraculous. Isaiah, in more natural manner, prescribed a poultice for the sick King Hezekiah (Is. 38:21). Jeremiah evidently entertained a high regard for medicine when he exclaimed: "Is there no balm in Gilead? Is there no physician there? Why then is not the health of the daughter of my people recovered?" (13:22.) To be sure, the voice of opposition to secular medicine did not fail to be raised among the Jews as well as elsewhere. The priestly Chronicler censures King Asa, who suffered from foot disease, "yet in his disease he sought not to the Lord, but to the physicians" (II Chron. 16:12). In the main, however, while resorting to prayer in illness as in health, the Jewish people did not reject physical aids to health. The Temple had a special health officer.[79] The rabbis believed strongly in the efficacy of prayer in sickness. A number of saintly men, like Honi Hameagel and Hanina b. Dosa, were believed to have wrought miracles by their petitions. At the same time use was made of whatever medical knowledge was available.

---

* Ezekiel Kaufman maintains that the priests only offered sacrifices for lepers, etc., but did not engage in healing. The healers were the "men of God," like Moses (Num. 12:10–13; 21:8–9); Elisha (II Kings 5:1–14); Isaiah (20:7; 38:21). *Toledot Haemunah Hayisreelit*, I, 551. Sickness is not caused by demons, but by God Himself. (Lev. 26:16; Deut. 28:22, etc.)

Some of the leading representatives of Judaism in the Middle Ages distinguished themselves also as physicians. The vast contribution of the Jews to medicine, surgery and pharmacology testifies to the high regard in which the ministry of health was held by Judaism.[80] Even Jewish practical mysticism, as represented by Hasidism, made no vain escape from evil and disease by the short cut of identifying them with unreality and error. Though the wonder-working Tzaddikim resorted to exorcism of malignant spirits and to magical procedure as well as to mental healing, they neither denied the phenomenal reality of disease nor hesitated to recommend the consultation of physicians and surgeons.

While invoking God as the "Faithful Physician" and as the source of all blessings, the Jewish people have been taught to look for His aid to come through human as through natural agencies. Ben Sira counsels:

Cultivate the physician in accordance with the
    need of him.[81]
For him also God ordained.
It is from God that the physician getteth wisdom. . . .
God hath created medicines out of the earth,
And let not a discerning man reject them. . . .
My son, in sickness be not negligent;
Pray unto God, for He can heal.
(Turn) from iniquity, and purify thy hands; . . .
Give a meal-offering with a memorial,
And offer a fat sacrifice to the utmost of thy means.
And to the physician also give a place. . . .
For there is a time when successful help is in his power;
For he also maketh supplication to God,

To make his diagnosis successful,
And the treatment that it may promote recovery.

—38:1ff.

Ben Sira's attitude still reflects the old notion of sickness as a direct manifestation of God's retributive justice as expressed in Exodus 15:26. Hence the emphasis on the need of proper atonement as a first step to healing, and the concluding statement: "He that sinneth before his Maker shall be delivered into the hands of the physician" (v. 15). Popular Jewish belief retains this notion to the present day, as evidenced by the gifts of charity which are dispensed on behalf of the sick or by the sick themselves. However, since Job's searching critique of the popular conception of suffering, there always has been some reluctance to consider all sickness as the result of misbehavior or sin, although in many instances this may be the case. If, then, in sickness as in health, God's help is invoked, while utilizing all the aid of human skill, it is because of the conviction that to a considerable—though not exclusive—degree the right mental attitude contributes to physical well-being.

The attitude of Judaism to medicine is strikingly expressed in the following story, recorded in the late Midrash Temurah, in connection with the words of Ps. 103:15: "Man's days are as grass." "R. Ishmael and R. Akiba were walking through the streets of Jerusalem, and a certain man accompanied them. They were met by a sick person, who appealed to them: 'My masters, advise me wherewith to be cured.' As they prescribed for him, their companion asked: 'And

who smote him?' To which they replied: 'God.'
'Then, why do you interfere in something that is not
your affair? He smote and you cure! Are you not
transgressing His will?' In reply, the Rabbis asked him:
'What is your occupation?' 'A farmer,' he answered,
'as you see from the sickle in my hands.' 'And who
created the soil?' they asked. 'God,' was his reply.
'And you interfere in something that is not your
affair?' they demanded. 'He created it and you cut its
fruit!' 'If I did not go out to plow, hoe, fertilize, and
weed the soil, it would not yield anything.' The Rabbis
said: 'Most foolish man, from your work do you not
understand the saying of the Scripture, "man's days are
as grass"? Even as the plant, if not weeded, fertilized
and plowed, does not grow, and if it begins to grow
and is not properly watered and cared for, cannot
thrive and withers, so is the body of man. The ferti-
lizer is the medicine and the husbandman is the physician.' " [82] They in nowise conflict with God's provi-
dential care of man. The rabbis further maintain that a
city without a bath-house, physician and bloodletter
is not fit for a scholar to live in. [83] Rab Aha teaches that
on being cupped one should pray: "May it be Thy
will, O Lord, my God, that this action may serve me
as healing, and mayest Thou heal me, for Thou art a
faithful healer and Thy healing is certain for it is not
the way of human beings to cure, but this is their
custom." *

* Ber. 60a. See "The Physician's Prayer" in the *Selected Poems
of Judah Halevi*, ed. Brody-Salamon, p. 113. The "Physician's
Prayer" ascribed to Maimonides is in reality the creation of

The official view of Judaism on medicine is summarized in the *Tur Yore Deah*, §336: "The School of
R. Ishmael derived from the words *Verappe yerappe*
('and the offender shall cause the victim to be thoroughly healed,' Ex. 21:19) that permission is granted
the physician to heal. The physician may not say
'Why borrow trouble? I may err and appear like one
who killed a person unwittingly.' He shall indeed be
exceedingly careful in exercising his art even as a
judge must be careful in deciding criminal cases. In
like manner, the physician may not say: 'God smites,
and shall I heal?' This is not the way of men with regard to healing, as we find Asa in his sickness consulting not God, but physicians. Hence Scripture came to
teach us that the physician is permitted to heal. Indeed,
healing is a duty; it is saving life. He who is zealous
in the work of healing is praiseworthy; and he who
refuses to heal is a shedder of blood." *

Repeated in the *Shulhan Aruch*, this represents the
law of traditional Judaism. The *Kitzur Shulhan Aruch*

Marcus Hertz. See G. Deutsch, *Jew and Gentile*, 1920, pp.
93–95. Sifre Deut., 247 refers to Hilchot Rofeim from which
laws are derived. See also Sefer Noah in Yellinek's *Beth
Hamidrash*, III, 155–6; Eisenstein, *Otzar Midrashim*, pp. 401 f.

* On the other hand, Hezekiah's act of hiding the Book of
Medicines was accounted praiseworthy because that made
the people turn to God for help (Ber. 10b). The same reason
underlies the saying: "The best of physicians is destined for
Gehinnom" (Kid. 82a). Rashi comments that relying upon his
knowledge he is not afraid of sickness and shows no contrition
before God. In addition he occasionally causes the death of
his patients, and denies healing to the poor who cannot pay
him for his services. See Friedenwald, *op. cit.*, I, pp. 11–13.

places the responsibility upon the patient. In time of sickness it becomes a religious duty to consult a physician. The neglect of calling for medical aid constitutes an act of presumption on the part of the sufferer, for he seems to presume such righteousness as to merit the direct miraculous help of God.[84] It is instructive that medical means for checking pestilence were not regarded by the masters of Judaism as interference with the will of God. While teaching man to submit to the inevitable, they urged him to resist the things that blight life and to promote human health and welfare.

As to the use of magical aid to health opinions differed. Authorities like Rabbi Abahu, Abaye and Raba held that whatever has medicinal value cannot be prohibited as magical practice.[85] Others were opposed to such practice. R. Joshua ben Levi, for example, prohibited the use of words of the Torah for purposes of healing. Maimonides condemns the employment of Scriptural texts, Torah scrolls and *tephillin* for healing purposes. He classes those who engage in such practices not only with sorcerers and magicians but also with heretics, for "they turn the words of the Torah into means of healing the body whereas they are intended to serve as means of healing the spirit, as it is said, 'They shall be life unto thy soul'" (Prov. 3:22). At the same time he permits whispering a charm in case of snake bite, even on the Sabbath, despite the worthlessness of the procedure, in order to relieve the patient's mind.* [86]

* It is instructive that the ban which the Anti-Maimunists issued against the study of science and philosophy by men

In either view, Judaism is not a system of medicine but a *torat haadam*—a law for the whole man. While it has certain therapeutic value for the sick and suffering, it is not confined to healing. Its concern is with the enrichment and sanctification of life and with the establishment of society upon the foundations of righteousness. It is not an art of healing but an art of living for the sound and healthy as well as for the ailing. It is the agency of personal and of social morality.

under twenty-five years of age specifically excluded medicine on the ground that it was permitted by the Torah. (First Letter by Solomon of Montpellier, Kahana, *Sifrut Hahistoria*, I, 258.)

# THE
# ETHICAL LIFE

# IX. RELIGION AND ETHICS

THE ETHICAL AND THE RELIGIOUS LIFE. Morality and religion may have grown out of different roots in the human psyche, but in the course of their development they have grown closely together. The Kantians, rejecting the ideas of their distinct origin, derive the religious from the moral. In M. Arnold's phrase, religion is "morality tinged with emotion." Even those who construe religion as the fruitage of a distinct consciousness of the holy fully recognize the prominence of the moral in the texture of every religion.

Judaism links the two into an indissoluble union in its character of ethical monotheism. As with religion in general so with Judaism opinions differ as to which of the two elements is primary. The followers of Kant, like the older rationalists, have taken ethics to be the soul of Judaism. "Sanctification is moralization"—so runs the fundamental thesis of M. Lazarus' work, *The Ethics of Judaism*.[87] Religion is identified with morality in the philosophy of Hermann Cohen. Leo Baeck finds the principle, essence and nature of Judaism in ethics. For Edmond Fleg "religion in its deepest essence is conscience, the morality of the soul that takes man to ever higher planes in the pyramid of all things living." Others uphold the contrary position that the religious element is the root of the moral in Judaism. This view goes back to ancient reflections on Judaism, and may be read in the pages of Josephus. Rejecting, as J. Montgomery puts it, "the Hellenizing

temptation to regard religion as an ethic or a handmaid
to the ethical, he stoutly insists that the excellence of
Judaism lies in this, that religion in that system is prior
and superior to ethics." In his polemic against Apion
he writes: "Moses did not make religion a department
of virtue, but the various virtues—I mean justice,
temperance, fortitude, and mutual harmony between
the members of the community—departments of religion. Religion governs all our actions and occupations
and speech; none of these things did our lawgiver
leave unexamined or indeterminate." [88] The masters
of the Synagogue, who refused to reduce the commandments of the Torah to mere rules of reason,
shared the same viewpoint. Historical analysis supports
their position. Judaism did not derive its religious
sanctions from morality, but rather based the laws of
morality upon the authority of religion.

Dr. K. Kohler, while announcing that "the basis of
Judaism is Jewish ethics," proceeds to demonstrate the
contrary, that the basis of Jewish ethics is Judaism.
"Cut loose from religion, ethics is but a broken cistern
that holds no water. However delicious the fruit, you
cannot make it grow without stem and blade. Call
your conscience a magnetic needle in the direction of
the right and the good, but forget not that without
some great magnetic power around and above, no
needle will work." [89]

While from the purely ethical side Judaism may be
treated as a moral tradition, its essential nature transcends morality. In its descriptive formula of "ethical
monotheism" the noun forms the ground for the adjec-

tive. *Judaism is the living faith of the Jewish people and its consecration to the Holy One.* "Historically," G. F. Moore well observes, "the epithet [Holy] was not applied to God because He was conceived to be morally perfect, but the meaning of moral perfection attached to the word because such perfection belonged to the character of the Holy One [i.e., of God]." [90] Judaism is not a mere *code of conduct* but a code of conduct conditioned by the *creed* and *cult* of the *Jewish community*.

Philo properly classed the teachings of Judaism into those which regulate man's conduct toward God by means of piety and holiness, and man's conduct toward his fellow men by the rules of humanity and justice. [91] The rabbis, too, distinguished between the obligations of man's relation to God and of man to his fellow men. [92] As in the Decalogue so in the rest of the Torah the duties of man to man are consequent upon the duties which he owes to God. The first five commandments were viewed as the exact parallel of the other five. [93] In post-Talmudic writings the commands of the Torah are often grouped into (1) rational or ethical, and (2) traditional or ceremonial.

Morality is neither the whole of religion nor something distinct from religion. It is an integral part of the way in which religion translates itself into life and character. God is worshipped when moral duties are discharged faithfully. Psalms 15 and 24 present ethical behavior as the condition of communion with God. The Mekilta cites the comment of R. Eleazar of Modiim on Ex. 14:26, "and wilt do that which is right

in His eyes," as consisting of honesty in business relations. "He who transacts his business honestly and is
pleasing to his fellow men is accounted as having fulfilled the entire Torah." [94] Morality becomes a form
of worship, but not the whole of it. By the side of
"doing justly and loving mercy," the prophet emphasizes "walking humbly with God" in his program of
the religious life. To the fulfillment of moral duties
must be added devotion, reverence, faith, knowledge
and conviction. Love of God with all the heart and
soul and might and love of one's fellow men must be
combined. Ethics forms neither a substitute for nor an
addition to, but a phase of the religious life.

The moral and the religious are two inseparable
aspects of the spiritual life. As in Stoicism, obedience
to the law of Nature or reason, so in Judaism, obedience to the will of God constitutes the highest good.
God, the rabbis say, entrusted Israel with the Torah
as a manifestation of His goodness. Its moral and
ceremonial commands alike express His will. Though
some of them seem inexplicable, obeying them is
virtue.

NATURE OF JEWISH ETHICS. Though the terms *morality*
and *ethics* often figure as synonyms, a difference between them may be discerned. Morality, true to its
Latin derivation, stresses practice, while ethics, retaining its Greek flavor, is theoretical. Ethics is the analysis, reflection, and judgment of the principles, standards and goals of morality. Hence it ranks variously as
a normative science and as a philosophy. It starts with

human nature, the springs of human conduct, and the sphere of their operation, and seeks to discover the ends which man has set for himself, for his group or nation, and for humanity. In its application to life, ethics like religion assumes the nature of an art. In its study of human character and the ways in which it may be directed toward the attainment of its goals, ethics takes into consideration not only the facts of biology, psychology, economics, and politics, but also of religion and philosophy. Man's beliefs regarding himself and the universe enter into the shaping of his conceptions of the supreme good. An ethical system has for its basis a considered metaphysic of life and reality.

Jewish ethics starts with the principles of Judaism, i.e., with the monotheistic view of the world and of life, with Torah and with Israel, and with man as a free and responsible agent. It does not rule out other systems of ethics, predicated upon other religious and even non-religious conceptions. In the measure in which they humanize man they serve a high end. However they lack the transforming quality which derives from religious sanction, from being related to the all-encompassing spiritual reality. The relation of religion to ethics is that of motive power to action, of faith to performance, of consecration and promise to endeavor. Religion as shown above, integrates, strengthens and purifies the spirit, and thereby prepares it for the ascent to higher planes of conduct. It brings man a courage, a determination, a devotion to duty, a seriousness, zeal and joy, and a radiant hope in the face of insurmountable difficulties and dangers which he is unable to get from purely scientific analyses of naturalistic and utilitarian considerations and behavior patterns. An old moralist writes:

"Whoever desires to acquire moral qualities must blend fear of God with every virtue, for the fear of God is the bond which unites the virtues. It is like a string passed through the holes of the pearls and tied into a knot to hold them together. No doubt that by loosening the knot, the pearls fall apart. Even so the fear of God links all virtues. When it is loosened the virtues disintegrate. Lacking the virtues you can have neither Torah nor Mitzvot, for the entire Torah depends upon the perfection of man's moral qualities." [95]

The ethics of Judaism did not become a subject for reflective thought until the Jewish masters of Alexandria came into contact with Greek speculations on this subject. Even then it did not form an independent field for research, but continued to be a branch of religion. The authors of the *Letter of Aristeas, Wisdom of Solomon,* and the *Fourth Book of Maccabees,* and the most distinguished representative of the Hellenistic school, Philo, did not construct independent systems of ethics. With the aid of Greek methods and technical terms, they undertook to demonstrate that the moral teachings of the Torah are in perfect harmony with the highest conceptions of philosophy. The same apologetic method actuated the labors of the Jewish thinkers of the Middle Ages. They had the advantage of basing their work upon the Oral as upon the Written Torah. Consequently their writings appear more indigenously Jewish, and their classifications and analyses of moral principles more systematic. This may be observed in Saadia's tenth chapter of the *Emunot Vedeot*, Bahia's *Hobot Halebabot*, Gabirol's *Tikkun Middot Hanefesh*, Maimonides' *Hilchot Deot* and *Shemone Perakim*, etc.

The non-philosophical ethical teachings show even more directly their dependence upon religion. In the Bible the moral elements are embodied in the historical narratives, in the law, in prophecy, in the Psalms, and in the Wisdom literature. In the presentation of the events of history and of the character of Israel's heroes and in direct precepts, they set forth the way of life demanded by Judaism. While the Wisdom books base their aphorisms upon observation of experience, the Torah and the prophets announce their doctrines as Divine commands. The book of Ben Sira, the tractates *Abot, Abot of Rabbi Nathan*, and *Derech Eretz Zutta*, and other portions of Talmudic Haggadah and Midrashim merely combine human reflections on moral conduct with the teachings derived from the Torah. While the Haggadah is marked more by its poetic qualities than by ordered thought, attempts at the organization of its teachings are in evidence. Some of the Midrashim represent fairly coordinated homilies on moral and religious questions. The principles of Scriptural interpretation, frequently employed to establish doctrine, display considerable ingenuity.

The Halachah as the authoritative guide of Jewish life is more practical than the Haggadah in its definition of human duty and obligation. It ever deals with the concrete rather than with the general. Rooted in the Torah, it flowered as an ethic of the finest type. It seeks to translate into practice the ethical and spiritual aspirations of Judaism. Whether it deals with criminal, civil, matrimonial or ritual law, the ethical element is always in the foreground.[96]

The *Musar* literature of the Middle Ages, whether in the form of ethical wills or in special works, like the *Sefer Hasidim, Orhot Tzaddikim, Menorat Hamaor, Reshit Hochmah,* etc., follows the earlier models. Haggadah and Halachah are combined and sometimes flavored with philosophical and mystical conceptions, and enriched with profound observations regarding human virtue and frailty. The varied customs of the Jewish people, the glories and tragedies of the Jewish past were employed as means of inculcating moral ideals. As the name indicates, *Musar,* which literally means "chastisement," moral discipline, or correction, seeks to train and to fashion man into a moral and religious personality. Perfection of character is its chief concern. The term was used in the Bible and in rabbinic literature in the sense of moral instruction, and came to apply to the whole of ethics. For ethics as a science or philosophy there is no corresponding term in Hebrew. Sometimes the combination *Torat Hamusar* or *Torat Hamiddot* is used in this sense. Modern Hebrew took over the term *Ethica.*

JEWISH ETHICS AND THE ETHICS OF JUDAISM. Jewish ethics may more properly be termed the ethics of Judaism. It is the science and art of conduct of a religion rather than of a racial or national group. The moral obligations of the Torah are conceived as commands of God—Mitzvot, which a man must fulfill in obedience to His will.[97] The Halachah, deriving its authority from its connection with the Written Law, presents itself as religiously binding. Its observance betokens obedience. Hence Rabbi Hanina teaches: "Greater is he who is commanded and does than he who acts without being commanded."[98] Other masters stress the dependence of the Torah upon the heart. Jeremiah's ideal of the Torah is that it shall not remain an external code but be inscribed upon the hearts of men (Jer. 30:31–34). Though the law is given to man, it gains no control over him until he voluntarily accepts its rule. "Since you have accepted My Kingdom," God says, "accept My decrees."[99] It is left to man to reject the Torah or to accept it as his standard of conduct. "Everything," R. Hanina says, "is within the power of Heaven excepting the fear of Heaven."[100] God Himself does not compel a man against his will to be religious. Religion is a matter of inner choice and commitment. The duties which it implies must be self-imposed or they fail of their purpose. "We imposed on ourselves obligations," reads the declaration of the people in Nehemiah 10:33. Though the Torah as a body of norms appears heteronomous in form, it does not deprive man of moral autonomy. His moral and religious behavior is not a matter of economic, racial or physical determinism, but of free choice.

While Jewish ethics is based upon the authority of the Divine Lawgiver, attempts were made to establish its claims on the ground of human reason and conscience as well. The authors of the Wisdom books of the Bible consistently justify their precepts by appeals to reason and to experience. The Haggadists often follow their example, illustrating and enforcing their teaching from history and from nature. Significant is the saying of the rabbis regarding the moral and spiritual as distinguished from ritual laws—viz., prohibition of idolatry, incest and murder, robbery and blasphemy—that had they not already been written in the Torah it would have been necessary to write them.[101] Aiming to benefit the individual and society, they naturally recommend themselves to reason independent of external legislation and sanctions. The moral consciousness is autonomous, bearing the moral law within itself.[102]

NATURAL AND JEWISH ETHICS. As the ethics of a religion that strives after sanctification of life rather than its suppression, Jewish Ethics does not set itself up in invariable opposition to nature. Much that is natural and material is good. Indeed, according to the Genesis account, the whole of creation was appraised by the Creator as very good. Nature's laws are viewed as divinely implanted. The laws that control heaven and earth, sun, moon and stars, the sea and the deep operate also in the lives of men. The laws of the Torah have their counterpart in the laws of nature.* Such, for

* Josephus was of the opinion that everything in the Torah "is in keeping with the nature of the universe." Ant. I, 24. Cf. Philo, On Creation, 3. "Think of the sacred ties of nature

example, is the law of retribution.[103] At the same time, the rabbis recognized that the moral laws cannot always be identified with the laws of nature. A man steals a measure of wheat and sows it in his field. From the standpoint of the moral law, the wheat should not grow, but nature pursues its own course in total oblivion of the legitimate or illegitimate ways in which the grain was secured.[104] Furthermore nature has to be curbed before it serves the purposes of man. It is cruel, destructive and wasteful of life. The typhoon and the earthquake, the tiger and the python are parts of nature as well as man. The laws governing them obviously cannot apply to human beings. Human life itself is torn between conflicting tendencies. Savage instincts are no less real than good impulses. Cannibalism, murder and bestiality are matched by self-sacrifice, charity and humanity. Egotism, avarice and lechery exist by the side of altruism, generosity and self-discipline. Tendencies of destruction thwart the tendencies of construction. The passions, while neither good nor evil in themselves, may be employed as instruments of either godly or satanic ends. In other words, morality is the creation of man and represents the flower of his reason, conscience and religious spirit.

While for analytical purposes ethics is content with the study of the springs of human behavior and their expression, for practical ends of directing the lives of men, it is more exacting. Not what *is* being done, but what *ought* to be done constitutes its measure of value.

and the constancy of affection which she instils even into the beasts." Wars I, XXIII, 465.

Whereas science speaks in the indicative mood, religion uses the imperative. Its characteristic expressions take the form of commands and prohibitions, thou shalts and thou shalt nots.*

EVOLUTION OF JEWISH ETHICS. The ethical aspect of Judaism has been shaped by the experience of the Jewish people in the course of more than three millennia. The soul of the Jew, which is reflected in religion, is reflected also in its twin-growth, ethics. What has evolved through long stretches of time naturally displays the variety of changing national and geographical conditions, the growing idealism of its forward-looking leaders, and the interchange of ideas with other peoples. The Jewish moral consciousness has kept pace with the general spiritual and cultural advances. Whereas in its early stages it accepted the *lex talionis*, under the influence of progressive religious ideas, it evolved a conception of justice free from vindictiveness and tempered with love. Slavery, recognized as a legitimate institution through long ages, was gradually curbed and ultimately eliminated by changing economic and political as well as by ideo-

* " 'This is your wisdom and your understanding,' says Deuteronomy 4:6, with reference to the law. When Kant calls the force that decrees, teaches, makes demands, by the term 'practical reason,' he but uses another expression for morality. Call it law, principle, idea, what you will, it is always an objective norm, in nowise dependent upon the pleasure of man, but constraining him as he knows himself to be constrained by the laws of logic when he thinks, by the laws of mathematics when he computes." Lazarus, *op. cit.*, p. 117.

logical factors. Polygamy, long representing the form of marriage, similarly yielded to monogamy. The inferior status of woman in the home, community and synagogue has been corrected in part—since the last century—by the ever-growing recognition of the equality of the sexes.* In turn the growing moral sense exercised a vivifying influence upon religious thought. Ideas of the holy that failed to gain the approval of conscience could not maintain themselves as true.

Within the same age lower standards and motives of conduct exist by the side of the higher. If from a historical standpoint neither the one nor the other may be overlooked, the practical ends of life demand that we discard the lower, the outworn and the obsolete, and pursue what appear to us as the higher and nobler standards, whether they be of ancient or of modern origin. Numerous conceptions of moral idealism have been adopted from the outside, as by Philo from Plato, by Maimonides from Aristotle, and by Steinthal, Lazarus and Hermann Cohen from Kant. Grafted upon the tree of Judaism, they have yielded beautiful fruit of character. Adjusted to the fundamental attitudes and teachings of Judaism, they form part of the ethical tradition of Judaism. To the degree to which they help us solve our moral problems, they are vital for us today.

---

* Even in Reform Judaism women are still unable to find admission into the rabbinate. Neither is it common for them to hold the highest offices in the synagogue. In Orthodox and Conservative synagogues they do not count in a quorum.

# X. MOTIVES AND SANCTIONS

Moral ends. "Which is the right course that a man should choose for himself?" is a question which every person who wishes to master the art of life must answer for himself. So many failures result from failure to apply intelligence to the affairs of life, from the neglect to think out either the ultimate or proximate goals and directions of conduct. Like dumb-driven cattle multitudes of men are the playthings of their emotions and appetites, consuming their years in the search for food, sex and amusements. Motivated by low aims, their lives are circumscribed and narrow. Their thoughts and their strivings are harnessed to the steeds of their physical desires. Matters that do not directly affect their skin-bound existence fail to touch them.

Some of more reflective turn of mind rationalize these pursuits and place them as the conscious aims of all human striving. The driving forces of life, they maintain, are personal happiness and utility. That which yields the maximum of satisfaction recommends itself as ideal. The good is the pleasant or useful. Conversely, things that are painful or useless are neither good nor valuable. Human occupations, social relations and political interests are invariably determined by considerations of personal advantage. Everything is reduced to a hedonic plane. Self-interest determines every enterprise and situation. Friends are selected for the advantages, social, economic or political, which they are expected to bestow. Even charity is not disinterested. It is dispensed out of the desire to rid oneself of sights and situations that communicate pain and distress, with a view to securing public recognition, or for the pleasure of playing patron to the poor and forlorn, thus experiencing a sense of importance and of power. Religion itself often recommends charity as an investment, yielding dividends both in this world and in the next. Love of man and woman is stripped of all romance, glamor, and ideal, and reduced to mere sexual gratification. The love of parent for child becomes nothing more than a matter of self-benefit. As the child clings to the mother because it is helpless without her, so the mother is attached to the child because she needs the child. All other ideal relations turn out to be expressions of self-love.

Some form of self-gain or of happiness is doubtless "the tacitly implied ultimate end" and impelling force of all endeavor. Only by advancing their own interests do men also advance the welfare of society. However, men are better than their theories. The reduction of the aims of human endeavor to a calculus of profit and loss, to pleasure and pain, or to the craving for power leaves out of thought much that is heroic in human nature. There are times when man flings personal considerations to the winds and sacrifices his life for others. Considerations of personal welfare sometimes vanish even from the minds of otherwise selfish creatures when the imperative call of duty comes. Hardened criminals have on occasion evinced tender regard for others. A news item, which is not wholly out of the ordinary, reports that a child was taken to a hospital for an operation. The surgeon found a transfusion of blood indispensable. In response to an announcement, more than a dozen young men, who had not even known the little sufferer, came to offer their blood. The action of men in disasters at sea, with the rule of "women and children first," and with the crews and captains last, demands a different measure of conduct than the physical self. Men by the thousands, in every civilized land, devote their energies to painstaking tasks in laboratories, struggling to extend the boundaries of knowledge and to overcome disease and danger at the cost of their lives. Responding to an inner call, they lay down their lives in the effort to alleviate pain, misery and suffering, in order that others may live a fuller and a happier life. The Father Damiens, the Florence Nightingales, the Grenfells, Pasteurs, Ehrlichs, and Noguchis cannot be left out from any balance sheet of human character. The martyrs of religion, science and patriotism, whose name is legion, show that considerations other than those which end in self often shape the lives of men.

With Leslie Stephen we conclude that "the attempt to establish an absolute coincidence between virtue and happiness is in ethics what the attempting to square the circle or to discover the perpetual motion is in geometry and mechanics." [105] The universality of suffering and its presence in the lives of the noblest of men suggest that happiness cannot be the highest end of human existence. Those who refuse to gauge life by the yardstick of profit and loss, of pleasure and pain, or of animal satisfactions, find their highest goal in their self-realization as spiritual personalities, in the actualization of their capacities for goodness, truth, beauty, and holiness, and in the cultivation of good will and in its translation into a dynamic of character and of action. Some are enthralled by the vision of intrinsic goodness or are overawed by the majesty of God, finding the meaning of life in sacrificial service of Him. Even on the theory that happiness is the chief end of man, it cannot be overlooked that there are different kinds of happiness. Not all men can be satisfied with the happiness of the snail. There are those whose happiness must be that of the soaring eagle, ever aspiring, ever striving for the heights.

Spencer contends that "no school can avoid taking for the ultimate moral aim a desirable state of feeling called by whatever name—gratification, enjoyment, happiness. Pleasure somewhere, at some time, to some being or beings, is an inexpugnable element of the conception. It is as much a necessary form of moral intuition as space is a necessary form of intellectual intuition." [106] It has been well observed that while pleasure may be the form, it is not the substance of moral intuition.[107] The sense of right, obligatoriness, and goodness stems from deeper roots of our being.

The logic of experience demands that the hedonic ideal be shifted from the egoistic to the universal plane. It is the greatest good to the greatest number that looms as the moral ideal in the teaching of men like Bentham and John Stuart Mill. The happiness which forms the standard of right conduct "is not the agent's own happiness, but that of all concerned." [108] Personal impulse, pleasure, desire, and judgment are not purely private matters, springing wholly from within and operating independently. In great part they are evoked and molded by external pressure. We are ushered into a social life consisting of hereditary and environmental, economic, political, and cultural factors and of group habits, laws, and beliefs. Forming the condition of social existence, these forces exert continuous pressure upon us, directing our thought and our conduct. Adjustment to them assumes the form of social obligation and duty. Deviation from them is frowned upon and stigmatized as anti-social, i.e., immoral, disloyal, and dangerous, whereas conformity to them is recognized as moral, loyal, and helpful. Our actions, instead of being wholly our own, are conditioned by the requirements of our group or people. While we feel ourselves free human beings, we submit, whether consciously or unconsciously, to the dictates of our society as expressed either directly or through its leaders. Aside from such adjustment to the public good there can be neither sharing in social life nor self-preservation in the struggle against the forces of nature and of a world in which tribes and nations are often set against one another. Private interest thus coalesces with social well-being, defining for us the sphere of duty and of right. The laws which the group promulgates and which maintain its life resemble, in some respects, the laws of nature. A breach of the social order appears anti-natural.

Behind the social imperatives there is the religious

command and sanction. Ever playing a social role, religion sustains and reinforces the claims of the group upon the individual, even as it protects the individual against the undue pressure of the group. Primitives fancied the spirits and gods as bound up with their tribes and peoples, acting as guardians of the tribal mores and standards. The religion of Israel, too, regarded God as the keeper of the covenant and guarantor of justice, demanding and enforcing right conduct from individuals and from the nation.

The moral *ought* thus reveals itself as something different from the dictate of reason. Intelligence dawned comparatively late in man's development and introduced orderliness and consistency into conduct, which by its very nature is subordinated to the needs of society. The real root of obligation, however, is non-rational and social. National crises generally bring this fact into clear light. The ends of the nation become the goals of the individual. Private opinions and judgments are silenced before the concrete situation of a people facing the perils of war and defeat. Only exceptional personalities, filled with the sense of Divine vocation or dowered with rare mental powers of foresight, rise beyond the confines of the immediate community to vision the needs of other communities as well, and to recognize duties to humanity at large. Rising above the mass of their fellow men, these commanding figures strike at the old and disclose the new, they wound and they heal, liberate and transform. To use Bergson's figure, like an "army of conquerors," these prophetic spirits, founders and reformers of religion, enthusiasts and mystics, sages, saints, break through the crust of habit and convention, blaze new roads of moral progress and raise humanity to a new destiny. Obligation becomes through them "the force of an aspiration or an impetus," urging men onward to lofty ends and spurring them to heroic deeds beyond those dictated by nature.[109]

While moral ends attain clarity through reason, they grow into power through the sanctions of religion. As considerations of reason, they are subjected to conditions and limitations, and thus are ultimately reduced, in practice if not in theory, to prudentialism, whereas religion endows them with absoluteness. Recognized as the will of God, they claim man's complete and unquestioned obedience. They become the unconditioned law of his being, a categorical imperative.*

---

* Unless we assume that the foundations of morality rest in the will and the wisdom of God, transcending group interests, economic conditions and temporal exigencies, the ground of obligation crumbles and all social reform and democratic claims lose their force. Galloway writes: "The truth is, the ethical conception of life cannot stand by itself: we must either try to reduce it to the natural or carry it up into the spiritual. The former attempt cannot possibly succeed. The alternative is the frank recognition that the ethical view of man and his vocation, when its implications are thought out, leads up to the religious view." (*The Idea of Immortality*, p. 221.) To this we may add W. E. Hocking's consideration: "Unless the universe has a central and unified life in which our destinies are involved, and which gives these destinies a higher importance than they can have for our finite vision, the notion of obligation loses the degree of dignity which we, in fact, ascribe to it. When we speak of the rights of man and the duties of man, the respect we accord them is measured

THE GOOD. The evolving conceptions of the moral ends
and of obligation have translated themselves into corresponding standards of good or value. The primitive
man has no existence aside from his tribe. His good is
limited to that which serves his family, clan, tribe,
nation, and humanity. This may consist in habits,
customs, skills, and knowledge. On an advanced level,
attained through awakened intellectual leadership, that
which has proved good or beneficial for the individual
and for the group becomes the norm for good in itself
or universal good. In its reasoned form, it serves as a
standard of moral conduct and judgment. Behavior
prompted by impulse, appetite or passion, without being guided by mind, is found injurious. Gluttony,
overindulgence, self-assertiveness, anarchy, etc., come
to be acknowledged as evil. Restraint, sobriety, purity,
modesty, consideration for others, fair-play, kindliness, and uprightness recommend themselves as good.

Living the good life means to follow the standards
which society approves as good, of seeing oneself as
others see him and of reflecting in one's conduct
genuine concern for their welfare. To his instinctual
cravings, desires, will, and thought, man applies the
moral and spiritual standards, judgments and insights
of his group. He avoids doing unto others what he
would not have them do unto him. He judges himself
as he would judge others. He thus awakens within

by our belief that they belong to man as a metaphysical entity, a ward of the universe. The work these 'rights' have
done in history may testify to the truth of this statement."
(*Human Nature and Its Remaking*, p. 425.)

himself the faculty of judgment or conscience (the Latin *conscientia* means "joint knowledge," i.e., knowledge shared with others, and more particularly the knowledge of good and evil). Respect for law governs his whole being. A sense of duty and responsibility is born within him. He feels obligated to uphold the moral standards and ideals of the community even when they hurt him and call for sacrifices. He no longer does good merely because it is profitable or because he is coerced by external pressure but because he has been transformed by it. The good has become the inner law of his being, and responds to the deep of his soul.

The new-born sense of moral judgment or conscience may lead man to vision higher levels of conduct and of value than those held by his people, and even to declare war on prevailing lower standards in the interests of the higher. This is the story of the prophets of Israel and of the great champions of moral progress everywhere. In his struggle, the moral idealist is sustained by his vision of morality transcending local and temporal limitations. Beyond the relativism of tribal mores and tabus, of practices and habits imposed by geographic and economic factors and of standards imposed by tyrants and conquerors, he discerns basic moral laws. He sees the steady play of cause and effect in the lives of men and of nations, the universal struggle to shatter the shackles that bind men to secure freedom, the persistent gravitation of society toward stability, order and harmony, despite all barriers and disruptive forces. He recognizes the interdependence of men and their responsibility for one another. He is awed by the majesty and sanctity of truth, of right and of love, and he puts his confidence in them. The good recommends itself to him not as a mere invention of man but as grounded in the very nature and context of the universe. Despite the moral chaos, moral laws operate. They seem as real as the laws which govern his physical being or the rest of nature. Man does not invent them; he only discovers them. They are manifestations of the universal order-producing principle or of the will and purpose of God. As the compass introduces us into the world of space so the good introduces us into a divinely governed universe. Understanding the true implications of the moral ideal, loyalty to its imperatives and perseverance in rendering it, the rule of conduct for oneself and society constitute the supreme good. In this sense, the good merges with and becomes part of the holy. In the words of the prophet: "It hath been told thee, O man, what is good, and what the Lord doth require of thee: only to do justly, and to love mercy, and to walk humbly with thy God" (Micah 6:8). The ethical ideal of the good as shown in justice and in love is not a mere social figment or utilitarian device. For the religious soul it is charged with spiritual value, as a revelation of the will of God. It is to this Divine element in morality that the prophets and the Torah appealed and to which the sages directed their searching minds. It is also the element which constitutes the beacon light of man's undying aspirations.

While the highest good transcends the immediate

interests of both the individual and the community and is conceived as having its source in God, it is bound up with the lives of men and of nations. Devotion to the supreme ideals of one's people and of humanity represents its corollary. However, the ideals of one's class or nation may not coincide with those of humanity (e.g., wars between classes and nations). The growth of the individual may be arrested by class, tribal, national, or racial mindedness. The lesser "loyalties" to one's particular race, nation, class, or group may tend to grow into exclusivism, narrowness, and combativeness, and ill will toward others, and thus may defeat the greater loyalty toward universal humanity. To preserve the gains of moral progress and, at the same time, to respond to the claims of one's own community is a task of the greatest difficulty. In the light of such conflict man's freedom consists in enjoying the right of judgment as to which loyalty has the highest claim upon him, i.e., which demands serve the highest good. These he must learn to judge not on the ground of external pressure, personal whim or temporary expediency but on the ground of the permanent and universal well-being. Freedom of decision means the unhampered exercise of reason and conscience in the determination of what constitutes right and good. Anything that impairs the free workings of reason and of conscience and interferes with man's moral autonomy marks a defeat of the aspiring spirit of man. On the other hand, with personal freedom preserved, every voluntary sacrifice of self-interest upon the altar of the common good represents a victory of the spirit.

MOTIVES OF CONDUCT. The consideration of moral aims may serve as a key to the motives, i.e., of the psychic and rational grounds, of conduct which figure most prominently in Jewish thought. In general they may be said to have varied with the advancing viewpoints of Judaism, although some of the older and less ideal motives appear by the side of more progressive standards, either as survivals or as pedagogic means to higher ends.

The *profit motive* has persisted throughout the development of Judaism, keeping pace, however, with its changing outlooks. In the Bible, where the unit of consideration is the nation, and where the moral horizon is bounded by this world, the law of compensation plays the leading role. The acts of the individual have their bearing not only upon his own but also upon his people's future. Achan, by breaking a tabu, brings guilt upon the entire people (Josh. 7). Jonathan tastes the honey of the forest, in unconscious violation of Saul's oath, and thereby brings defeat to the army of Israel. On the other hand, righteous men are the bulwark of the community. A faithful remnant insures the nation's future (Gen. 18; Is. 10:20 f.). Obedience to the commands of God guarantees prosperity, plenty and security for oneself and for the nation. Disobedience, on the other hand, entails sorrow, grief, misery, defeat, suffering, and death (Deut. 11:13–21; 28; Lev. 26). "That it may be well with thee" and "that thou mayest prolong thy days upon the earth" are the recurrent themes of Deuteronomy and are implied in the other books of the Bible. The well-being referred to

is both communal and personal. The second commandment appeals to this principle of Divine retribution
(Ex. 20:5–6; Deut. 5:9–10). Jeremiah speaks of God
as "great in counsel, and mighty in work; Whose eyes
are open upon all the ways of the sons of men, to give
everyone according to his ways, and according to the
fruit of his doing" (Jer. 32:19). This belief hardened
into a ruling dogma. Though challenged by Job as
inadequate to explain the vicissitudes of life, it maintained itself as part of Jewish religious belief because
of its ready appeal to common sense and to the un-
critical demands of justice. Moral behavior further
recommends itself as a form of group loyalty. A good
act benefits the entire people; an evil deed injures all
of them. Hence the rabbis emphasized that "all Israelites are responsible for one another." [110] Jewish unity
often has been enforced by the harsh conditions under
which they lived. The entire people was held ac-
countable for the misdeeds of individuals.

In response to the deeper craving for a moral balance
in the affairs of men, the principle of retribution was
extended also to the hereafter. The injustices of this
life will be adjusted in the next. Divine judgment
awaits all creatures. The good which a man does will
not fail of a harvest in the hereafter. Evil, too, is stored
up for his future punishment. Man's conduct, whatever
its temporal reward, comes to a final accounting in
the beyond. [111] The Mishnah enumerates certain duties,
like respect for parents, the practice of charity, prompt
attendance at worship, hospitality to wayfarers, visiting the sick, dowering the bride, etc., as yielding

fruit in this world, while their stock remains for the world to come.[112] "A portion in the future world" or "future bliss" has figured as an incentive for religious conduct. Doing good came to be regarded as storing up treasures in heaven.[113] Man's meritorious acts transcend personal, and even national well-being, and assume universal significance. They condition the salvation of the whole world. In the opinion of the rabbis, "The Messiah will come only in a generation which is either wholly meritorious or wholly steeped in guilt." [114]

The doctrine of *grace* aims to encourage men in righteousness. No one need despair. A share in future bliss awaits even those who have but little merit of their own. "All Israelites have a portion in the world to come." [115] It is assured them as an act of grace, a grace first extended to Abraham and continued to his seed after him. The merit of the fathers aids their children and mitigates the severities involved in the strict application of justice.

The wage motive of righteousness is fed by the twin psychological roots of *expectancy* of reward and of *fear* of punishment. The fear grows out of the certainty of God's avenging wrath for evil doing. In the words of the sage: "The wicked flee when no man pursueth; but the righteous are secure as a young lion" (Prov. 28:1). Conscience plagues the wicked. They dread the effect of their misdeeds (Gen. 3:10; 4:13–14). This motive operates in both personal and national life. Disobedient Israel is threatened with dire calamities, while prosperity and peace are held out as the prize of obedience to the word of God (Is. 3:10–11; Deut. 11:13–17; 28; Lev. 26).

Fear of the consequences of evil serves a disciplinary purpose. "A wise man feareth and departeth from evil" (Prov. 14:16). "Fear the Lord and depart from evil" (Prov. 3:7) represents the typical admonition of the sages. Identified with religion, fear of God figures as the beginning and the end of wisdom, as the condition of true knowledge of God and of blessedness. The way to escape the fear of death and of other evils is to fear and to trust in God (Ps. 56:4). The fear of God, as we noted earlier, is by no means a depressing emotion. The Psalmist uses it in the sense of reverence and of awe, when he calls, "Serve the Lord with fear, and rejoice with trembling" (2:11). When approached in awe, God puts gladness in the heart. To them who fear (=revere) Him "shall the sun of righteousness arise with healing in its wings" (Mal. 3:20). Fear thus came to be coupled with *love* as the great commands of religion. Both lead man to hate and to depart from evil (Deut. 10:11–12; Ps. 97:10). Ben Sira summarizes the Jewish attitude toward these two motives of conduct:

> They that fear the Lord will seek His good pleasure,
> And they that love Him will be filled with [His] Law.
> They that fear the Lord will make ready their hearts,
> And will humble their souls before Him.
> —2:15–17; see also 1:11–20; 2:7–11

Though fear and love came to be used in combination, the rabbis call attention to their root differences. Commenting on Deut. 6:5, "Thou shalt love the Lord thy God," the Sifre observes: "Scripture has distinguished between one who serves God from love and one who serves Him from fear. . . . Sometimes, a man who is afraid of his fellow will leave him when he becomes troublesome and go his way. But act thou out of love, for there is no love where there is fear, nor fear where there is love, except in relation to God alone." [116] R. Simeon b. Eleazar teaches: "Greater is he who acts from love than he who acts from fear." Abraham is the prototype of God-loving men; Job of God-fearing men, though on the ground of Job 13:15 and 27:5 he too was claimed to have served God from the motive of pure love.[117]

The wage motive of righteousness easily empties itself of its religious character. The service may become entirely subsidiary to the reward. Posthumous compensation only represents the postponement of sensuous gratification. The rabbis, therefore, felt the need of a purer motive to direct man in his religious life. Thus Antigonos of Socho teaches: "Be not like servants who minister to their master [solely] upon condition of receiving a reward; but be like servants who minister to their master without the condition of receiving a reward; and let the fear of heaven be upon you." [118] The religious life must be actuated by genuine reverence for God rather than by self-interest and material considerations. Only such a religion can stand the test of life. Not that the practice of religion is barren of results. Josephus, giving a Hellenistic tinge to the Pharisaic doctrine, writes: For those "who live in accordance with our laws the prize is not silver or gold, no crown of wild olive or of parsley (i.e., as in the Olympian or the Isthmian and Nemean games) with any such public mark of distinction. No; each individual, relying on the witness of his own conscience and the lawgiver's prophecy, confirmed by the sure testimony of God, is firmly persuaded that to those who observe the laws and, if they must needs die for them, willingly meet death, God has granted a renewed existence and in the ages the gift of a better life." [119] As far as this life is concerned, Ben 'Azzai states succinctly: "The reward of a precept is a precept and the punishment of a transgression is a transgression." [120] The real compensation for either good or evil is in the acts themselves. Good leads to more good, and evil is trailed by evil. R. Eliezer comments on Ps. 112:1, " 'Happy is the man who feareth the Lord, that delighteth greatly in His commandments,' i.e., who delights in His commandments themselves and not in the reward of His commandments." [121] The Sifre comments on Deut. 11:13: "Lest you say I shall study Torah in order that I may become rich, that I may be called Rabbi or that I may be rewarded in the hereafter, Scripture specifies 'to love the Lord your God'; whatever you do, do from love." [122] R. Eleazar b. Zadok taught: "Do things for the sake of doing them; engage in them for their own sake." He taught further: "If Belshazzar, who made common use of the vessels of the sanctuary, which were already profaned (cf. Ezek. 7:22), was plucked out of this world and of the next, he that makes profane use of the instrument wherewith this world and the next were created (i.e., the Torah) will surely be uprooted from both this world and the next" similarly. R. Benaah teaches: "If you have fulfilled the words of the Torah for their own sake they are life unto you (Prov. 4:22), but if you do not fulfill them for their own sake they slay you." [123] In the same spirit R. Zadok taught: "Make not of the Torah a crown wherewith to aggrandize thyself, nor a spade wherewith to dig. So also Hillel used to say, 'He who makes a worldly use of the crown of the Torah shall waste away.' Thus you learn that he who derives a profit for himself from the words of the Torah removes his life from the world." [124] The belief that the Torah must not be a means of gain led the masters of Judaism in the course of many centuries to earn their livelihood by ways other than through remuneration for teaching Torah. A salaried rabbinate is a comparatively late institution.

With deep insight into human nature, Rab counselled: "Let man ever engage in the study of Torah and the performance of its commandments even if not for their sake, for engaging in them for ulterior considerations may lead him to engage in them for their own sake." [125] Expectancy of rewards and fear of punishments may serve as pedagogic aids to perfection. Maimonides writes: "In order that the common folk might be established in their convictions, the sages permitted them to perform meritorious actions with the hope of reward, and to avoid the doing of evil out of fear of punishment. They encourage them to these conceptions and their opinions become firmly rooted, until eventually the intelligent among them come to comprehend and know what truth is and what is the most perfect mode of conduct." [126] The true lover of God must outgrow these pedagogical crutches. He must love truth and follow virtue not because of any worldly or other-worldly emoluments but because of their intrinsic value. As a child of God, man attains his full self-realization by leading a godly life. Without demanding clear tariffs of merits and demerits, man must offer his deeds, his strivings and his ideals at the altar of God and live in the hope of Divine approval. Albo similarly emphasizes that while retribution is a cardinal principle of religion, the true lover of God is motivated neither by considerations of compensation nor by fear of punishment but solely by the desire of fulfilling the will of the Beloved One. [127]

Man must aspire after the highest, which alone is fit to serve as his ideal. His deeds should be prompted by motives of pure religion. This is expressed in the saying of Antigonos by the words, "and let the fear of Heaven be upon you." Fear of Heaven, as we have seen, came to denote piety or religion. It is fear mingled with reverence and love. Sometimes the religious motive is expressed by the phrase Leshem shamayim —"for the sake of Heaven" or Lemaan hashem—"for God's sake." In the words of R. Jehudah Hasid: men should be guided not by fear of punishment in this life or in the next but by fear of not being whole-hearted with God. [128]

The religious rule of conduct is: so act that your action may have the approval of both man and God

(Prov. 3:4). Possibly this is the meaning of R. Hanina b. Dosa's dictum: "He in whom the spirit of his fellow-creatures takes delight, in him the spirit of God takes delight; and he in whom the spirit of his fellow-creatures does not take delight, in him the spirit of God takes no delight." [129]

The religious motive assumes different forms. It appears as obedience due God on several grounds. The oldest of them is the covenant relationship between Israel and God. God chose Abraham and his seed as His people. This covenant was renewed on a larger scale at Sinai, where it was embodied into a code of law. As God's people they owe Him unquestioned service and undivided loyalty. Under prophetic preaching the religious motive was moralized. Man must do God's will because it represents the moral good (Is. 48:18–19). God demands righteousness and mercy, for through them men attain true life. The motive of obedience was further moralized through fusion with the motives of gratitude and love. The prophet Hosea denounces the immorality of his day as a form of ingratitude to God (2: 11). The Deuteronomist, too, pleads for devotion to God out of gratitude for all He has done for the people in the past, by choosing them from among all peoples, delivering them from bondage and revealing to them His law. Justice to one another and sympathy for the poor and the unfortunate are claimed as an acknowledgment of their indebtedness to God (10:12–22).

Obedience to God in the view of Malachi (1:6) is prompted by man's relationship to Him as *servant,* on

the one hand, and as *son* on the other. The first conveys the idea of subordination to God. In the words
of the Torah: "Unto Me the children of Israel are
servants; they are My servants whom I brought forth
out of the land of Egypt" (Lev. 25:55). While servitude to man is degrading, service of God is the highest
honor. All worship constitutes service of God. The
idea of Divine sonship derives from the sense of identity with the higher order. To be a son of God is not
the prerogative of one favored individual—as is
claimed by Christianity for its founder—but of every
God-conscious being. In the words of R. Akiba: "Beloved is man, for he was created in the image of God;
by special love it was made known to him that he was
created in the image of God, as it is said, 'for in the
image of God made He man' (Gen. 9:6). Beloved
are Israel in that they were called children of God;
by a special love it was made known to them that they
were called children of God, as it is said, 'Ye are children of the Lord your God' " [130] (Deut. 14:1). As sons
and servants of God, the Jewish people are called upon
to act as God's witnesses (Is. 43:10–12). This privilege is not limited to Israel. All men shall ultimately
testify to Him (Is. 45:23). This is the substance of the
belief of the establishment of the Kingdom of God on
earth.

The consciousness of Divine sonship is coupled with
the sense of *human brotherhood* as motive powers of
moral conduct. The two, as will be shown later, are
inseparable in Jewish thought.

# XI. THE DIVINE IN MAN

KIDDUSH HASHEM. What ground does Judaism posit for the ethical ideal? To be valid, it must have its source outside itself. Man cannot be expected to sacrifice personal desires and satisfactions for others unless he is motivated by an ideal transcending his own self. The basis for the obligation which he feels is not in his skin-bound existence, in the social herd or in blind custom, but rather in the nature of the spiritual environment in which we live, in God and in the Divine quality of the human spirit. From this source alone come the urges to love, to sacrifice and to aspire beyond physical well-being and necessity. The basis for living as moral beings, i.e., to respect each other's life, honor, and personality, to do justly, to love mercy and to cherish peace is not only because we are social animals, but principally because we are brothers by virtue of being children of God. Our moral nature points to a world of spirit or God. He forms the ground of our moral gravitation. Consequently our moral values are not mere outgrowths of prudentialism, utilitarianism, or eudemonism, but rather manifest a Divine endowment in our natures. Our whole moral and religious life thus assumes the character of witnessing unto God, or, in traditional Jewish phraseology, of a sanctification of God's name, a *Kiddush Hashem*.

Through the long centuries of Jewish history, Kiddush Hashem figured as the dominant ideal of religious life. R. Simeon b. Eleazar says: "When Israel does God's will, His name is magnified in the world (Jos. 5:1, 2:10–11), but when Israel fails to do God's will, His name is profaned in the world." [131] Israel's well-doing was believed to affect God Himself. Accordingly in the development of the idea of Kiddush Hashem two aspects must be noted, one Divine and one human. Ezekiel announces that in view of Israel's failure, God himself will hallow His name by revealing His Divinity in triumphant might before the nations and thus vindicate His justice. His punishment of Israel led to a profanation of His name, for man said of them: His own people have been exiled from the land. In pity for His holy name He will restore them back to their land, and thus sanctify (vindicate) His great name (Ezek. 36:20–37; 39:7–8; so Is. 48:9). God will thus compel the acknowledgment and the reverence of the nations. "Thus will I magnify Myself, and sanctify Myself, and I will make Myself known in the eyes of many nations; and they shall know that I am the Lord" (38:23). These words, embodied in the opening of the Kaddish, sound the Messianic hope of the ultimate establishment of the Kingdom of God on earth. [132]

In this light the rabbis interpret the Divine part in the whole drama of Israel in Egypt, of the Exodus, and of the conquest of Canaan as having had for its object the sanctification of God's name. The miracles shown to Daniel and his companions were intended to serve as means of bringing the nation to acknowledge God. The sole purpose of giving the Torah to

Israel was to sanctify God's name. Remnants of Israel will be spread in many lands, "and they shall declare My glory among the nations" (Is. 66:19).[138]

The uniqueness of the doctrine of Kiddush Hashem derives from its human side as the supreme ideal and obligation of the Jewish people. It makes its first appearance negatively in Amos 2:7, where the infraction of moral laws is denounced as a profanation of God's name. Isaiah demands of Israel the sanctification of God (8:13; cf. 19:21f.; 29:23) and defines the idea of sanctification in moral terms. "The Lord of hosts is exalted through justice and the Holy One is sanctified through righteousness" (5:16). This idea is central in the priestly writings in the Bible. By means of ceremonial deeds as well as through moral actions men sanctify and honor God. Priests, prophets and the whole people of Israel must so conduct themselves as to reflect credit upon the God they worship. "Through them that are nigh unto Me I will be sanctified, and before all the people I will be glorified" (Lev. 10:3; cf. Num. 20:12; Deut. 32:15). When they fail to honor Him properly, His name is profaned. Ezekiel charged Israel with violation of the Torah, profanation of the Sabbaths, and despising the holy things (32:8, 26). Idolatry in any form constitutes a profanation of God's name, which God will not tolerate in Israel (Lev. 20:3; 22:32). Religion is judged by the conduct of those who profess it. Not by words of mouth alone but by their whole lives men must witness to God. One's behavior must reflect the Divine, and render Him beloved by other men. The commandment "Thou shalt love the Lord thy God" (Deut. 6:5) is interpreted in the Sifre: "Make Him beloved by your fellowmen."

Kiddush Hashem forms the subject of the third benediction in the 'Amidah. The Kedushah calls upon Israel to sanctify the name of God even as the angels sanctify it on high (Is. 6:2–3). This thought is stressed in the mystic Haggadah and in numerous *piyyutim* for the High Holy Days. Kiddush Hashem came to form the ruling objective of religious and moral conduct, not only in public but also in private. R. Isaac Abravanel construes the saying of R. Levitas in Abot 4:4 that man should be exceedingly humble, as aiming against hypocrites, who, under the cloak of humility, plot to take advantage of their fellow men. Their secret pride is an offense against Heaven. R. Levitas' saying applies further to all who give the appearance of modesty but who are proud of heart. Of them the prophet says: "For the Lord of hosts hath a day (of judgment) upon all who are proud and lofty, and upon all who are lifted up and lowly" (Is. 2:12, with deviations from the literal translation). The rabbis say that he who profanes God's name in secret crowds out the Shechinah, for the two "cannot live in the same premises." [134] Samuel de Uzida adds to these observations of Abravanel, that every offense, whether inadvertent or presumptuous, does not escape from being something of a profanation of God's name, inasmuch as His word is despised. [135] Conversely, each virtuous deed, whether private or public, constitutes an act of Kiddush Hashem.

Obviously witnessing to the Divine in public is rated more highly, because of its effect upon others. Thus R. Simeon the Hasid observes that Joseph, for sanctifying God's name in private, merited that the second letter of the Tetragrammaton (Ps. 81:6— Jehoseph) be added to his name; Judah for sanctifying God's name in public (Gen. 38:26) merited that all the four letters of the Tetragrammaton be embodied in his name.[136] God's name is sanctified by the observance of ceremonial as well as of moral laws. Thus strict regard for the Sabbath serves as a testimony to God.[137]

The question, "What constitutes Hillul Hashem?" is variously answered by a number of rabbis. Rab holds that God's name is profaned by a scholar when he makes a purchase and does not pay immediately. Abaye modifies this statement as applying only where no selling on credit system obtains. R. Johanan applies it to a scholar who walks four ells without studying Torah and without wearing phylacteries. Isaac of the school of Jannai thinks that God's name is profaned when one renders himself an object of shame to his friends. R. Nahman b. Isaac expresses the similar opinion that a man has profaned God's name when people have to say: "May God forgive him." The ideal of conduct, according to Abaye, is that it may render God's name beloved. A scholar who deals pleasantly with his fellow men reflects honor upon his father and teacher, and evokes the emulation of others. Conversely, a person, who by his conduct belies the Torah which he studied, brings down denunciations upon those who taught him, and becomes an abhorrence to his fellow men.[138] A scholar who teaches, "do not lend on usury," and exacts exorbitant interest; "do not rob," and proceeds to flay his fellow men; "do not steal," and engages in thievery, profanes God's name.[139] It becomes a duty to expose hypocrites in order to prevent the profanation of God's name.[140] "Though one profaned God's name in secret he is made to pay the penalty in public. No distinction is made between inadvertence and presumption in such instances.[141] Retribution follows both types of action, even though in differing degrees corresponding to the gravity of the offense.[142]

Consequently, a man of piety, scholarship or prominence must strive to be above reproach in matters of business, in his food and drink, and in his relations with his neighbors in general. He must keep himself free from pretense and duplicity, and exercise patience and forbearance. Above all he must avoid giving ground for offense against his faith.[143]

This consideration renders robbery of a non-Jew a graver offense than robbing a fellow Jew. Even in accidental cases one must not permit himself to take advantage of a stranger.[144] The story is told about Simeon b. Shetah, who bought an ass from an Ishmaelite, and found a precious stone on its neck. His disciples congratulated him on his good fortune, but he ordered the stone returned to its owner. "I bought an ass," he explained, "not a precious stone." Whereupon the Ishmaelite exclaimed: "Blessed be the God of Simeon b. Shetah." Once rabbis bought a heap of grain from an army and found in it a bundle of dinars. When they returned the money, the soldiers exclaimed: "Blessed be the God of the Jews." [145]

The *Sittenbuch* (a Yiddish paraphrase of the fourteenth century Orhot Tzaddikim) teaches: "Also with a gentile one should not deal falsely or deceptively, for that is a hillul hashem. For when gentiles see that the Jews deceive them, they begin to hate the Jews and to say that since the Jews practice falsehood, their faith, too, must be false. Thus God's name is profaned. When one deceives a gentile he may not be able to repent of the evil, for the Creator, praised be He, cannot tolerate lying and deceiving even when directed against a gentile. On the other hand, he who deals truthfully and faithfully with gentiles sanctifies His holy name. Thereby they come to love us and they grow pious. Seeing the righteousness with which Jews deal with them, they say: 'How pious are they and what a good faith they have!' Thereby God's name is sanctified." [146]

The same motive is invoked by this moralistic work for raising the standard of Jewish devotion: "When gentiles enter the synagogues and hear and see how we talk and babble with one another [during the service], it is a hillul hashem. For when they behold such levity, they say: 'The Jews themselves do not think much of their prayers.' Could there be a greater hillul hashem than this? Similarly with all the mitzvot. When the gentiles note how careless we are in observing them, they conclude that we have little regard for our faith. However, if the gentiles see that we are upright and

observant, they praise us, saying: 'The Jews are more
devout than we gentiles are.' Then we become sancti-
fiers of the name of God." [147]

Though religion in its truest form is what man does
with himself in his solitude, as a social phenomenon it
must reckon with its public practice, especially because of its effect upon others. Accordingly R. Abahu
teaches in the name of R. Hanina that it is better for
man to commit a transgression in secret than to profane God's name in public (Ezek. 20:39). R. Ilai the
Elder goes to the extent of saying: "If a man sees
that his evil inclination is overpowering him, let him
go to a place where he is not known, attire himself in
black and do his heart's desire, but let him not profane
God's name in public." [148] A scholar must be particularly careful, for if God's name is profaned through
him, "he is not afforded the opportunity of re-
penting." [149]

This doctrine of Kiddush Hashem became the
touchstone of Jewish practice. Lev. 18:5 reads: "Ye
shall therefore keep My statutes, and Mine ordinances,
which if a man do, he shall live by them: I am the
Lord." The Sifra comments: "He shall live by them,
not that he shall die because of them. R. Ishmael
taught: Whence do we know that if a man is told pri-
vately, 'Worship an idol that you may not be killed,'
that he may transgress the Law in order to escape
death? Because it is written: 'He shall live by them,'
i.e., not that he shall die by them. Does this imply that
even if he is forced to embrace idolatry in public, that
he should submit? Hence it is written: 'And ye shall

not profane My holy name; but I will be hallowed among the children of Israel: I am the Lord who hallow you' (Lev. 22:32). If you sanctify My name, I too shall hallow My name through you as I did through Hananiah, Mishael and Azariah who, at a time when all the nations prostrated themselves before Nebuchadnezzar's idol, stood upright like palms." [150] Where there is danger of public profanation of God's name the Jew must uphold his faith at the cost of his life. Thus in time of religious persecution, martyrdom became a duty even when the transgression that was demanded was of a minor nature, both in private and in public. Prior to the Maccabean uprising, the Hasidim permitted themselves to be slain rather than violate the Divine law by taking up arms in self-defense on the Sabbath. The II Maccabees embodies these experiences of martyrdom in the stories of the aged Eleazar, who submitted himself to death by torture rather than break the law by eating swine's flesh, and of the mother and her seven sons who offered themselves as sacrifices upon the altar of faith in the One God.* In the war against Rome, martyrdom again became the Jewish badge of honor. Like Samson and Saul, the Jewish soldiers who were besieged at Masada destroyed themselves rather than fall into the hands of the Romans. During the Hadrianic persecutions, a law was passed that to save his life a man may transgress

---

* The rabbinic version of the story of the mother and her seven sons gives as the cause for martyrdom the demand that they worship an idol. Cf. II Macc. 7; Gittin 57b.

all the laws of the Torah, excepting only idolatry, incest and murder.[151] In practice martyrdom was undergone in other circumstances as well. In the time of the Crusades and during the Cossack massacres in the seventeenth and eighteenth centuries, Jews sought refuge from the brutality of the vicious mobs by destroying themselves and their dear ones. R. Jehudah Hasid comments on Ps. 95:7, "He is our God and we are the flock of His pasture": "When do we know Him as our God? When we are slaughtered like sheep to sanctify His name." [152] To escape the danger of forced conversion to Christianity and to Islam the Jews of Spain and the Orient resorted to migration to other lands where they could enjoy freedom of worship.[153] The ghastly pogroms, incited by the forces of dying Czarism before the First World War, and the slaughter of countless thousands in the Ukraine and other parts of Russia after the war, and the methodical extermination of millions of Jews by the satanic forces of Nazism during the Second World War added new chapters of horror to the tragic record of Jewish martyrdom. Though they were massacred not so much because of their religion as on account of their very existence—as part of a fiendish method of political and racial warfare—their death, too, constitutes a Kiddush Hashem. They fell as victims of the eternal struggle for human dignity and for the right of every individual to life and to freedom against the forces of tyranny, hatred and bestiality. In their death, these victims of human depravity guarded the tortured image of God in man.

The honor of Judaism is entrusted not only to the Jewish community as a whole, but also to each individual Jew. It is within the power of each one of us to demonstrate its truth, dignity and beauty or to drag it into the mire.

Israel continues to pray: "Our Heavenly Father, help us that by our lives we may sanctify Thy name before men, and testify of Thee and of Thy holy law. . . . Put into our hearts the love and fear of Thee, that we may consecrate our lives to Thy service and glorify Thy name in the eyes of all men." [154]

THE MORAL PATTERN: IMITATIO DEI. In the art of living as in the art of sculpture or of painting we must reckon not only with aims and motives but also with patterns. Moses, we are told, was shown at Sinai a fiery model for the lamp which he was to make for the tabernacle. The rabbis took this to be symbolic of the fashioning of human lives as well. Of them, too, it is said: "Look thou and work after their pattern which was shown thee in the mount" (Ex. 25:40). Like a star a man's ideal is high in heaven. Though he may never quite succeed, he must strive to hitch his wagon to the star. In the very endeavor he finds scope for the expansion of his powers and for the growth of his spirit.

The person whose eye is set on the highest cannot be satisfied with a pattern derived from the lower order of being. He refuses to regard life as a "strange interlude," composed of nothing but predatory impulses, sex hungers, and animal satisfactions. Neither is he content with a pattern of utilitarian type. His mind has been fired with a higher vision. He strives to fill his life with richer meaning. He no longer lives in the physical tracts of the body. He is conscious of soul life, of reason, of love of truth, of justice, of goodness, of beauty and of holiness. He is a child of the Divine order, created in the very image of God. While his physical being demands care, it must not dwarf the spiritual side of his being, if he is to work out within himself the pattern revealed to him on the height of religious vision. The Midrash comments on the words of Psalm 100:3, " 'It is He that made us, and not ourselves'—we do not make ourselves." Rab Aha adds: "We do not complete our souls." Our perfection as human beings is attained through our consciousness of the Divine.[155]

Herein lies the chief service of religion to morality. Plato recognized that morality based upon considerations of reward and punishment or similar ideas of prudentialism lacks intrinsic worth. True morality consists in assimilating man to God. He puts these words into the mouth of Socrates: From the evils of earth let man take refuge in the divine order. "To fly away [from the earthly] is to become like God, as far as possible; and to become like Him, is to become holy, just, and wise. . . . He is perfect righteousness; and he of us who is most righteous is most like Him. . . . There are two patterns eternally set before them [men]; the one blessed and divine, the other godless and wretched; but they do not see them, or perceive that in their utter folly and infatuation they are growing like the one and unlike the other, by reason of their evil deeds; and the penalty is, that they lead a life answering to the pattern which they are growing like." [156]

Not all religions hold out the same heavenly pattern for man. Plato was impelled to question the moral value of the Greek myths concerning the behavior of the gods to one another. "Whether these stories have in other ways a good or bad influence," he writes in the tenth book of the *Laws*, "I should not like to be severe upon them, because they are ancient; but, looking at them with reference to the duties of children to their parents, I cannot praise them, or think that they are useful, or at all true." The great dramatists of Greece and the Stoic thinkers were not less outspoken in their condemnation of the immoral myths upon which the people were raised. The Jewish propagandists in Graeco-Roman times saw in them a source of corruption.[157] R. Levi bar Hama dwelt on the kinship that is established between the worshippers and their deities. "He who follows an idol becomes like it, as it is said (Ps. 115:8): 'They that make them shall be like unto them; yea, every one that trusteth in them.' " [158] The clay can assume no finer form than is provided by the mold.*

---

* The thought appears in Philo. He ridicules idolators as persons so demented that we might well say to them, "Good sirs, the best of prayers and the goal of happiness is to become like God. Pray you therefore that you may be made like your images and thus enjoy supreme happiness with eyes that see not, ears that hear not, nostrils which neither breathe nor smell, mouths that never taste nor speak, hands that

It is instructive to note the contrasting relations of
man to deity in primitive and in advanced religions.
Whereas the primitive religions seek to win over or to
coerce the gods, by means of magic, to do man's will,
the advanced religions strive to direct man to do the
will of God and to imitate Him. On a somewhat lower
plane this appears also in the mystery religions. In
Egypt the Osiris cult provided for each man to become an *osiris* after death. By identifying oneself with
the god, the worshipper died with him and rose with
him to new life, i.e., through magical imitation of him,
men acquired immortality. The idea reappears in
Christianity (Acts 2:38; Rom. 6:5–11; Gal. 2:20). In
Judaism, as in the theistic philosophy of Plato, men's
imitation of God assumes purely ethical forms.*

neither give nor take nor do anything at all, feet that walk
not, with no activity in any parts of your bodies" (F. H.
Colson comments that Philo clearly has in mind Ps. 115:5–8;
cf. Spec. Leg. II, 256), "but kept under watch and ward in
your temple-prison day and night, ever drinking in the smoke
of the victims. For this is the one good which you imagine
your idols to enjoy." (Decalogue 15, 73–74.) The Egyptians
who worship animals run the danger of being "transformed
into the nature of these creatures . . . as they pass before
him (the animal deity), they become beasts in human shape."
(*Ibid.*, 16, 80.)

* Mahayana Buddhism makes the imitation of Buddha the
chief end of its teaching. "Every one is potentially a Buddha,
and by the thought of enlightenment he may begin to become
one by passing through numberless existences in which his
aim is not merely to become a Buddha in order to teach, but
also to acquire merit, which may be transferred to others.
He is then a *bodhisattva*." (Edward J. Thomas, art. Righteousness, Buddhist, *H.E.R.E.*, X, 779.)

The immoral attributes of the pagan deities drew the attack of Christianity as well as of Judaism. Salvation, it maintained, can come only through faith in Jesus, who is the embodiment of the Divine. However different their constructions, the innumerable sects of Christendom are at one in looking for the ideal of human personality to Jesus. He is the mediator between God and man in the ethical as in the metaphysical sense. In him God became flesh, claim the orthodox. He is the ideal type of manhood, assert the liberals. Aside from the mythological coloring of his character, the unhistorical elements in its portraiture and the Messianic claims made for him, Judaism has refused to consider him, any more than any other individual, as the absolute ideal for all the ages. Neither Moses nor Jesus, Socrates nor Hillel, Buddha nor Mohammed, Epictetus nor St. Francis can serve as an infallible standard of conduct for all the generations of men of all times and of all lands. Servile copying of one figure proves cramping for individuals who lack his traits and temperament. In view of the growing mental outlook and changing standards of moral behavior under ever-varying needs and conditions, the ideal of one age may be the aversion and despair of the next. The problem is further complicated by the fact that the historical figure of Jesus is shrouded in dense obscurity. Indeed, the conceptions of his ethical character have been variable rather than constant. Each age, land and sect has molded its own image of Jesus. Such idealization of one man has appeared to the Jewish people as inconsistent with pure monothe-

ism. It gives to man the honor that consistently may
be given only to God.*

While refusing to idolize any one person as the pattern of morality for all men and all times, Judaism
recognizes the value of ideal types in the moral education of man. The Bible is replete with noble characters
whose lives no less than their words have acted as
levers of moral progress. The Haggadah dwells upon
their traits and interprets them in the light of Jewish
standards of righteousness. The Midrash to Psalm 15
finds each one of its moral ideals first in God and then
in one of Israel's heroes of faith. The righteous are the
true witnesses to God on earth. Their faithfulness
manifests the greater faithfulness of God. Hence
they constitute the foundation of the world (Prov.
10:24). "The soul of one righteous man outweighs the
whole universe." "God saw that the righteous are
few; He, therefore, planted them in each generation.
. . . The world can be maintained by even one righteous man." According to another statement, there are
no less than thirty-six righteous men in each generation who receive the Shechinah.[159] Jehudah Halevi extols the men of fame "on whose tongues are God's
praises and whose inner beings are free from oppression and deceit, whose nights are spent in prayer and
their days in fasting, in whose hearts are paths unto

* David Friedrich Strauss maintained that the historical Jesus
is simply a problem, and a problem cannot be an object of
faith and an example of life. See *The Old and the New Faith*.
The Bible applies the term "man of God" to Moses, Samuel,
David, Shemaiah, Elijah, Elisha, etc., without ascribing perfection to any one of them.

God and who have places in His throne, whose ways form a ladder ascending to the Lord thy God." [160] Bialik, too, sings of these masters of the art of life and witnesses unto the Divine: "Your lives are your best vision, and your glory is your very being. You are the faithful keepers of the image of God in the world." [161]

Judaism rules out all deification and all worship of saints. Holy men are witnesses unto God, but not gods. They are not divine, but pathfinders to the Divine life. Their virtues light up the dark avenues of human life. In some ages their examples make a stronger appeal than in others. Only in God can each generation, in accordance with its own needs and lights, find the embodiment of its supreme aspirations and ideals, in God not as reflected in the life of one outstanding personality, but in Himself, super-personal, infinite and holy. Hence the call of Judaism: "Be ye holy, for I, the Lord your God, am holy" (Lev. 19:2). To become Godlike is the highest aim of man. [162] When the Torah was translated into Greek, this verse was rendered: "Be ye perfect as I, the Lord your God, am perfect." A pure religious idiom was replaced with an ethical one. The loss in meaning is compensated by uniting the moral and religious aims of man in the single program of *imitatio dei*. We have noted that this ideal forms the basis of Plato's ethico-religious system. By identifying deity with the idea of the good, he rendered the doctrine of *imitatio dei* both intelligible and practicable. In Judaism, too, this doctrine serves as the basis of the ethical life. While God transcends the man-derived moral attributes, He can best be approached by man through them. Holiness, justice, love—are the very essence of man's soul life whereby man is joined unto God. The world's supreme values are set up as the ultimate goal of human striving. Man's will is directed into harmony with the will of the morally perfect Lawgiver and Creator. Man's moral ends are identified with the ends of the Holy One.

*Imitatio dei* becomes the equivalent of Kiddush Hashem. The comment of the Sifra on Lev. 19:2, which we have quoted in part, may form the starting point of rabbinic teaching on this subject. " 'Be ye holy, for I, the Lord your God, am Holy.' If you sanctify yourselves I account it unto you as if you have sanctified Me, but if you have not sanctified yourselves, I account it as if you have not sanctified Me. Lest you imagine that only if you hallow Me am I holy, but if not I am not holy, Scripture specifies: 'for I, the Lord your God, am Holy.' I abide in My holiness irrespective of whether you sanctify Me or not." Sanctification is a human rather than a divine necessity.[163]

Though transcendent, God can be approached through moral conduct. The thirteen attributes of God, revealed in the theophany to Moses (Exodus 34:6–7), set forth standards of human behavior. Haggadists, rationalists and mystics alike employ them to trace the chart of life for man. To be like God one must act like Him.[164] Abba Saul, who is the first to use the words "imitate the King," [165] interprets the words of Exodus 15:2, "This is my God, and I will glorify

Him" (*veanvehu—ani vahu*, i.e., I, man and He, God), as meaning: "Be like Him. As He is merciful and gracious so be thou merciful and gracious." [166] Similarly, the command "to walk in His ways" (Deut. 10:12) is explained as following the thirteen attributes of God.[167] R. Hama b. Hanina comments on Deut. 13:5, "after the Lord your God ye shall walk": How can man walk after Him who is said to be "a devouring fire"? The verse must be taken to mean that man should pattern his life after the Divine attributes. Like Him he must clothe the naked, visit the sick, comfort the mourners, and bury the dead.[168] Commenting on the same verse, another Midrash states: The people asked Moses how they may go after God whose way is in the whirlwind and the storm and in the mighty waters (Nahum 1:3; Ps. 77:20). He replied: "I shall declare unto you His ways. 'All the paths of the Lord are mercy and truth' (Ps. 25:10); mercy means lovingkindness, and truth the Torah." [169] Seder Elijahu Rabba amplifies these views in connection with Deuteronomy 28:9, "Thou shalt walk in His ways." "As God shows mercy unto the wicked and receives them in repentance, so must you practice mercy to one another. Another explanation is: As He is gracious, extending bounties to those who know Him and to those who do not know Him, so must you be generous one to another. A further explanation states: As He is long suffering with the wicked and receives them in repentance, so must you be patient with one another in matters that lead to good, but not in things which lead to punishment. Still another explanation is: As He is abundant in mercy, i.e., He inclines toward mercy, so should you prefer good rather than evil." [170] By manifesting love and consideration for our fellow men we show our Godlikeness.

Solomon Schechter remarks that man's "Godlikeness is confined to his manifestation of mercy and righteousness, the rabbis rarely desiring the Jew to take God as a model in His attributes of severity and rigid justice, though the Bible could have furnished them with many instances of the latter kind." [171] Exaltation, jealousy, revenge, and retribution are left to God, but man must be humble, just and merciful.

To the rationalist the doctrine of *imitatio dei* presented itself as the ideal of reason. Maimonides identified it with the Golden Mean. [172] Bahia b. Asher included under *imitatio dei* the pursuit of truth. [173] R. Obadiah of Sforno taught that man should imitate God by means of reflection, knowledge and the exercise of free will in a manner acceptable to God. [174] The mystic, R. Moses of Cordovero, devotes his treatise "Tomer Deborah" to an exposition of the thirteen attributes as means of attaining the Divine image and likeness.

Traditional Judaism conceived of the Divine attributes as heaven-revealed patterns of conduct. We recognize them rather as reflexes of the God-illumined soul, as the crystallized expressions of the religious aspirations of the Jewish people, and as potent means of leading us into the realm of religious values and of endowing our lives with worth. *Imitatio dei* does not mean for us a slavish imitation of certain anthropomorphic patterns, which tradition has identified with the Divine nature, but our submission to the influences of the Divine, permitting our emotions, intellects and wills to be shaped and controlled by it. The consciousness of God must permeate man's moral values, and irradiate his whole life, adding dignity to his relations with his fellow men, and zest to his striving after the realization of his goals. Far from urging him to become a duplicate of another, *imitatio dei* stimulates man to grow into an original ethical personality. Not only the individual but also the community and the entire people of Israel attain their moral and spiritual status and individuality through their relation to God. His holiness is mirrored in them and is marked by the elevation of their lives. Inherent in the Divine nature, holiness constitutes complete freedom from all moral and spiritual defects and represents the supreme expression of moral sublimity and perfection. A Divine attribute, it serves as the principle and ideal of human conduct.

The pattern of the Menorah, according to the Midrash, was fashioned out of fire, even as everything heavenly is symbolized as fiery. Herein lies one of the vital differences between secular and religious ethics, to which attention was called in a previous chapter. The one is a matter of scientific exposition, formal and dispassionate. It deals with human conduct as physics deals with the laws of motion and gravitation. But religion from one standpoint is "morality tinged with emotion," and from another a special category of the spirit. It is charged with the fire of consecration, and communicates its enthusiasm to the morality which it inspires. Like poetry it appeals to the feelings and to the imagination as well as to the intellect. It conceives of questions of human conduct as of infinite moment. In its view, problems of good and evil are bound up not only with the individual and the race but also with the cosmic order and with God. Hence religion calls upon man to heed the good not merely on prudential grounds, because it yields the best returns or the greatest measure of happiness, but principally because the good is God's way. Though it temporarily plays havoc with our lives, it is still the ultimate good and therefore commands our undivided allegiance. "Though He slay me," the suffering patriarch declared, "yet will I trust in Him" (Job 13:15). Morality based upon social pressure and enforced by the policeman's club is better than no morality at all, but it falls lamentably short of a morality growing out of the inner conscience, of the free and joyous spirit of faith and devotion to God. Man's morality must be founded neither upon compulsion nor upon promised rewards but upon whole-hearted love of truth, goodness and righteousness as manifestations of the Holy One.

SANCTIFICATION OF LIFE. The chief goal of Jewish ethics reveals itself in the nature of Judaism as a religion based upon *Kiddush Hashem* and *Kiddush Hahayyim*, the sanctification of God's name and the sanctification of life. In the idea of sanctification, as we have pointed out, the Divine mingles with the human. The elements which are conceived as Divine are singled out as patterns to be worked into the tapestry of life. The ethical goal presents a new light in which to view the nature of man and of his relations to his fellow men.

If man were not distinguished from the rest of the animal world, or if he were no more than a mechanical combination of matter and energy, pleasure, physical health, and efficiency would have represented his supreme good. But being endowed with mental and spiritual gifts, his life does not reach its highest level of good until it takes on a rational and spiritual character. His mind discloses traces of intelligence at the heart of existence. His impulses for ideal ends point to a source beyond himself of goodness, truth, beauty and holiness. His life is radiated by a spark of the celestial energy which throbs throughout the cosmic order. Stamped with the image of the Creator of all being, man is enabled to achieve sanctity. In the words of the Flemish mystic Ruyersboeck: "Ye are as holy as ye will be holy."

Epictetus asks: "If what philosophers say of the kindred between God and man be true, what has anyone to do but, like Socrates, when he is asked what countryman he is, never to say he is a citizen of Athens or of Corinth, but of the world? Why may not one who realizes his relation to the cosmic order and to God call himself 'a citizen of the world'? Why not a son of God?" [175] The Jewish people have been taught to consider themselves sons of God (Deut. 14:1), and to extend Divine sonship to men of all creeds and races. This doctrine has carried the most far-reaching consequences.

As a child of God, man may not be degraded to a mere cog of either the industrial or the political order. He forms a center of human value and is an end in himself. The worth of the individual is fundamental to the democratic spirit of Judaism. Every person, irrespective of the accidents of birth or station, is regarded as divinely endowed, as the possessor of a soul. Says R. Elazar: "The whole world was created only for the sake of man." R. Abba b. Kahana adds: "Man outweighs the whole world." [176] The significance of these statements lies not in the realm of empirical fact but of ideal value. "Man was created alone," so runs another Talmudic saying, "to teach you that whoever destroys a single soul in Israel is accounted by Scripture as if he has destroyed a whole world; and whoever preserves a single soul is credited with having saved an entire world." [177] Each individual represents the whole universe. Philo comments similarly that the Decalogue was addressed not in the plural but in the singular to teach that "each single person, when he is law-abiding and obedient to God, is equal in worth to a whole nation, even the most populous, or rather to all nations, and if we may go still further, even to the whole world. And therefore elsewhere, when He praises a certain just man, He says, I am thy God, though He was also the God of the world." [178] The great God "could not brook to despise even the humblest, but deigned to banquet him on holy oracles and statutes, as though he should be the sole guest, as though for him alone the feast was prepared to give good cheer to a soul instructed in the holy secrets and accepted for admission to the greatest mysteries." [179]

Crushing of the human spirit offends holiness. Schemes of efficiency, whether industrial, economic, or political, must serve human needs; they must never turn Molochs to which human beings are immolated. Man must not be treated as a mere tool of another's desires but must be assured the means of growing into a free person. Whenever his essential humanity or freedom is crushed, the foundations of the social order are shaken. The social unrest which frequently breaks out in many lands may be traced to the disregard of the sanctity of human life and to the infringement upon the rights of the individual to life, liberty, and the pursuit of happiness in the interests of a particular class, race, party or the state.

Human life, like personality, forms an end in itself and is sacred. Life is an attribute of God, who is visioned as "the source of life" and as "delighting in life." Coming from God, it is man's highest good, which he must cherish as a trust. Life is identified with the good, and death with evil (Deut. 30:15, 19). Shedding of blood, say the rabbis, defiles the land and causes the Shechinah to depart from Israel.[180] Preservation of life has recommended itself to the Jew as the supreme duty of man. The laws of Sabbath observance, of fasting on Yom Kippur, of *kashrut*, etc., are set aside when life is at stake. Even where it is not certain that life can be saved, these laws may be set aside. "There is naught that stands in the way of saving life, except apostasy, incest and murder," [181] i.e., life obtained at the cost of the desecration of its supremest values is not worth having. In the history of Jewish martyrdom, pious women preferred death to defilement.[182]

Suicide under any other circumstances is condemned as a form of murder.* [183] A crime whether against oneself or one's fellow men is an offense against God.[184] "Surely," the priestly writer declares in the name of God, "your blood of your lives will I require; at the hand of every beast will I require it; and at the hand of man, even at the hand of every man's brother, will I require the life of man. Whoso sheddeth man's blood, by man shall his blood be shed; for in the image of God made He man" (Gen. 9:5–6). This harmonized in early times with the practice of blood revenge and subsequently with the legal execution of criminals. An exception was made in the case of self-defense.[185] Philo writes: "Though the slaughter of enemies is lawful, yet one who kills a man, even if he does so in self-defense and under compulsion, has something to answer for, in view of the primal common kinship of mankind." [186] R. Akiba deduced from the verses of Genesis that "whoever sheds blood is regarded as if he has diminished the Divine image. What is the reason for inflicting capital punishment upon one who killed his fellow man? Because man has been made in the

---

* Among the causes that have made for the rapid growth of suicide, the decay of religious faith undoubtedly plays a leading role. Dr. Elwood Worcester expresses the conviction of religious people of all creeds that "when God goes out of a man's life, hope and courage, fortitude in adversity, and a sense of responsibility are apt to go with Him." *Body, Mind and Spirit*, p. 188.

image of God." * Murder is an affront to holiness, for which one forfeits his right to the enjoyment of the Divine gift of life.

Actuated by the belief in the sanctity of human life, the advanced religions of the world have variously proclaimed the commandment: "Thou shalt not murder!" Not alone negatively, but also positively they have persevered in the endeavor to preserve, to protect, and to perfect life, to eliminate pain, misery and sorrow, and to render life more abundant and healthful. They have created homes for the aged, the orphaned and the forlorn; and they have built hospitals and asylums for the care of the sick and the feeble. Compassion for one's fellow man grew out of the conviction of the sanctity of human life. Prompted by this conviction, religions have raised their voices not only against war but also against capital punishment. Though bound by the Biblical law, which sanctions the execution of criminals, R. Akiba and R. Tarfon stated that had they been members of the Sanhedrin they would not have permitted the execution of a single human being.†

* Genesis R. 34:13–14; Yebamot 63b; Tos. Yeb. 8:5; Yalkut Shimeoni, Samuel, 134; Targum Jonathan, Deut. 21:23 states that the reason for not permitting the body of an executed man to remain all night upon the tree is "because he was made in the image of God."

† Makkot 1:10. Carried to the logical extreme, this belief would lead to the condemnation not only of war and of capital punishment, but also of self-defense and of the protection of society against those who seek to destroy its very existence and to crush its highest values, like right, truth,

*Asceticism.* The recognition of the sacredness of human life has rendered Judaism an affair of this world. No unbridgeable gap exists between body and spirit, nor is the flesh vile and corrupt. Not that Judaism has escaped the extravagances of asceticism. The Rechabites and the Nazirites of old, the Essenes and the Therapeutae of Alexandria under Greek influence, and the Mourners of Zion after the fall of the Temple [187] renounced the ways of the world, which lead to sin and to misery. Indeed, the entire institution of Christian monasticism was in some measure affected by the Essenes and the Therapeutae. For Philo, too, mystic union with God was attainable through flight from the world, thus liberating the spirit from its bondage to the flesh.[188] Respected leaders of Pharisaism may be included in this fraternity of saints who sought spiritual salvation through the mortification of the body. The Pharisees were derided by their opponents for mortifying themselves in this world and being destined to disappointment in the next. Men like Hanina ben Dosa, R. Zadok, R. Simeon ben Yohai, Abba Saul and many others that might be named, regarded suffering as signs of Divine love in the most literal sense of the word.

Bahia devotes a chapter of his *Hobot Halebabot* to

religion, compassion, etc. Human experience calls for a reservation of the principle of the sacredness of life, by limiting it to life that is free from criminality. See L. R. Farnell, *Attributes of God*, pp. 159–162. For the application of this idea to war, see Samuel S. Cohon, *Judaism and War*, Popular Studies in Judaism, Union of American Hebrew Congregations; art. War, *Universal Jew. Enc.*, 10, pp. 449–452.

*Perishut* which he defines as self-restraint and abstention from the enjoyment of things which are within
one's reach. He distinguishes, on the one hand, between restraints imposed by the government, those
prescribed by physicians for the sick and those imposed by one's own reason. On the other hand, there
is the distinctive *Perishut*, which the Torah and reason
teach to prepare the soul for the hereafter. It grows
out of God's desire to chastise and to test the human
soul in this world and to purify it that it might par-
take of the character of the holy angels. While asceticism is a necessity for all men, if universally practiced,
it would destroy the world. Accordingly some men
specialize as ascetics in order to act as witnesses to
God.

The Cabbalists of the Middle Ages and the groups
of *Perushim*, that appeared from time to time in various communities to the present day, further show the
extent to which this spirit worked in Jewish life. Long
fasts, "annihilation of the flesh," wandering on foot
away from home and kindred (*Galut*) was the usual
form of ascetic practice. Thereby men hoped to fit
themselves for revelations of Divine truth, to hasten
the Messianic end, and to bring universal salvation.

Nevertheless, it may be stated that in the main Judaism rather discouraged these excesses. As a religion
rooted in the optimistic spirit, it refused to regard
matter as inherently evil, and it checked the tendency
to other-worldliness and the "enjoyment" of unhappi-
ness. On the contrary, it taught man the duty to be
happy. Special benedictions were provided for every

enjoyment. The rabbis frequently quote with approval the comment of R. Simeon ben Eleazar that the sin-offering of the Nazirite (Num. 6:11) was due to his abstention from the use of wine.[189] Rab taught that "man is destined to give account for every legitimate pleasure which he denied himself." [190] A would-be ascetic is told: "Hast thou not enough of the prohibitions of the Torah that thou addest new ones of thine own invention?" [191] R. Jose teaches that "an individual is not allowed to afflict himself by fasting, for he might become dependent upon the public [by reason of incapacity for work] and find no mercy on their part." The Biblical ground for his opinion is found in the verse (Gen. 2:7): " 'And man became a living soul'; the Torah means to say, keep alive the soul which God gave you." [192] Fasting on the Sabbath was condemned as sinful. A fast day other than Yom Kippur which occurs on the Sabbath is postponed to Sunday. The leaders of Hasidism fought excessive asceticism as a species of melancholy. The discipline which Judaism recommends must enhance and enrich life. Anything that blights life and its joys possesses no religious value.

In contrast to the melancholy mood of asceticism, Jehudah Halevi extols the joyous element in Judaism: "Know that our Torah is constituted of the three psychological states: Fear, joy, and love. By each of these thou mayest be brought into communion with God. Thy contrition in the days of fasting does not bring thee nearer to God than thy joy on the Sabbath and on festivals, provided thy joy emanates from a devotional and perfect heart. And just as prayer requires devotion and thought, so does joy, namely, that thou wilt rejoice in His commandments for their own sake [the only reason for this rejoicing being], the love of Him who commanded it, and the desire of recognizing God's goodness towards thee. Consider these feasts as if thou wert the guest of God invited to His table and His bounty, and thank Him for it inwardly and outwardly. And if the joy in God excites thee even to the degree of singing and dancing, it is a service to God, keeping thee attached to Him." [193]

The way to God, in the view of normative Judaism, is not through flight from the world and through self-mortification. Holiness, as we have indicated, while representing a unique category of the spirit, is realizable in man's earthly life. The physical, far from being antithetical to the spiritual, may serve as its vehicle. Holiness is attained through molding the human into the patterns of the Divine. It consists not in the extirpation of the natural instincts and desires, but in their refinement, discipline and direction toward godliness and social as well as personal welfare.

*Marriage and Family Life.* The attitude of Judaism toward sex well illustrates its idea of sanctity. Condemning both libertinism and morbid asceticism, it does not regard the sex instinct as an evil. Only when abused and debased as an instrument of lust and vice, does it lead to human corruption and degradation. As the natural means for the preservation of the race, it has the benediction of the Torah. Marriage is treated not as a mere concession to the flesh,[194] but as a divinely established institution (Gen. 2:18). The command, "Increase, multiply, and fill the earth" (Gen. 1:28), was construed by the rabbis as the first of the 613 Pentateuchal commandments. While the chief aim of marriage is procreation of offspring, sexual gratification was likewise recognized as one of its aims. Woman was to be not merely a child-bearer but also a sex-partner. Far from enjoining abstention from legitimate cohabitation, the Halachah orders both man and wife to respect each other's conjugal rights. However, sanity and consideration must characterize their relations.[195]

The highest interests of the race demand that the well-springs of life be kept pure and undefiled. Hence Judaism sanctions sexual relations only between husband and wife. Any other form of sex experience constitutes *Zenut*, lewdness or immorality. Irregular relationships unsettle the foundations of the family and of the social order. Prostitution, in particular, menaces human well-being. Aside from its danger to health, its unfortunate victims are reduced to the status of slaves, serving as the mere tools of lust.[196]

Marriage must be based not only upon physiological instinct but also upon psychic factors, such as the desire for companionship, affection and love. In a polygamous age, the wife was spoken of as a man's helpmate (Gen. 2:18). The marriage relation is referred to in Prov. 2:17 as a Divine covenant. C. H. Toy comments: "The old polygamy or bigamy (the rule up to the Exile) is ignored; monogamy is assumed as the established custom. The husband is the trusted friend;

the marriage-tie has a Divine sanction (cf. Mal. 2:14). The expression *covenant of God* may refer simply to the general idea of sacredness involved, or it may possibly allude to a religious marriage ceremony." [197] The primary meaning of the rabbinic term for marriage, *Kiddushin*, is setting the wife apart for the husband alone, rendering her tabu to any other man.[198] But it came to convey the idea of consecration in the ethical and religious sense.

Though marriage did not assume, in Judaism, the nature of a *sacrament*, i.e., an outward sign or channel of inward and Divine grace (as in the Church, on the ground of the term *mystery* in Ephesians 5:32), it was viewed as sacred. The basis of the family and the home, it is of the utmost social significance. Its violation through adultery constitutes a violation of a Divine order which cannot be condoned by the offended party. According to Jewish law the court must compel the husband to divorce his wife who had been found guilty of adultery.[199] *Gilluy 'Arayot* (i.e., both incest and adultery), like idolatry and murder, must be avoided even under the threat of death.[200] Fidelity, purity, and chastity form the conditions of marriage.

The Jewish family is based not only on economic and biological considerations but also on a religious foundation. "Man cannot exist without woman, nor woman without man, and both of them without the Shechinah." [201] No conflict, therefore, is envisaged between one's duty to his family and to God (as in 1 Corinthians 7:25–40), for through family life one serves God. Celibacy was regarded with disfavor.[202]

The high priest who was to perform the atonement rites was expected to have a wife.[203] Isserles prescribes that the officiating *hazzan* during the penitential season must be a married man.[204] Orthodox congregations generally refrained from having unmarried rabbis, a practice diametrically opposed to that of Roman Catholicism.

The family is the nursery of the race. The parents stand in the place of Providence in relation to their offspring. They are obligated to care not only for their children's physical well-being but also for their moral and spiritual development. Education represents a cardinal Jewish duty. In turn, children are commanded to honor their parents, to revere them and to care for them in sickness and in old age. The duty to honor parents extends beyond the grave, and expresses itself in the tender remembrance of the dead and in the observance of the anniversaries of their departure by the recitation of the Kaddish.[205] "There are three partners in man: God, father and mother. When men honor their parents, God says: 'I account it unto them as if I were dwelling among them and they honored Me.'" [206] As no other factor, the pure and tender family ties helped to preserve the Jewish people and to keep them on a healthy and moral plane.[207]

*Dietary Laws.* A further illustration of the application of the sacred to Jewish life is afforded by the dietary laws. While they have exerted beneficial effects upon the health of the Jewish people, their hygienic value is but incidental. Their primary aim is to train the Jews in holiness. Derived from ancient tabus and intended at first for the priests (Ezek. 4:14; 44:31), they were subsequently extended to all Israel as the priest people of God (Ex. 22:30; Deut. 14:21; 12:13–27). Their purpose is summarized in Leviticus 20:26: "And ye shall be holy unto Me; for I the Lord am holy, and have set you apart from the peoples, that ye shall be Mine." The Pharisees carried the rules of priestly purity from the Temple into the home (with ablutions before meals and with benedictions), thus turning it into a sanctuary and the table into an altar. They took over the temple mode of slaughtering and inspecting the sacrificial animals for the preparation of their meat (*Shehitah* and *Bedikah*).[208] The dietary laws were invested with the absoluteness of Divine commands. They were to be observed not because of personal taste, but as an expression of obedience to God. In the words of the Sifra to Lev. 20:26: "Say not, 'I do not like swine's flesh'; but rather 'I do like it, but abstain from eating it in accordance with the decree of my Father in heaven.'" These laws are classified by the rabbis as *hukkim* (statutes), which transcend human reason, and must be observed—despite the derision of gentiles—as means of consecration to God. Rab suggests a moral ground for their observance. "What difference does it make to God whether one slaughters the animal by cutting the neck in front or in the back? Or what matters it to Him whether one eats pure or impure things? This shows that the commandments were given only for the purpose of testing men." [209] The ritual minutiae of shehitah and of the other laws of *kashrut* are thus conceived as serving the purpose of trying and purifying human character. They were interpreted as safeguards against cruelty to animals, as measures to train men in self-discipline, and as means of distinguishing the Jews as a priest people and of submission to God's will.[210]

Maimonides concludes his treatment of the dietary laws in his Code with the comment: "Whoever is careful in the observance of these matters invests himself with added holiness and purity, and cleanses his soul for God's sake, in keeping with the words (Lev. 11:44): 'Sanctify yourselves therefore, and be ye holy.'" In his Guide he writes that the object of observing them "is to restrain the growth of desire, the indulgence in seeking that which is pleasant, and the disposition to consider the appetite for food and drink as the end [of man's existence]."[211]

As long as the Jews lived apart from the rest of the world, the dietary laws presented effective means of holding the Jews together as members of a holy community. Partaking of swine flesh, for example, was equivalent to apostasy (II Macc. 7:1ff.). With the break-up of the ghetto and the growth of social intercourse between Jews and Christians, the restrictive rules of diet began to present serious difficulties for the modern Jew. The motive of isolating the Jews from their neighbors, which inspired them in the past, now became the chief reason for their neglect by ever-growing numbers. With the struggle of the Jewish people for social as for civic equality, any custom or law that preserves barriers between them and their neighbors is resented. Furthermore, their economic as well as their social welfare requires that they maintain table-fellowship with their neighbors. Jewish separateness must not be too general if Jews are to share in the common life of the countries of which they form a part. Whatever distinctiveness inheres in their self-preservation as Jews must be limited to the sphere of religion and the cultural and social elements associated therewith, as is the case with Catholics, Episcopalians, Quakers, or Unitarians.

Under these conditions some doubt the value of maintaining the dietary laws, with their emphasis on outward purity and holiness, as part of spiritual religion in modern times. Others take the position that with some modifications, these laws still fulfill a vital function and should be preserved. Judaism, embracing the whole of life, cannot exclude from its consideration questions of diet any more than it can ignore questions of personal well-being or of family and social relations. As a way of living it must stress temperance and moderation in the use of meats and drinks and the avoidance of excessive luxuries, etc. Even the health aspect of the question—while primarily belonging to the sphere of hygiene—may not be wholly excluded from the concern of religion if we recognize the interdependence of spiritual states and the physical and mental health of men. But it is the religious needs of modern Jewry that make at least part of the dietary laws necessary. No one who is familiar with the masses of men will fail to recognize that where abstract religious and ethical teachings fail, concrete observances may prove effective in inculcating the spirit of holiness. As in the past, the dietary laws train men in obedience to religious demands; and inasmuch as they evoke obedience to some things they may stimulate obedience to others as well. They also foster self-restraint and self-discipline. They further identify the Jew not only with his past, but also with his fellow Jews of all parts of the world today.

The danger of their acting as barriers between the Jew and his environment may be met by relaxing their rigorism. Accordingly, it has been suggested that only the Pentateuchal laws of diet (Lev. 11; Deut. 14) be kept, and that the more burdensome and seemingly arbitrary extensions and modifications of these laws by the rabbis be dropped. This would exclude from the Jewish diet not only the flesh of a diseased animal or of one that died a natural death or that was killed by a beast (*nebelah* and *terephah*)—which have come to be prohibited by the sanitary laws of all civilized lands —but also the meat of swine, wild animals, and of birds of prey, as well as shell-fish. It would relax the prohibition of eating milk and meat together and the requirements of ritual slaughter and of the extraction of the sinews and the blood from the meat.

Despite the difficulties in distinguishing between the Pentateuchal laws and their rabbinic modifications—especially since centuries of observance have drawn them together into one whole—there is merit in the effort since it saves the basic purposes of the dietary laws, of strengthening the Jewish consciousness of the individual and of maintaining the religious character of the home.[212]

The sacred combines ritual with moral elements. It also contains a tinge of the aesthetic. According to the rabbis, to be holy means to be not only consecrated to God, but also to be separated from objects and ways that defile.[213] "Separateness leads to purity, and purity to holiness." [214] The emphasis is on pure acts and also on pure feelings and thoughts and on pure speech. Purity is a virtue of the mind as well as of the body. It is both an aesthetic and an ethical matter. The Torah, Maimonides teaches, seeks to promote purity and holiness among its followers "by teaching them to suppress sensuality, to guard against it, and to reduce it to a minimum." Sanctification further spells restraint in drinking, eating, and other forms of enjoyment. "Cleanliness in dress and body by washing and removing sweat and dirt is included among the various objects of the Law, but only if connected with purity of action, and with a heart free from low principles and habits. It would be extremely bad for man to content himself with a purity obtained by washing and cleanliness in dress, and to be at the same time voluptuous and unrestrained in food and lust. . . . The chief object of the Law is to [teach man to] diminish his desires, and to cleanse his outer appearance after he has purified his heart." [215] Even within the limits of the Law, one must avoid extremes. The rule for the religious person is: *Kaddesh atzmecha b'muttar lach*—sanctify thyself in the enjoyments that are permissible to thee.[216] Despite the current popularity of the cult of self-expression, the religious way calls for sanity in the enjoyment of the natural pleasures of life, for restraint even in legitimate sexual relations, and in the use of food and drink. The golden mean avoids both extremes of self-indulgence and of indiscriminate self-denial, and strives after a life of reason and of faith.

COOPERATION WITH GOD: LABOR. Man is most like God when he engages in creative work. He lives in two worlds. As a citizen of the physical kingdom, he must take orders. He is subject to all the physical laws that govern all other creatures. He must submit to the laws of birth and death, of bodily health and sickness. Like a Prometheus he is chained to the rock of natural circumstance. But as a citizen of the kingdom of the mind, man also gives orders. By means of his intellect and will, he obtains partial freedom from the fetters that shackle him. He can overcome nature's laws that menace his well-being by arraying against them another set of laws that work to his advantage. Disease and pestilence threaten him. He checks them with the aid of medical science and sanitation. He bridles the destructive powers of electricity and bids them give him light, carry his burdens, propel his machines, and transmit his voice. He tames the elements and makes them his servants. The very laws of gravitation, which pull him down, he turns into wings for his flying through the air. Through these endeavors man attains the fulness of his powers. In the language of the rabbis, he becomes a *Shutaph* or co-worker with God in tasks of creation.[217] Every human being is both an instrument and an agent of creative life.

Man's true vocation is to be a creator. He is called

upon to complete that which God has initiated. Nature is full of thorns and thistles. It is for man to make it blossom as a rose. Nature is infested with deadly bacilli and with pestilence. Man must render it healthful. By properly exercising his talents and gifts, he carries forward the work of God. He can call new worlds of his own into being. He creates worlds of art, poetry, music and science. He builds cities and countries, and produces civilization. As George Eliot's poem, "Stradivarius," makes the great violin maker say:

> My work is mine,
> And heresy or not, if my hand is slackened
> I should rob God—since He is the fullest good—
> Leaving a blank instead of violins.
> I say, not God Himself can make man's best
> Without best men to help Him. I am one best
> Here in Cremona, using sunlight well
> To fashion finest maple till it serves
> More cunningly than throats, for harmony.
> ............... 'tis God gives skill,
> But not without man's hands: He could not make
> Antonio Stradivari's violins
> Without Antonio.

As the scientific and artistic so the moral and the religious universe is the construct of man's inventive and creative spirit. We are citizens of God's kingdom, subjects of the Supreme Power who guides the universe in ways which are hidden from us. We feel, however, that in some way, not always clear to ourselves, we are agents and instruments of the Divine power and will, which keep the universe going. In this consciousness of participation in the creative labors of God we find our full self-realization. The noblest goal that we can possibly set up for ourselves is "the full employment of our nature in harmony" with the Divine, to eradicate evil and to increase the good, to create new values and to add to the well-being of the world.

This task is within reach of the humble as well as of the great. To a certain degree every person is a creator of some kind, the bricklayer even as the master-builder, the farm-hand as well as Burbank, the ordinary music maker as well as Beethoven, the telegraph operator and electrician as well as Edison, and the housewife as well as Madame Curie. The more of the creative spirit we are able to bring with us to our tasks, the greater is the happiness that we derive from them ourselves and the greater the joy which we transmit to others. The consciousness of having accomplished worth while tasks is the source of truest happiness. In the words of "Stradivarius":

> 'Tis rare delight: I would not change my skill
> To be Emperor with bungling hands,
> And lose my work, which comes as natural
> As self at waking.

The sage teaches: "Whatsoever thy hand attaineth to do by thy strength, that do; for there is no work, nor device, nor knowledge, nor wisdom, in the grave, whither thou goest" (Eccl. 9:10). Work alone makes life meaningful and blessed. The joy that comes from it is contagious. It increases the happiness of the world.

To translate the ideal of cooperation with God into a life of industry in cooperation with one's fellow men has been one of the chief ethical goals of Judaism.

The conception of man as co-worker of God furnishes the key to the Jewish attitude toward labor. Work is the vocation of man, the chief instrumentality of his joy and salvation. However, it is not only the joy of labor but its pain that is sounded in Jewish literature. The second chapter of Genesis reechoes the cry of the weary that labor is a curse. The tillers of the soil in southern Palestine, who struggled against the desert influence and against the thorns and thistles that overcrowded their arid land, naturally felt the bitterness of their toil. The Biblical author, voicing their sentiments, explained labor as the consequence of Divine displeasure. Due to a grave sin on the part of the father of the human race, the soil was cursed and man was made to wrest bread from it through the sweat of his brow.

Conditions have been at work that made this sentiment universal. Whether one tills the ground or tunnels the rocks, whether one builds with brick and stone, or carries heavy burdens, his labor is accompanied by a pain that frequently leaves a deadening effect upon him.

Though doing the world's work, laborers were kept in fetters and were bought and sold like cattle. That pall of servitude has not been entirely lifted from them even in these days of supposed freedom. No sooner were they liberated from physical bondage than economic and industrial progress forged new shackles for them. Before the great industrial revolution was ushered in by the invention of steam power, the workers bound or free, for the most part, had the opportunity of doing skilled work. The carpenter, the blacksmith, or the tailor was called upon to produce a complete article. Therein his personality often found room for self-expression. His labor, even if attended by much pain, also afforded him some pleasure, for through it he displayed his creative power, his skill and his taste, i.e., his free personality. This joy of work well done and of self-expression, in a great measure, has been removed from the toilers through the introduction of steam, gas, and electric power and the subsequent division of labor. Instead of creating a whole object, the worker is assigned a small part of it by turning the wheel of a machine which does the work for him. From morning to evening he drives the wheel "to mold a pin or fabricate a nail." The days lengthen into weeks, the weeks into months and the months into years, finding him at the same task of boring holes in buttons or turning studs. Thus "the iron wheels go onward grinding life from its mark." The modern methods of division of labor have immeasurably increased the wealth of the world, but they also have impoverished humanity by transforming the laborer into an appendix to a machine, or even into a small cog in the wheel of the machine. Humanity is knocked out of him. Little room is offered for the exercise of mind or will. He is but a "factory hand." His whole skill is concentrated in tending and keeping pace with the machine.

In centers of distribution no less than in the places of the production of goods the same routine prevails. Though his task may be less onerous, the clerk is not wholly relieved of monotony and grind. His whole day passes in tying bundles, pasting labels and assorting goods. If he is more fortunate, he is entrusted with the task of making entries or of manipulating the counting machine or typewriter. To a certain extent, his personality, too, is submerged. Only instead of being a "factory hand" he is an automatic machine. Weary of his routine, he looks upon the time spent at work as the price which he is forced to pay for the few moments of leisure which may be his at the end of the day's labor.

So it is throughout the field of endeavor. Not the love of work, but the fear of starvation and the craving for a bit of pleasure drive men into the fields and mines, into copper works and stock-yards, into foundries and ammunition plants. Men expose themselves to unbearable heat and to poisonous gasses, and run the risk of occupational diseases and accidents in order to save themselves and their dependents from the pangs of hunger. Eating their bread in the sweat of their brows, workers naturally feel resentful of a social order that robs them of the joy that comes of free creative labor.

The exploitation of man by man in the form of slavery deprived the ancient nations of the true nobility and joy of work. Even so highly gifted a people as the Greeks failed to discover the true meaning of labor as the means of human self-realization. Its philosophers

and poets no less than its masses rated work beneath
the dignity of free men. Not only rough, common and
hard toil, but all handicrafts and even works of art,
which lend so much luster to the name of Greece, were
relegated to slaves. Free men, supposedly made of finer
clay, were destined for leisure, pleasure and revelry.
The only occupations worthy of them were hunting
and fighting. The Germanic nations, too, were more
attracted to the sword and the spear than to the plough
and the sickle. Leaving their work to the women and
slaves, the heroic Teutons engaged in the chase and in
battle.

Of all the nations of antiquity, Israel alone recognized that labor holds the secret springs of joy, and
emphasized the greater dignity of labor than of warfare. Work alone is truly honorable. The monition
"chose life" (Deut. 30:19) means: choose a handicraft.
"Love labor and hate lordship" is the text of rabbinic
teaching. The most offensive labor is not as degrading
as idleness. It is better for a man to flay a carcass in
the public square than to become a public charge.[218]
Work, no matter of what nature, provided it be honest
and legitimate, exalts and dignifies man, and renders
him a true child of God, who Himself is pictured as a
Master-Worker. The father of the human race, according to the legend of Genesis, was placed in the
Garden of Eden not for idle play but for the purpose
of tilling and caring for the Garden. As a child of
God, he was to assist in God's work. It is only when
Adam was lured into sin that labor lost its charm and
became a curse. But even this curse the rabbis viewed

as a blessing. They said that when Adam heard the words of God announcing that the ground would yield thorns and thistles and that he would have to "eat the herb of the field," he cried: "What! Shall I and my cattle eat from the same manger?" But when God added that in the sweat of his brow he would eat bread, Adam was relieved and blessed the hallowing power of labor, whereby he would be able to rise above the brute world.[219]

This exaltation of labor marks all Jewish literature. The leaders of the people are pictured not as hero-warriors, but as hero-workers, brave toilers, cheerful shepherds and ploughmen. In whatever field they engaged they served their Maker by performing their tasks in His spirit. The story of the building of the Tabernacle tells that God put His spirit into Bezalel to enable him to perform all manner of work. The same spirit that prompted the prophets to prophesy, Psalmists to sing, and kings to rule, also prompted artisans to work.

Rabbi Eliezer well characterizes labor as a form of Divine worship and adds: "great is labor for even as the people of Israel were enjoined concerning the Sabbath, so were they commanded to labor, for it is said (Ex. 20:9): Six days shalt thou labor, and do all thy work, and the seventh day shall be a Sabbath unto the Lord thy God." [220] Indolence on week-days leads to the profanation of the Sabbath. Scripture says: "The Lord thy God will bless thee in all the work of thy hands" (Deut. 14:29). "Shall I infer from this statement that the Divine blessing will come even to him who stays idle? Therefore the verse continues: 'which thou doest.' " [221] Where there is no labor there is no blessing. Hence the rabbis rated the merit of industry above idle piety. In the words of the Psalmist:

> When thou eatest the labor of thy hands,
> Happy shalt thou be, and it shall be well with thee.
> —128:2. [222]

While there are drones in every hive who fatten on the work of others, they are to be pitied rather than envied. Idleness is a curse which leads to ill health and to immorality. [223] A good share of honest toil has recommended itself to moderns as a cure of many an illness and as the best way out of mischief. "He who does not teach his son a trade is as if he taught him robbery." [224] A person of sound health has no right to live on that which he has not earned. Adam, while still in the Garden of Eden, was not allowed to eat before he earned his bread by work. [225] In the wilderness, too, the manna was given to the Israelites only upon the condition that they would perform some kind of labor. Should man say: "I am a scion of a distinguished family and, therefore, ought not degrade myself through work," he is to be reminded: "Foolish man, your Creator has preceded you; He worked long before you were born." "Great is work, for it honors those who engage in it." All the prophets engaged in labor. The Shechinah rested upon the Children of Israel only after they labored. The men of piety sustained themselves by work, no matter how menial.[226]

Labor is not only the means of personal self-expression, but also of the stability and the happiness of the family and of the well-being of the community and the nation and of humanity at large. Rough and unpleasant tasks, while trying on the worker, may be necessary for the health of society. The menial tasks on the farm or in the factory, in the city streets or in the market-place, in sick rooms or in kitchens—though unheralded and unsung—are indispensable to the preservation of society. Hand labor and brain work are equally needed and honorable. The greatest benefactors of mankind spent their energies in unselfish and sometimes trying work. The great songs of the world have not been composed by butterflies. Men gave their hearts and their brains that music might be. Their pain has secured the world's joy. All that is best in the world—the proud structures of antiquity, the glories of medieval art, and the exploration of new lands, the discoveries of scientific truths and their application to practical purposes—all that makes up our complex civilization; is the product not of idleness but of hard and back-breaking toil. The struggle for the maintenance of life on our planet is so strenuous that it demands the combined efforts of all humanity. To this struggle every human being has something to contribute. The tiny contributions of all individuals form the monument which each generation leaves behind and whereby its memory is kept for future ages.

Man's vocation is to achieve the good through honest toil. It is his task to remove the pain of labor, by removing the unnecessary drudgery and hardship connected therewith, and to eliminate the cancers of slavery and ruthless exploitation that feed upon it. The economic depression that came in the aftermath of the First World War and which contributed to producing the Second World War demonstrated that the curse from which men suffer is not labor but lack of labor. The task of securing gainful employment for the millions of men who may be forced into idleness has come to form one of the major problems of the world's governments. How to remove the conditions which fill labor with pain and turn it into a source of joy, how to eradicate the elements of bitterness that all too often mingle with toil, and how to create conditions under which men and women shall be able to engage in fields congenial to their natures, and to eat the fruit of their labor in gladness, represents the foremost task of humanity today. Around the solution of this problem revolve the social, economic, and political issues of our time.

# XII. SOCIAL RIGHTEOUSNESS

THE INDIVIDUAL AND SOCIETY. The ethical ideal of Judaism is attainable by pursuing the twofold path of personal and social advancement. The individual forms the unit of all human relationship. The whole social order, whether economic, industrial and political, or cultural, ethical and religious, begins with and centers in the individual. All difference between happiness and misery, prosperity and failure, perfection and degradation, responsibility and shiftlessness, thrift and parasitism, derive from him. Indeed, the moral world may be said to exist for the individual.

Individuality is a slow fruitage of maturing humanity. It emerged gradually out of the mass of ancient society and slowly acquired a measure of freedom from the mores and tabus of the tribe and people. After long struggle, to live his own life, to think his own thoughts, to aspire after ideals that fire his mind, and—to a more limited degree—to act in accordance with his own convictions, came to be recognized in progressive lands as the highest good of man. In some countries the individual still has no existence aside from the nation, and no freedom aside from that which is granted him by the head of the state or the political party in power. Even in free states, emancipation from crowd-mindedness has been achieved by the veriest few. Constitutional freedom for the individual in political, commercial and religious spheres is more common. In the economic realm, it still figures chiefly in the theories of some idealists, but finds little room in actuality. Totalitarian schemes, far from offering the individual relief in this regard, threaten to deprive him of the modicum of freedom which he enjoys under the competitive system, and to reduce him to a mere cog in the machine of planned society or of self-contained national economics.

Inasmuch as society is not composed of Robinson Crusoes, the freedom of the individual can never be absolute but only relative. As a creature of sense, he is bound up in his own skin and is absorbed in his interests and needs. Shutting his eyes to reality, he may imagine himself a world apart, differing from all the rest and independent of them, creating out of his inner resources the conditions for his being. In the world of fact no person is his own parent. Life may manifest itself in the single cell, but its full growth and development is contingent upon the entire organism of which it is a part. The propagation of life, while expressing itself through the individual, is inseparable from the preservation of the species. At his lowest biological level, man is a creature of society. He has no existence apart from his family, people and race.*

Allowing for the inexactness of the analogy, the individual may be compared to a branch on a tree, which, while separated from the other branches at one end is united with them through the common trunk

* Bergson observes that this "can only be a comparison, for an organism subject to inexorable laws is one thing, and a society of free wills is another." *Two Sources of Morality and Religion*, p. 1.

and roots. At the root of our being, we are all part of one another. The blood that streams in our veins, the physiques that distinguish us from one another, the surges of emotion that well up within us, our very endowments of mind are not of our own making. They are heritages from a racial past that link us to fellow heirs. The rich gifts of language, of culture, of ideas, of knowledge, of taste for beauty, of customs and habits, the notions of truth and the standards of right and of goodness come to us from the society in which we were born and in which we were nurtured and live. In turn these gifts unite us with that society. We are products of a certain group, children of a particular people, citizens of a definite state and country. The inexorable laws of heredity and environment in great measure dictate to each individual the particular place which he must hold in society.

To recognize his dependence upon society and to discover, at the same time, the measure of independence that he may enjoy by virtue of his rational and spiritual nature, i.e., his freedom, is man's true course to self-realization. Such recognition is indispensable to securing the proper harmony between the individual and his community as well as of the balance between his rights and duties. In his own fashion each person must translate Hillel's saying into his life: "If I am not for myself, who will be for me? But if I am only for myself, what am I?" [227]

The recognition that our lives are shaped by the patterns of our social heritage carries far-reaching implications. We were not consulted regarding the conditions in which we were born and in which we spent the impressionable years of our early youth. Yet it was within those conditions that our minds and spirits were fashioned. Our personalities, characters and consciences were to a considerable degree cast into the molds supplied by our heritage of custom and of moral and religious idealism and practice. Whatever freedom we enjoy to modify our lives and to find our place in the world is generally attained through our identification with the forces and elements of our environment. We express our gifts and talents and discover our tasks within the group of our birth or of our choice and adoption. As we grow we not only adjust ourselves to the standards of our people, but in turn affect them whether for good or ill. We may become destructive parasites adding to our people's woes and miseries, or we may become bearers of their burdens, creative sharers in the social process, economic, political and cultural. In either case we feel the strain of communal and national ills, of insecurity, poverty, exploitation, war, etc., and benefit from social prosperity and well-being. Our lives receive meaning from the life of our people. Its welfare spells also our welfare, and their misery is our own.

Loyalty to the particular people to which we belong by birth and upbringing forms the means of our cultural, moral and spiritual growth. The examples of our leaders supply the standards of our personal conduct. Our people's visions and tasks direct our thoughts and deeds. Its joys and triumphs inspirit us, its sorrows sober and discipline us, and its hopes lift our hearts.

By identifying ourselves with our own people and sharing their destiny we take our proper places in the advancing ranks of bearers of its moral and religious values.

As with the people so with the country. Though its government sometimes pursues courses to which we cannot give our fullest assent, it is our home, with which all we cherish for the present and future is bound up. "Seek the peace of the city whither I have caused you to be carried away captive," Jeremiah counselled the Judean exiles in Babylon, "and pray for it unto the Lord, for in the peace thereof shall ye have peace" (29:7). However, experience teaches that "patriotism is not enough." Unless patriotism is founded upon ethical principles, it may turn into a tyrannous force in the lives of men. It is therefore of transcendent importance for all men to guard the laws that govern their country and to see to it that its national and international policies be justly conceived and faithfully executed. The personal well-being of the individual depends upon the scrupulous and impartial administration of the government. His freedom calls for the freedom of others, and is restrained by their freedom. He must do justice to others if he is to receive justice from them. He must treat others as brothers if he is to be treated as a brother. The love which he craves he must manifest to his fellow men. Thus personal freedom, justice and love are universalized and socialized. The enslavement of one individual is a potential threat to all members of the community.

Social-mindedness thus conditions personal well-being. While demanding from society to be treated as an end in himself, the individual may not regard himself as the end. His search for personal happiness is doomed to failure unless he regards the welfare of society. Thus the contrast between the individual and society loses its poignancy in the ethical sphere. A person's conduct can never be something apart from the interest of the group. His actions, no matter how seemingly private, have definite social bearing. The drunkard, the drug addict, the libertine and the would-be suicide cannot claim that their actions concern only themselves. From the cradle to the grave, we live and move among fellow men, and are affected by their thoughts and deeds even as they are by ours. Consequently, while attaching the greatest value to individuality, to the free and unhampered development of personality, we must recognize that individuality itself is socially conditioned. Our characters are molded by the society of which we are a part. The ethics of Judaism, therefore, concerns itself not only with the springs and motives of personal behavior but also with their relations to the community.

The integration of individuals within the community is conditioned by their natural differences of physical and mental endowments, of race and sex, and by their social, religious and occupational affiliations. While stressing the obligations of their common humanity, Jewish teaching stresses their respective duties. Man's tasks begin wherever he happens to be. The strong have obligations toward the weak, parents toward their children, even as children toward their parents, employers toward their employees, employees toward their employers and both of them toward the public. This interdependence extends not only to the social, economic and political fields but also to the spheres of general culture, art and religion. The individual may be at once a consumer, a producer, a member of society, a seeker of truth, a creator of things of use or of beauty, and a believer. He associates himself with others to promote these varied interests. Under normal conditions these manifold relationships blend into a harmonious whole. However, circumstances arise when man as a scientist, thinker, writer, or artist stands in opposition to the claims made upon him by the state, which demands that he subordinate his visions to its policies. A choice must then be made between duty to truth and to goodness and duty to the political order, and between his professional or religious associations and the state.

The conflict assumes explosive proportions in the realm of religion. During the existence of the Jewish commonwealth, for example, the prophets were often pitted against the heads of the state. The clashes between Elijah and Ahab, of Amos and Jeroboam II, of Isaiah and Ahaz, of Jeremiah and Jehoiakim and Zedekiah concerned the character and destiny of the nation. Was the nation to subordinate itself to the will of its kings or to the rule of God? Was its life to be determined by political expediency or by the eternal law of righteousness? The Hasidim combined with the Maccabees in resisting the Hellenization of the Jewish spirit. The Pharisees similarly struggled against the secularized Sadducean rulers to preserve the character of Israel as a religious people.

With the fall of the Jewish state the relation of the individual to the community was greatly aggravated. In the Diaspora, he was confronted not only by the pressures of his own people, but both he and his people found themselves under the rule of alien governments and alien religions. Following Jeremiah's teaching, they recognized their duties to the governments of the lands in which they lived, and especially of the countries where they settled by their own choice. At the same time, they were committed to the way of life dictated by their religious heritage. The conflict was resolved by the common sense rule of Mar Samuel that "the law of the land is binding—*dina d'malchuta dina*." * Even where the Jews had their own courts, they recognized the judiciary system of the state. This rule applied only to *civil* legislation (*dina*). In ritual law (*issura*) or in religious belief, they rigidly adhered to their inherited standards and defended them with their lives against all encroachments by either temporal or ecclesiastical rulers.[228]

This compromise between religious and civil law

---

* R. Samuel b. Meir comments, B.B. 54b, that inasmuch as all the subjects accept the laws of the government of their own volition, the laws are binding upon them. R. Nissim adds that the laws of the government are binding only if they are followed by the governmental authorities themselves, but not when they act contrary to the laws. Such instances constitute violence, and hence are not binding. Comment on Gittin 10b. R. Moses Sofer invests the rule of Mar Samuel with religious sanction. (Note to Yoreh Deah, 314.)

placed the Jews at a grave disadvantage under medieval conditions in which the Church and the Mosque
dictated the laws of the lands in which the Jews constituted a voiceless minority. Conditions changed with
the dawn of Jewish emancipation in Europe and in
America. The Jews were now placed on a par with
their Christian neighbors in shaping and in administer-
ing the laws of their lands of birth or adoption. Under
the new conditions the civil law of the land rightly
constitutes the law of the Jew as well as of the Christian. Only in strict matters of religious life, e.g., ritual
and belief, do Jews and Christians retain their separateness.

Except, therefore, where governments are discrim-
inatory and tyrannical, running counter to the laws of
God and humanity, and violating the most sacred convictions of faith, right and truth, individuals and
groups owe them loyalty and cooperation. While giving whole-hearted allegiance to their country, men of
different faiths and professions often devote themselves to the advancement of the welfare of fellow believers or associates in common enterprises in other
lands. The Catholics of the world are bound by religious ties to one another and to the Vatican. The
Protestants, to a lesser degree, are similarly linked up
by their missionary endeavors and by the efforts to
build up an ecumenical Christianity. Scientific, humanitarian, and trade union interests, too, cut across
the barriers of government and geography.

So the Jews, while identified as nationals of various
lands, are drawn together by several factors. Foremost

among them are the common heritage of faith, common descent and the common historical memories and associations. Wherever Jews live they organize themselves into free communities or congregations for religious, cultural and social purposes. Jewish philanthropic activities generally aid the needy and the distressed, not only of the local and national community, but also of all parts of the world. In the face of a cold and often irresponsive world, Jews are compelled to rely upon one another in sorrow and travail. "Redeeming captives" in medieval times and helping victims of pogroms and refugees from lands of despotism in modern times have claimed the concern of the Jewish people. The virulence of anti-Semitism even in democratic lands further calls for concerted defense on the part of the Jews. Even non-religious elements are drawn into these endeavors, and are thereby brought closer to their fellow Jews. The rehabilitation of Palestine as a haven for the homeless and as a center of cultural and spiritual life has acted as a unifying force in world Jewry, despite the sharp cleavage which the political program of Zionism has evoked. The creation of the state of Israel in Palestine will call forth the generous sympathy and cooperation of Jews in other countries, without affecting their loyalties and obligations as citizens of their respective fatherlands. Such interrelations widen man's horizon and draw closed national groups into a universal society.

RIGHTEOUSNESS AND JUSTICE. Judaism builds the moral world upon the foundations of justice and love. We have noted that man emerges as an individual through his social contacts, through his self-assertion both physically and mentally, and through his embodiment of the strivings and aspirations of his fellow men. He is a product of social forces and throughout life he sustains unbroken relationships with them. He accordingly takes his rightful place in society as an ethical being.

The firm foundation of the social order is justice. It probably dawned early in man's development as the simple rule which places all members of the tribe as equals before the chief and before the deity. In its forensic form it is embodied in the *lex talionis*, of "an eye for an eye and a tooth for a tooth." "As one does so shall it be done unto him" (Ex. 21:24; Lev. 24:19–20). The rule of like for like applied only to tribesmen. To strangers the rule of the jungle applied, of doing to them whatever was within one's power. With the widening of social relations and sympathies, justice extended the sphere of its operations beyond the limits of the group and became intertribal and national, and it steadily strives to become international.*

Under prophetic teaching, justice came to be the touchstone of religion. Conceived as an attribute of God and the ideal pattern of human behavior, it was

---

* The primitive nature of the *lex talionis* showed itself in the mechanical mode of its execution, which ignored the total effect of its operation upon the victim. Pharisaic Judaism mitigated its harshness by introducing monetary compensation for physical injuries. "An eye for an eye" was interpreted to mean payment for the loss of the eye.

identified with righteousness, the all-inclusive moral category of Judaism. The Hebrew words for righteousness, *tzedek* and *tzedakah*, like the Latin *rectus*, may have had in their earliest uses the physical meaning of straightness or soundness, but came to be applied to moral conduct in the sense of conformity to norm, vindication and justification. They represent faith and truth in action. With all life and religion based upon covenants between two parties—whether between man and man or between man and God—"righteousness meant fidelity to the terms of these covenants." [229] Thus Amos views with alarm the wrongs and iniquities of his people as an offense against God (2:9ff.) who is their deliverer and benefactor. Social iniquity cannot be expiated with ritual piety. "Let justice (mishpat) well up as waters, and righteousness (tzedakah) as a mighty stream" (v. 23). God holds a plumb-line wherewith He tests Israel's rightness (7:7ff.). Moral crookedness imperils the whole structure of national life. A. R. Gordon defines the position of Amos: "With him righteousness is no mere body of customs, still less a legal status conferred by a fallible authority; it is the living essence of social ethics, embracing alike honesty in business—fair weights and balances, standard wages and prices—and impartial justice in the law courts. It may be defined, in a word, as 'the straight thing' (*nechoho*) by which alone the nation can be saved." [230]

As for Amos so for Hosea righteousness represented the foundation of social morality and the bond of Israel's union with God. He brands Israel's unright-

eousness and immorality as harlotry and infidelity to
God. The national apostasy consists not only in wor-
shipping the Baalim, but also in disregarding virtue,
truth, kindliness and decency (4:1–2). The nation will
enter into a new and lasting covenant and betrothal
with God by means of righteousness and of justice, of
lovingkindness and compassion. The rigor of righteousness in its forensic sense is mitigated by Hosea's
tempering of justice with love. "Keep mercy and
justice," he pleads, "and wait for thy God continually"
(12:7).

Isaiah more clearly than his predecessors visions
righteousness as the supreme moral ideal, which is
rooted in the holiness of God and forms the focusing
point of all human relations, personal and social, national and universal. "The Lord of hosts is exalted
through justice, and God the Holy One is sanctified
through righteousness" (5:16). Justice is "the line and
righteousness the plummet" wherewith the Great Ar-
chitect tests the structure of national life (28:17). The
prophet's idea of Zion is that of a city righteous, "Zion
shall be redeemed with justice" (1:26–27). Justice
implies equality of all members of the community, including the stranger (Lev. 19:33ff.). There is the
commutative justice of the judge toward the litigant
which consists in vindicating the innocent and punish-
ing the guilty (Is. 5:23; also Ex. 23:7; Prov. 17:15).
There is also the distributive justice of the governor
toward his subjects, who in addition to exercising his
judicial function, rewards each according to his de-
serts. Equality implies equity, exact compensation,

free from personal or class preferment.* The ideal king shall be girded with righteousness and with faithfulness. Under the reign of justice the struggle between the rich and the poor will cease. None shall hurt or destroy the other. A just social order will leave no room for strife either among the warring classes or peoples. "And the work of righteousness shall be peace, and the effect of righteousness, quietness and confidence for ever" (Is. 32:17).

Jeremiah 9:23 may serve as a summary of pre-Exilic prophecy on social morality. "I am the Lord who exercises mercy, justice and righteousness in the earth; for in these things I delight, saith the Lord." The new covenant, which God will form with the Jewish people, will consist in inscribing the law upon the hearts of men, so that they will practice justice of their own accord without any external restraint (31:26–33). Ezekiel, while foremost in advocating individual responsibility, is no less emphatic regarding social justice (18; 45:9–12; 46; 16–18; see also Zech. 8:16–17; Mal. 3:5).

For Deutero-Isaiah righteousness is not merely a matter of even-handed justice, fair-dealing and honesty, and regard for the poor and needy; it is above all God's vindication of the Jewish people and their restoration from captivity. Unrighteousness was Israel's undoing and disgrace. Righteousness will restore it as God's elect people.[281] While the redemption of

---

* The Greeks represented justice as holding the scales and weighing impartially the merits of men. Cf. the Latin *pensare*, to weigh, to judge.

Israel will come as an act of Divine grace, Israel must prove worthy of it by fidelity to God's purpose (45:22–25; 48:17–19; etc.).

The prophetic pleas for justice, integrity, mercy and benevolence were embodied into the legal codes of the Torah. Here they were translated into concrete laws to govern the affairs of men. Animated by faith, the law was so formulated as to serve the ends of morality and was to be so administered as to have justice done to all. To insure the rights of poor and rich, of home-born and strangers alike represents the duty of the judges, rulers and kings. God Himself is the guarantor of justice. "Ye shall not respect persons in judgment; ye shall hear the small and the great alike; ye shall not be afraid of the face of any man; for the judgment is God's" (Deut. 1:17). Most striking are these laws in the Code of the Covenant: "Thou shalt not follow a multitude to do evil; neither shalt thou bear witness in a cause to turn aside after a multitude to pervert justice; neither shalt thou favor a poor man in his cause" (Ex. 23:2–3). Geiger calls attention to the uniqueness of the last law. The rich man must receive no advantage because he is rich, nor should the poor man have preferential treatment because he is poor. "Sympathy and pity are emotions that have their proper place and use, but even those noble feelings must be silent before justice." [232] The full significance of this law is brought out by its sequel: "Thou shalt not wrest the judgment of the poor in his cause" (vs. 6). It is more important that he get justice than that he be favored. Inequity in any form is iniquity. The

Code of Holiness states similarly: "Thou shalt not respect the person of the poor, nor favour the person of the mighty; but in righteousness shalt thou judge thy neighbour" (Lev. 19:15).

With the adoption of the Torah as the foundation of Jewish life, righteousness came to be regarded as strict observance of its laws and ordinances (Deut. 6:25). Identified with the revealed will of God, the laws of the Torah exercised supreme authority over the Jewish people. The rabbis continued the ideals of the prophets and of the Torah. R. Simeon b. Gamaliel taught that "the world (social order) rests upon three things: upon truth, upon justice and upon peace." [233] The Gemara adds "And the three of them are one. When justice is done there is truth and there is peace." "Every judge who applies the law truthfully even for a short while is considered a co-worker with God," and "he causes the Shechinah to rest upon Israel." [234] "The sword comes to the world because of the delay of justice and the perversion of justice and because of those who interpret the Torah not according to the Halachah." [235] Justice implies respect for one's fellow men and for their possessions. "Let the property of thy neighbor be as dear to thee as thine own." [236] "He who robs his neighbor of the worth of even a *perutah* is as if he took his soul from him." "He whose hands are stained with robbery calls to God and is not answered." [237] Robbing a Gentile is as heinous an offense as robbing a Jew.[238] Deception and trickery are as bad as stealing and robbery.[239] "There are seven thieves; the first of them is he who deceives his fellow men." [240]

Whoever offends against righteousness and justice offends not only against man but also against God. This is the heart of the social doctrine of Judaism.

> Righteousness and justice are the
> foundation of Thy throne;
> Mercy and truth go before Thee.
> —Ps. 89:15.

These are not artificial human constructs but abiding forces in the Divine government of the universe. Light may as well be considered the product of the seeing eye as righteousness and justice the mere creation of the human spirit. They constitute the moral equilibrium of humanity. God is "the power not ourselves that makes for righteousness." He deals with man on the principle of measure for measure (Ps. 18:21–28). If righteousness yields abundant life, evil destroys the wicked (Ps. 34:22).

The doctrine: "Resist not evil" (Matthew 5:39),* in its literal form, has not appealed to the Jew. While teaching forbearance with the wicked, Judaism calls for resistance to wickedness in every form. "Let all wickedness perish as in a moment" reads the Jewish prayer.† Not to resist evil often means to let it triumph over the good, to let it crush virtue and to trample upon purity and nobility. Such an attitude may

* It also reads: "Resist not him that is evil." Moffatt renders it: "You are not to resist an injury." So, too, Goodspeed.

† Singer, P. B., p. 48. Some editions read: "all doers of wickedness." The New Year's prayer reads: V'chol harish'ah, all wickedness.

amount to a withdrawal of religion from life and to surrendering the affairs of society to the devil. The Jew, when true to his religious heritage, has felt himself bound to fight all forms of evil, to exterminate its poisonous seed and flower, and to clear the hearts of men from its infections. At the same time he has been taught to draw the line between evil and evil doers. The learned Beruriah corrected her husband, R. Meir, when he prayed against outlaws who annoyed him. "What is your idea," she said to him, "is it because of the verse (Ps. 104:35): 'Let sinners cease out of the earth'? Does the text read *Hoteim*, sinners? It reads *Hataim*, sins. Furthermore, turn to the end of the verse, which states: 'And let the wicked be no more.' With the eradication of sin there will be no sinners. Rather pray that they repent." [241] The human heart should harbor no hate against the misguided worker of iniquity but against the causes which actuate them, lest it succumb to the same poison. The wicked must be disarmed and rendered harmless, and when possible won over to the good. Resolute efforts must be made to maintain the balance of justice or the cause of humanity is endangered.

In fighting evil we run the danger of resorting to its methods, on the supposition that the end justifies the means. Experience teaches that generally the means condition and determine the end. The Inquisition was based on the premise that it is proper to sacrifice the bodies of sinners in order to save their souls. Many an aggressive war was justified on the grounds that it was waged in order to secure some moral end, though its real purpose was loot and robbery. Each despotism in its effort to win popular support promises to bring about some ideal state, and succeeds only in adding to the woes of humanity. Thus far unholy methods have not led to holy goals. There is no alchemy whereby wrong may be transmuted into right. Enslavement of mind and body, tyranny, violence and war (whether among classes or nations) are poor instrumentalities of freedom, humanity, universal welfare and peace. The notion that might makes right, whether the might is in the hands of kings, militarists, and capitalistic over-lords or of the proletarian masses, plays havoc with the highest interests of humanity. There can be no hope for the humanization of man until he learns to pursue justice in ways that are intrinsically just.

LOVE AND BROTHERHOOD. The attribute of justice is supplemented, in the ethical view of Judaism, by the attribute of mercy. A legend tells that God first considered creating the world by the attribute of mercy alone. Seeing that in such a world sin would go un-checked, He thought next of creating it by the attri-bute of strict justice. But recognizing that such a rigid world, too, could not abide, He combined justice with mercy in order to endow the world with endurance.[242] Neither principle by itself can furnish the foundation of the social order. Justice, forming the touchstone of the Torah, proves creative because it is tempered with mercy, including active beneficence and kindly con-sideration for others.

Ahad Haam suggests that the distinction between

the two consists in this: Justice regards only the nature
of the deed, and judges the doer by it; mercy considers
first the character of the doer at the moment of the
deed, and judges the deed in the light of the circumstances.[243] Judaism, while upholding the objective
standard of right, concerns itself also with the lives
of men, with their weaknesses and their needs. As a
body of law, the Torah may be viewed as a system of
pure justice, but as an expression of religion, it draws
its life breath from the atmosphere of love. God's love
for man serves as the inspiration for man to manifest
love for his fellow man. Sympathy, kindness, good
will, helpfulness, and forgiveness are the indispensable
correctives of a world of men.

The Jewish doctrine of love comes to light in the
ideal of human brotherhood. The abstract term for
brotherhood—*ahavah*—appears only once in the
Bible, in Zechariah 11:14, and came into general use in
rabbinic literature. Its basic meaning is a relationship of
common family ties, descent or nationality, but it
came to express also relationship of common faith and
of common humanity. Among the Semites, the basic
bond of brotherhood was kinship. All who belonged
within the circle of the family or tribe considered
themselves as "one living whole, a single mass of blood,
flesh and bones, of which no member could be touched
without all the members suffering." [244] All who shared
this common life were bound to protect and care for
one another. Outsiders could lay no such claims. Every
stranger encountered in the desert was eyed as a
natural enemy. He had no protection against violence

save his own strength and the fear of his tribe's vengeance in case his blood was shed.

The fear which dominated the ancient world could
be overcome by an artificial extension of kinship
through a covenant. The most wide-spread form of
this rite was the blood covenant, whereby the cove-
nanters created a tie of kinship among themselves by
mixing a little of their blood. The covenants reported
in the Bible are generally of a sacrificial character in
which the blood of an animal was substituted for one's
own, with the deity figuring as the third party to the
alliance. A violation of the covenant was believed to
bring down the wrath of the deity. By the law of the
desert, when a member of the clan bound himself to a
stranger by a covenantal bond, he thereby extended to
him the right of kinship, which obligated all the members of the clan to treat him as one of themselves. Thus
kinship or brotherhood came to be not merely a matter
of birth but could be acquired through certain rites.
The life of such a "brother" was held sacred, i.e., un-
touchable, not because of itself but rather because it
was that of a kinsman. David asks Jonathan to deal
kindly with him because of the covenant of the Lord
which they formed (1 Sam. 20:8, 14–15).

The word "kindly" in this statement is covered by
the word *hesed*, which expresses the idea of goodness,
kindness, mercy, or favor, growing out of the sense of
brotherliness and involving mutuality of relationship.
When bestowed upon a person, tribe or people, it calls
for reciprocal helpfulness, born of sympathy and consideration. The covenant between Israel and God ex-

pressed itself by the same relationship of hesed between the deity and the people, on the one hand, and
of the people to one another.[245]

The prophet Hosea, in his denunciation of the low
moral and religious standards of his people, indicts
them particularly for disregarding hesed. "Your goodness (hesed)," he complains, "is as a morning cloud,
and as the dew that early passes away." The one thing
above all others which God demands is hesed. "I desire mercy, rather than sacrifice" (6:6, 4). In his
thought hesed is integrally related to faithfulness and
to knowledge of God.

Hosea's older contemporary Amos, though not using the word *hesed*, employs the related word *raha-
mim*, compassion, and emphasizes the sanctity of *berith
ahim*, the covenant of brotherhood (1:9, 11). The
master-word in his ethical teaching is, as we noted
above, *mishpat*, justice. Coming to believe in God as
all-just, Amos advanced to an enlarged view of human
brotherhood. In contradistinction to the popular notion that God concerns Himself primarily with the
affairs of Israel, fighting its battles and assuring it with
victory and plenty (Deut. 33:26–29), Amos sounded
a more universal note. God extends His help to the
Ethiopians, Philistines and Arameans as well as to Israel
(Am. 9:7). He applies the plumb-line of justice to all
of the nations. The stirrings of the Assyrian lion represent the measure of Yahweh's retributive justice for
Israel's neighbors because of their inhumanity. Doom
awaits Damascus for "threshing Gilead with sledges
of iron," and Ammon for "ripping up the women with

child of Gilead, that they might enlarge their border."
The Phoenicians and Philistines are threatened for
carrying on a trade of slaves obtained through kidnap-
ping raids on friendly people in violation of the brotherly covenant. Edom is denounced for its unrelenting
blood-feud with Judah. "He did pursue his brother
with the sword, and did cast off all pity, and his anger
did tear perpetually, and he kept his wrath forever"
(cf. Obadiah 10ff.). Moab is condemned for its barba-
rous burning of "the bones of the king of Edom into
lime." These cruelties, common to ancient warfare,
are denounced as such and not because they inflicted
suffering upon Israel. God's wrath falls upon these
nations because they have broken the universal laws
of fidelity, kinship and humanity. The prophet pre-
dicts doom upon Israel, too, for disregarding the laws
of brotherliness.*

*Hesed* and *mishpat* are linked in subsequent writings as patterns of behavior approved by God. Micah
declares that what God requires of man is doing
justice, loving mercy (*ahabat hesed*) and walking
humbly with Him (6:8). Jeremiah combines hesed
with mishpat, and tzedakah in his view of God's way
with men (9:23).

---

* As J. M. P. Smith observes, in the 53rd chapter of Isaiah,
the old principle of national solidarity is "expanded to the
bursting point and made to include the nations of the world
in general. Israel is suffering, a part for the whole, being in-
dissolubly bound up in the divine purpose with the world at
large. Such recognition of brotherhood among the nations is
past all praise and constitutes an ideal which is yet far from
realization." (*The Moral Life of the Hebrews*, p. 326.)

The prophetic emphasis on fidelity, kindness, humanity and brotherliness, as part of man's duty of faithfulness to God, underlies the legislation of the Torah. The Code of the Covenant tempers its rigorous and inflexible justice with the quality of mercy. It is solicitous that the stranger shall not be wronged and that the widow and orphan shall not be afflicted. It further enjoins that consideration be shown for the poor borrower and that a helping hand be extended even to the enemy who is in need (Ex. 22:20–26; 23: 4–9). The Deuteronomic Code makes active beneficence the keynote to its entire legislative system. The doctrine of God's love for His people serves as the basis of man's reciprocal love of God and for his love of his fellow man. While stressing the impartial and strict execution of justice and the elimination of social evil, great-hearted benevolence is urged upon the people. "Humanity is the author's ruling motive, wherever considerations of religion and morality do not force him to repress it." [246] The severe attitude toward the admission of Ammonites and Moabites into the Jewish fold is based upon their disregard of brotherliness toward Israel, "because they met you not with bread and with water in the way, when ye came forth out of Egypt; and because they hired against thee Balaam the son of Beor from Pethor of Aram-Naharaim, to curse thee." Israel is ordered not to hate them but to remain permanently indifferent to their welfare, because of the hostility which they so often manifested through history. On the other hand, the Edomites for all their cruelty toward Israel must be accorded greater consideration on account of the closer ties of consanguinity which united the two nations. "Thou shalt not abhor an Edomite, for he is thy brother; thou shalt not abhor an Egyptian because thou wast a stranger in his land" (Deut. 23:4–8). The remembrance of having sojourned in Egypt must outweigh the bitter memories of slavery endured there.[247] The spirit of philanthropy and consideration for others, which marks most of the provisions of the Code, breathes also from the introductory sections of Deuteronomy. Characteristic of the entire book is the following application of the doctrine of God's impartial justice: "He doth execute justice for the fatherless and widow, and loveth the stranger, in giving him food and raiment. Love ye therefore the stranger; for ye were strangers in the land of Egypt" (Deut. 10:17–19).

It is in the Priestly Code that the brotherhood of man may be said to have attained the status of a fundamental conviction. Here it appears in its characteristic form as corollary to monotheistic belief. The Divine process of creation reached its climax in Adam, whom God fashioned in His own likeness, and who became the father of the entire human race (Gen. 1:26ff.; 5:1ff.). When in consequence of their corruption, his descendants were swept away by the destructive flood, the righteous Noah and his sons were spared to become the progenitors of the new humanity. Shem, Ham and Japhet are presented as the fathers of all the nations of antiquity (Gen. 10:1 ff.). Consequently all men of whatever race, color or speech are basically brothers. The priestly genealogist seeks further to establish the bonds of kinship between Israel and the neighboring Semitic peoples, the Arameans, the sons of Keturah, the descendants of Ishmael, the offspring of Lot and the Edomites (Gen. 22:20–24; 25:1–18; 36). In addition the covenant relationships of the Patriarchs with the non-Semitic Philistines are stressed (Gen. 21:22–23; 26:26–31).

The doctrine of the brotherhood of man carried with it the obligation of universal benevolence. The most humane legislation regarding the treatment of the indigent, the handicapped and the stranger appears in Leviticus 19. The high-minded provisions reach the climax in the great commandments: "Thou shalt not hate thy brother in thy heart. . . . Thou shalt not take vengeance, nor bear any grudge against the children of thy people, but thou shalt love thy neighbor as thyself" (vss. 17–18). These laws not only apply to a brother Jew but also to a stranger. Going beyond Deuteronomy 10:19, Lev. 19:34 commands: "The stranger that sojourneth with you shall be unto you as the home-born among you, and thou shalt love him as thyself; for ye were strangers in the land of Egypt." Brotherly love must be extended to foreigners as well as to fellow Jews. The spirit underlying this legislation is strikingly expressed by the last of the canonical prophets. Malachi (2:10) pleads:

> Have we not all one Father?
> Hath not one God created us?
> Why do we deal treacherously every
>     man against his brother,
> Profaning the covenant of our fathers?

While the prophet naturally addressed himself to his Jewish contemporaries, his words assumed universal significance. Job 31, describing the ideal religious personality, speaks of the consideration which he manifests toward the servant:

Did not He that made me in the womb make him?
And did not One fashion us in the womb?—vs. 15.

For the masters of post-Biblical Judaism the belief in the Fatherhood of God spelt the common brotherhood of man. Philo, for example, teaches that if God who in want of nothing has regard for man's weakness and makes him a partaker of His gracious power and fills up his deficiencies, "how ought you to treat other men, your natural kinsfolk, seedlings from the same elements as yourself, you who brought nothing into the world, not even yourself? For naked you came into the world, worthy sir, and naked will you again depart, and the span of time between your birth and death is a loan to you from God. During this span what can be meet for you to do but to study fellow feeling and good will and equity and humanity and what else belongs to virtue, and to cast away the inequitable, unrighteous and unforgiving viciousness which turns man, naturally the most civilized of creatures, into a wild and ferocious animal!" He writes again: "A second time Moses calls our fellow creature brother, to impress upon the master that he has a tie with servant, so that he may not neglect him as a stranger. Nay, but if he follows the direction of the law, he will feel sympathy with him, and will not be vexed when he is about to liberate him." Discussing the two sets of five commandments which compose the Decalogue, the first dealing with God the Father and Maker of all and the other with duties to fellow men, Philo refers to some who devote their lives wholly to the love of God and to others who concern themselves exclusively with love of men, and observes: "Both come but half way in virtue; they only have it whole who win honor in both departments." [248]

Refuting the charges of misanthropy leveled against Judaism, Josephus proudly points to the equitable treatment of aliens enjoined by the Torah. "To all who desire to come and live under the same laws with us, he [Moses] gives a gracious welcome, holding that it is not family ties alone which constitute relationship, but agreement in principles of conduct. On the other hand, it was not his pleasure that casual visitors should be admitted to the intimacies of our daily life." (Reinach suggests that this alludes to the exclusion of aliens from Passover, Ex. 12:43.) Josephus continues: "The duty of sharing with others was inculcated by our legislator in other matters. We must furnish fire, water, food, to all who ask for them, point out the road, not leave a corpse unburied, show consideration even to declared enemies. He does not allow us to burn up their country or to cut down their fruit trees, and forbids even the spoiling of fallen combatants; he has taken measures to prevent outrage to prisoners of war, especially women. So thorough a lesson has he given us in gentleness and humanity that he does not overlook even the brute beasts, authorizing their use only in accordance with the Law, and forbidding all other employment of them." [249]

The Essenes, according to Philo, taught a threefold doctrine: love of God, love of virtue and the love of mankind.[250] A Hasidic work of the first pre-Christian century contains the monition: "Love the Lord through all thy life, and one another with a true heart." The entire work is filled with this spirit. Love of God and the neighbor, compassion for the poor and the weak and even for the beasts are urged as the duty of man. Man must be compassionate, "because even as man doeth to his neighbor, even so also will the Lord do unto him." [251] Jesus, therefore, followed well-established Jewish teaching when he combined the commands to love God and to love one's neighbor.[252] So, too, R. Akiba regarded the command "Thou shalt love thy neighbour as thyself" (Lev. 19:18) as the leading principle of the Torah.[253] This view is probably related to his emphasis on man as created in the Divine image. By loving one's fellow man, love is shown to his Creator.

THE GOLDEN RULE. Hillel, while teaching the duty of man to "love his fellow creatures and to bring them near unto the Torah," [254] also summarized the intent of the entire Torah in the words: "What is hateful unto thee, do not to thy fellow man." * Jewish and Christian scholars have sought to find in Hillel's negative

---

* Sab. 31a. So Jonathan b. Uzziel's construction of Lev. 19:18. It also occurs in the Armenian version of the *Story of Ahikar*, chap. 2:88, in Charles' A.P.E. and Hebrew Test. Naphtali

formulation of the golden rule the tendency of Judaism
toward justice in contradistinction to its positive statement by Jesus (Matthew 7:12 and in briefer form in
Luke 6:31), typical of the Christian emphasis on love.
The contrast drawn between Jewish and Christian
ethics on the basis of the differing formulations of the
golden rule ignores the fact that both versions derive
from the command of Leviticus 19:18, "Thou shalt
love thy neighbour as thyself." [255] Furthermore, both
forms appear indiscriminately in the literatures of the
Synagogue and the Church. The Jewish apocryphal
book of Tobit teaches: "My child, love thy brethren,
and scorn not in thy heart thy brethren and the sons
and daughters of thy people. . . . And what thou
hatest, do to no man." [256] The Didache, a first century
manual of instruction of proselytes, which early Christianity adopted from Judaism (and hence representative of both religions), teaches the duty of love in
both its positive and negative forms. Its distinctly

1:6b. Israel Al Nakawa cites Lev. 19:18 as Hillel's reply to
the gentile. The wording *L'reacho* in place of *et reacho* he
takes to mean that the Torah commands that one must
love and desire for his fellow man that which he loves and
desires for himself. (Menorat Hamaor, IV, 305.) R. Samuel
Edels interprets the verse in the light of the preceding statements, viz., in regard to hatred, vengeance and bearing a
grudge one must love his neighbor as himself and abstain
from injuring him. However, the command does not mean
that one must do good to his neighbor as to himself, for one's
life and welfare precede those of another (Maharsho, Sab.
31a). We may note that the Golden Rule and the Lex
Talionis exhibit the same pattern of thought—like for like.
Their difference consists in the motivation.

Jewish part is summarized in the opening two verses: "There are two ways, one of life and one of death; and wide is the difference between them. The way of life is this: Thou shalt love God thy maker; second, thou shalt love thy neighbour as thyself. Now the teaching of these two words is this: whatsoever thou wouldst not have done unto thee, neither do thou to another." [257] An early Christian work, the Apology of Aristides, does not hesitate to characterize Christian belief and practice by the negative form of the golden rule: "Whatever they do not wish done to them, they do not do to another." [258]

The charge that Judaism limits the law of love to Jewish neighbors is contradicted not only by Leviticus 19:34 and Deuteronomy 10:19 but also by the whole emphasis of Judaism on love and brotherhood as basic elements in its ethical tradition. Hillel's teaching that man must love his fellow creatures and bring them near unto the Torah clearly includes all mankind under the law of love. The charge of misanthropy, which, as we noted, was refuted by Josephus, reappeared in different form in the New Testament. Matthew 5:43 ascribes these words to Jesus: "Ye have heard that it was said, 'Thou shalt love thy neighbour and hate thy enemy,' but I say unto you, Love your enemies." Nowhere does the Torah teach hatred of the enemy. Instead, it commands that one must lend a helping hand to the enemy when he is in need (Ex. 23:4–5) and that hatred must not be harbored even in one's heart (Lev. 19:17). Though the Law deals with men on the principles of like for like, the individual must not take vengeance into his own hands. "Say not thou: 'I will requite evil,'" admonishes the sage. "Say not: 'I will do so to him as he hath done to me; I will render to the man according to his work.'" One must not rejoice when his enemy falls. "If thine enemy be hungry, give him bread to eat; and if he be thirsty, give him water to drink" (Prov. 20:22; 24:29, 17; 25:21–22).* Some Christian apologetes have tried to justify the statement in the Sermon on the Mount on the ground of the vindictive expressions in the Psalms and the antagonistic relations between the different classes in Jewish society.[259] However, their ingenuity can hardly be considered felicitous. The statement seems to stem from an erroneous interpretation of the original idiom on the part of the Greek translator of the *Sayings of Jesus.* Schechter well observed that after declaring his attachment to the Torah (Matt. 5:17–19), it is not likely that Jesus would proceed to show its inferiority. Jesus probably used the formula current in rabbinic teaching: *Shomea ani . . . talmud lomar*—"from the text I might infer so and so; therefore there is a teaching to declare," etc. As applied to the passage in question, Jesus may have said: "From the commandment, Love thy *neighbor,* you might infer

---

* R. Hanina bar Hama interprets Prov. 25:21–22 to mean that even if the enemy came to your house to slay you, and he is hungry or thirsty, give him food and drink; for thereby God will reconcile him to you, reading *yishl'menu lach* instead of *yeshalam lach,* Midr. Prov., *ad loc.* Compare the example of Joseph's forgiving his brothers who had sold him into slavery and of Elisha feeding the Aramean enemies (II Kings 6:21–23). For Paul's teaching on this subject, see Romans 12:17–21.

that you are to hate your enemies; therefore I say unto you that Scripture teaches: love also your enemies." [260] The misleading translation of the saying of Jesus gravely misrepresented the ethics of Judaism before the Christian world.

The Jewish ideal of love furnishes the basis of the doctrine of forgiveness. Ben Sirach counselled:

Forgive thy neighbor the hurt that he has done thee,
And then thy sins shall be pardoned when thou
    prayest.
Man cherishes anger against man,
And does he seek healing from the Lord?
Upon a man like himself he hath no mercy,
And does he make supplication for his sins? [261]

Still loftier heights are reached in the Testament of the Twelve Patriarchs which, Charles points out, anticipates the teachings of Jesus on many subjects. The whole book is filled with the loftiest Hasidic sentiments of love and forbearance. Joseph is pictured as the saint who bore no malice to those that hated him, and did all in his power to help them. His example is commended to all. "Do ye also love one another, and with long suffering hide one another's faults, for God delighteth in the unity of brethren and in the purpose of a heart that takes pleasure in love." God urges upon his children to remove hatred from their hearts, "for as love would quicken even the dead, and would call back them that are condemned to die, so hatred would slay the living, and those that have sinned venially it would not suffer to live, for the spirit of hatred worketh together with Satan, through hastiness of spirit, in all things to men's death. But the spirit of love worketh with the Law of God in long-suffering, unto the salvation of men. . . . Love ye one another from the heart, and if a man sin against thee, speak peaceably to him, and in thy soul hold not guile. And if he repent and confess, forgive him. But if he deny it, do not get into a passion with him lest, catching the poison from thee, he take to swearing, and so thou sin doubly . . . And though he deny it, ye have a sense of shame when reproved, give over reproving him, for he who denieth may repent so as not again to wrong thee. Yea, he may also honor thee, and fear and be at peace with thee. And if he be shameless and persist in his wrongdoing, even so forgive him from the heart, and leave to God the avenging." [262]

The noble sentiments of these passages are voiced also in other Jewish writings. Philo speaks of the Law's "teaching men by remote examples not to be delighted at the unexpected misfortunes of those that hate them." Through conferring a favor on an enemy, there "follows of necessity a dissolution of the enmity." [263] The rabbis teach: "From the commandment, 'Thou shalt not hate thy brother in thy heart,' you might infer that you may not strike him, slap his face, or curse him. Therefore Scripture specifies 'in thy heart,' i.e., you may not hate him even in thought." [264] "Judge every man favorably"; or still better, "Judge not your fellow man until you have come to his place." [265] He who causes his fellow man to suffer punishment is excluded from the immediate presence of God.[266] The Day of

Atonement does not remove a man's sin until he
has obtained his neighbor's forgiveness. Even if
he wronged his neighbor in word of mouth only, he
should endeavor to propitiate him. The neighbor in
turn must not nurse his wrong, but he should be ready
to forgive even as God forgives offenses against
Him.[267] They who forgive their fellow men may expect to be forgiven by God, but they who show no
mercy to others cannot expect the mercy of God.[268]

The Jewish ideal of conduct is voiced in the frequently cited passage: "They who are offended and
do not offend, who are insulted and do not reply (in
kind), who do God's will out of love and rejoice even
in suffering, of them Scripture says (Judges 5:31):
'His beloved ones are as the sun rising in might.' "[269]
The same spirit is voiced in the Talmudic prayer of
Mar bar Rabina (based on Ps. 34:14), which is appended to the 'Amidah. "To such as curse me, let my
soul be dumb, yea, let my soul be unto all as dust.
. . . If any design evil against me, speedily do Thou
make their counsel of none effect, and frustrate their
designs, in order that Thy beloved ones may be delivered."[270] R. Abahu teaches: "Let man ever be of
the persecuted rather than of those who persecute."[271]

Forgiveness and love purge man of the weakness of
pride and vainglory, and endow him with saintliness.
Hatred, on the other hand, is condemned as the equivalent of bloodshed.[272] He who hates an Israelite hates
Abraham, Isaac and Jacob, the grandsires of Israel.[273]
In the spirit of Hillel and Akiba, the Jewish masters
felt that he who hates any man hates God, in Whose

likeness man is made. R. Hayim Vital, emphasizing the belief that all souls root in God, wrote: "Let man love all creatures, including Gentiles, and let him envy none." [274] An eighteenth century commentator on Hayim Vital's *Shaare Kedushah* declared that true brotherly love recognizes no barriers of nationality or language, and is directed solely to man as man. If it is withdrawn from the savage or criminal, it is for the good of society as a whole, for social welfare may demand the execution of a criminal even as the health of a man's body may call for the amputation of a diseased limb. Brotherly love reduces the dangers of social misery, and improves the chances of social happiness. He concluded that whether viewed "from the standpoint of nature, reason, or tradition, love of one's neighbor appears as a permanent duty, taking precedence over the search after truth, and scientific pursuits; it is even more precious than wisdom and the honor of the holy Torah. . . . And do not wonder that there is anything superior to the Torah; for inasmuch as the Torah ordains and commands it, love is not extraneous to, but a part of the Torah."

"The love of your neighbor shall be literally as of 'thyself,' i.e., as each limb of your body responds to the needs of the other, so shall you conduct yourself towards your neighbor. It is, therefore, not sufficient for you to abstain from harming him yourself, but you must strive to ward off all evil from him, even when threatened from other sources." Thus the negative form of the Golden Rule is supplemented by the positive. The one asks that no evil be done to one's neighbor, the other demands that good be done to him. Our author argues that in its negative form the Golden Rule admits of no difference between oneself and one's neighbor: "What is hateful to thee, do not to thy fellow man." In the positive form, however, a certain difference between oneself and one's neighbor has to be recognized. While in duty bound to do good to his neighbor, a man cannot, by the very nature of things, be expected to do as much for his neighbor as for himself. Except for rare instances, one's own life precedes that of the neighbor. Consequently the duty of love towards one's fellow man assumes a somewhat restricted form: You must do for your neighbor what you would expect him to do for you, i.e., love him sincerely, respect him, sympathize with him, receive him kindly, judge him favorably, help him at the cost of sacrifice to yourself, never be overbearing with him.[275] Moses Hayim Luzzatto would recognize no such distinction: "The Torah teaches the all-inclusive principle: 'Thou shalt love thy neighbor as thyself,' i.e., as thyself without difference, as thyself without divisions, evasions, or devices." [276] Though differing in degree, the love of oneself and the love of one's fellow man do not differ in kind, for true love must be consonant with justice and self-respect.[277]

Mercy is a distinguishing characteristic of the children of Abraham. They are *rahamanim b'nai rahamanim*, "merciful sons of merciful fathers." They acquired this quality by their long training in the principle of *imitatio dei*, morality's supreme goal.[278] They have been taught that hatred shrivels men's souls, while love invests them with godly power. Men should not insist on the letter of the law, for on account of this sin Jerusalem was destroyed. Instead, they should ever follow the law of goodness. "Be careful not to be unmerciful, for he who restrains his compassion is comparable to an idolator and to one who casts off the yoke of Heaven from himself." [279]

CHARITY. The Jewish conception of charity stems from the ideals of justice and of love, as is indicated by the Hebrew terms *tzedakah* and *gemilut hasadim*. The idea of tzedakah itself, as we have seen, was not confined to either retributive or corrective justice, but included "large-hearted benevolence" as well. The judges, rulers and kings were not only to restrain the violent but also to aid their victims. This is the hope concerning the ideal prince as voiced by the Psalmist: He shall judge the poor of his people and save the needy, and crush the oppressor. He will pity the indigent, and redeem their soul from violence. "And precious will their blood be in his sight; that they may live, and that he may give them of the gold of Sheba, that they may pray for him continually, yea, bless him all the day" (72:12–15).

The earliest legislation of the Bible contains special provisions for the helpless, and for the amelioration of their lot (Ex. 22:20–26; 23:6–12). The still more humanitarian law of Deuteronomy is particularly insistent upon regard for those in want. It urges liberality toward the poor, the manumitted slave and the landless Levite and consideration for the hired servant, the fugitive slave and the unprotected foreigner. With grim realism coupled with deep sympathy, the Deuteronomic Code states: "For the poor shall never cease out of the land; therefore, I command thee saying: Thou shalt open thy hand unto thy poor and needy brother in thy land" (15:11). The enjoyment of God's bounties must be shared with those who are in need (16:11, 14). Acts of kindness rate as tzedakah (24:13).

The still more advanced Code of Holiness prescribes that the corners of the field, the gleanings and the fallen fruit of the vineyard shall be left unharvested. The original purpose of this legislation may have been, as Frazer suggests, to leave some of the corn for the spirits of vegetation on whom the following harvest depended.[280] That motive is wholly forgotten and the humanitarian purpose is announced: "Thou shalt leave them for the poor and for the stranger" (Lev. 19:9–10; 23:22; Deut. 24:21f.; Ruth). The legislation of the Sabbatical year provides that the produce which the land yields without human effort may be shared with the owners by his dependents and indigent neighbors, and even by the cattle and the beasts. The jubilee year has as its additional aim to check the double evil of the concentration of the land in the hands of the rich and of the enslavement of the poor. The land may be sold only until the next jubilee, but not in perpetuity; "for the land is Mine; for ye are strangers and settlers with Me. And in all the land of your possession ye shall grant a redemption for the land." The person who is forced by poverty to sell his property, and has no one to help him redeem it, regains its possession in the jubilee year. An Israelite, forced to sell himself into bondage on account of poverty, secures his freedom in the jubilee year. The object of this legislation is the prevention of poverty.

While benevolence may be as universal as humanity; * the Torah made benevolence a positive religious obligation. God Himself "executes justice for the fatherless and widow, and loveth the stranger, in giving him food and raiment. Love ye, therefore, the stranger; for ye were strangers in the land of Egypt" (Deut. 10:18–19). Philanthropy must mitigate the ills that grow out of social inequity and economic distress. As a phase of justice, its practice constitutes a duty both to God and to man. What God desires of man, says the author of Isaiah 58, is not a fast of self-mortification, of gestures of woe and of humiliation but a fast which quickens the sense of tzedakah in its double aspect of justice and of active beneficence.

The ideal religious personality as defined by Job (29, 31) serves as eyes to the blind and as feet to the lame. He acts as a father to the needy and as a defender of the wronged and the oppressed. He gives of his food and raiment to the orphan and the widow, and shares his roof with the wanderer. Similarly, the woman of valor, who calls forth the praise of the sage:

* "Hellenic ethics were fully conversant with the idea of mercy as a human virtue of divine sanction, but the religious ideal of this people does not comprehend any spirit of active philanthropy." Farnell, *op. cit.*, pp. 180–181.

Stretches out her hand to the poor;
Yea, she reaches forth her hand to the needy.
—PROV. 31:20.

The men of the Great Assembly placed *gemilut hasadim* by the side of Torah and worship as a pillar of the Jewish world.[281] Rabbi Elazar ranked tzedakah above all sacrifices and as a substitute for them. R. Asi held that charity outweighs all the commandments of the Torah. R. Judah extolled charity because it hastens the redemption. Its practice offers a concrete way of following the Divine attribute of love. (See ch. xi on *Imitatio Dei*.) "He who preserves a single soul in Israel is as if he preserved the whole world." [282] R. Joshua b. Karha says that "he who closes his eye to charity is like an idolator." [283] R. Judah says that he who denies lovingkindness denies God. The Deuteronomic law enjoins that when a person is found slain in a field and the murderer was not known, the elders of the nearest city were to behead a heifer in an uncultivated valley; and washing their hands over it, they were to say: "Our hands have not shed this blood, neither have our eyes seen it" (Deut. 21:1–7). The Sifre comments: "Does it occur to anyone that the elders were suspected of shedding blood? What their statement implies is this: he did not come to us and we dismissed him without food; and we have not seen him and neglected to escort him." Failure to help the needy may expose them to starvation. "The Torah," R. Simlai observed, "begins with lovingkindness and ends with lovingkindness." [284] A harsh and hostile world

taught the Jewish people to aid one another in distress.
Jewish communities considered it to be part of pru-
dence as well as of religious duty to care for their own
poor, and to prevent them from becoming burdens to
their neighbors.[285] Motives of humanity prompted them
further to come to the aid of the non-Jewish poor.
Philo considers charity a debt due to all men, including strangers, slaves, and even enemies.[286] Josephus
writes that Moses taught the following duties towards
one's neighbors, without distinction: giving them fire,
water and food, showing them the road and burying
their dead.[287] The Talmud teaches that indigent non-
Jews must not be prevented from sharing the gleanings, the forgotten sheaf and the corners of the fields.
They were to be supported along with the Jewish
needy; their sick were to be visited and their dead
given burial, for the sake of peace and good will.[288]

The rabbis distinguished between *tzedakah* and
*gemilut hasadim*. "In three respects lovingkindness ex-
ceeds charity. Charity represents giving of alms; lovingkindness is both alms and personal service. Charity
is meant for the poor, lovingkindness is for the rich as
well as for the poor; charity aims to help the living;
lovingkindness is shown to both the living and the
dead." Benevolence in the fullest sense of the term
comprised feeding the hungry, clothing the naked,
tending the sick, burying the dead, comforting the
mourner, ransoming the captive, educating the orphan,
and providing a dowry for the needy bride.[289] While
the practice of charity fills the world with love, its true
value depends upon the loving spirit which prompts it.

While it is blessed to give, it is embarrassing to receive charity. Men are exhorted to suffer privation rather than accept alms. "Flay a carcass in the street, and be not beholden to any one." [290] The Grace after Meals includes the petition: "Make us not dependent upon the gifts of men, nor upon their loans." Maimonides writes that the leading rabbis engaged in menial labor, as hewers of wood and drawers of water. "They asked nothing from the congregation, and received nothing when aught was offered to them." Independence and self-help are the ideals for man to follow. On the other hand, the aged, the sick and the sufferers, who cannot live without help from others and refuse to receive it, incur the guilt of bloodshed. The highest aim of charity is not almsgiving, but constructive relief and rehabilitation of the indigent as self-respecting members of society. Maimonides enumerates eight grades of charity, and ranks as the highest the help that saves the needy from further dependence upon others. Next to it is the charity dispensed in such manner as to exclude the benefactor's knowing the recipient or the recipient's knowing the benefactor. This was the practice in the ancient temple at Jerusalem. It contained a Chamber of the Silent, wherein the generous deposited their gifts and from which the needy were maintained, without knowing each other's identity. [291] The type of charity which inflates the ego of the giver but robs the receiver of his self-respect and reduces him to a miserable pauper does not have the benediction of Judaism.

THE MESSIANIC NOTE IN JEWISH ETHICS. If the doctrine of *imitatio dei* forms the basic pattern of personal conduct, Messianism constitutes the goal of social morality. The Messianic idea exhibits a threefold hope of (1) the establishment of the Kingdom of God on earth, (2) the reunion of Israel under the restored reign of the house of David, and (3) the inauguration of an era of universal peace not alone for Israel but for all mankind. Cloaked in political forms, Messianism represents the flower of Jewish optimism, growing out of the undying conviction of the ultimate triumph of justice over wickedness, of love over hate, and of social harmony over chaos.

The prophets are never more eloquent than when they vision the *aharit hayamim*, the far-off Divine event to which all history moves. Hosea declares in the name of God:

> In that day will I make a covenant for them
> With the beasts of the field and the fowls of
>     heaven.
> And with the creeping things of the ground;
> And I will break the bow and the sword and the
>     battle out of the land,
> And I will make them to lie down safely.—2:20.

Stripped of all legendary forms and poetic fancy, Messianism affirms the moral and spiritual regeneration of all humanity and the creation of a social order, wherein the evils which harass man in the present will be completely eradicated. "The sun of righteousness will arise with healing in its wings" (Mal. 3:20). All nations will go up to the mountain of the Lord

to be taught of His ways. Submitting to His arbitra-
ment:

> They shall beat their swords into plowshares,
> And their spears into pruning-hooks;
> Nation shall not lift up sword against nation,
> Neither shall they learn war any more.
> > —Is. 2:1–4; MIC. 4:1–4.

Within the nation, too, all strife will cease. The reign
of enlightened and benign justice will remove all
rapacity, greed and oppression.

> And the wolf shall dwell with the lamb,
> And the leopard shall lie down with the kid,
> And the calf and the young lion and the
> > fatling together;
> And a little child shall lead them.

Destruction will cease:

> For the earth shall be full of the knowledge
> > of the Lord,
> As the waters cover the sea.—Is. 11:1–9.

The Divine law will no longer be something extraneous to them, but will be written upon their hearts
(Jer. 31:26–33). The prophetic hope for the future
envisages the creation of new heavens and a new
earth, when sorrow and weeping shall vanish, and men
will live to ripe old age, and enjoy the fruit of their
labor in peace (Is. 65:17ff.).

In both its national and universal aspects, Messianism has affected deeply the destinies of mankind.
When the hope of its speedy realization was dimmed

in post-Exilic times, it was transferred from earth to heaven, from the affairs of men to the realm of dreams, and from the present to a visionary "world to come." Prophecy was replaced by apocalypticism. The legendary character of the Messiah and of the future world came to dominate the religious life of Jewry, and gave birth to Christianity. Nonetheless, solitary thinkers questioned the reality of the dream. Rabbi Hillel (third century) ventured the idea that Israel may expect no Messiah in the future, because the prophecies regarding him referred to the age of Hezekiah. Rashi correctly interprets this statement to mean that not a personal Messiah but God Himself will redeem and rule over Israel. Discounting the extravagant promises that came to be associated with the Messianic idea, Samuel taught that there is no difference between the present (*olam hazeh*) and the Messianic times (*yemot hamashiah*) save political dependence.[292]

Maimonides, while placing the belief in the Messianic advent among the articles of Jewish faith, conceives it in the sense of Samuel as marking "the restoration of political independence to the Jewish people." "All Israel, their prophets and sages longed for the Messianic age in order to be freed from political oppression which hampers the proper study of Torah and the practice of Mitzvot. They will then find rest and be able to devote themselves to the pursuit of wisdom in order to attain to immortality." "Let it not occur to you that in the Messianic age anything will be annulled in the natural world order, or that there will be any change in creation." It will differ from the present merely in this: Israel will then enjoy complete independence. This new freedom will not be for the sake of ruling over other nations or for the enjoyment of physical pleasures but for the purpose of cultivating the higher life of the spirit. "In that age there will be no famine and no war, no jealousy and no rivalry, for the abundance will be great and dainties will be as common as earth. The only concern of all mankind will be to know God." [293]

Commenting upon Maimonides' elimination of all eschatological notions from his conception of the *yemot hamashiah*, Hermann Cohen observes: "Messianism is fully understood only when every notion of other-worldliness is removed from the conception of the Messianic future. The future which the prophets portray under the symbol of the Messiah is the future of world history. It is the goal, it is the meaning of history, which presents the contrast to history in its isolated reality." [294]

The prophetic ideal, though the product of a distant age, holds out a great light for the turbulent present. Above the chaos of the modern world scene, with its economic, political and social conflicts, rises the hope of a coming kingdom of God and the brotherhood of man. Attempts have been made to identify the prophetic ideal with current social theories and panaceas, varying from Single Tax to Socialism and from Anarchism to Communism. An examination of its character shows that it is predicated upon moral and spiritual rather than upon political and economic laws.

It is based not upon materialistic determinism and the class struggle but upon the belief in the ethical nature of God and in the ultimate triumph of righteousness. Its watchword is not consciousness of class but of humanity. Its goal is not material plenty but "the perfection of the world through the establishment of the Kingdom of the Almighty," the spiritual regeneration of humanity, the investment of the life of the individual and of society with worth and with sanctity.

Fundamental to the Jewish social outlook is the belief in the perfectibility of the human race. Society is not a mere herd, whose interests end in procreation, and in the control of the food supply and of the physical scene. Despite frequent set-backs and relapses back to the jungle, humanity has moved forward. Amid the darkest nights of violence, oppression and hatred, we venture to wait for the dawn of a better day.

Messianism is universalistic. The hoped for future is not for Israel alone but for all humanity. Religion originally manifested itself in social life as an affair of the clan, tribe and nation. Each had its own spirits and deities and forms of ritual. What united one group into a tribal or national entity separated it from all others. As wars often raged between the groups, the religious rites and forms were put into the service of tribal and nationalistic ends. In Israel the tribal, national and geographic barriers were cut across, and the God of Israel was exalted as the God of all the nations of the world. Though Egypt, Assyria, Babylonia, and Persia warred on Israel and Judah, they were all considered by the prophets as the instruments of God's plan for mankind. Envisaging a united humanity, the prophet could look for the day when there shall be "a highway out of Egypt to Assyria, and the Assyrians shall come into Egypt, and the Egyptians into Assyria; and the Egyptians shall worship with the Assyrians.

"In that day shall Israel be the third with Egypt and with Assyria, a blessing in the midst of the earth; for that the Lord of hosts hath blessed him, saying: 'Blessed be Egypt My people, and Assyria the work of My hands, and Israel Mine inheritance'" (Is. 19:23–25).

We noted the conviction of the Bible that the white, black, and yellow races are brothers. Their diversity is but skin-deep, while their kinship is essential. The idea of caste which, in Egypt or in India separated the slaves from the free men, soldiers from priests and merchants, was foreign to the Jewish people. Absent, too, was the wide gulf which divided the "black heads" from the "red heads" in Babylonia and that made the Greeks call themselves "children of the sun" and the rest of the world "barbarians." Strangers were welcomed into the Jewish fold as brothers. In the tradition of the synagogue the *Ger* is known as a son of Abraham.

The doctrine of the kinship of the human race appeared as a purifying flame to burn out the vain pride of the thoughtless and the arrogant, and as a pillar of fire to lead the nation to moral heights. To those who interpreted the idea of Israel's choice by God in the sense of nationalistic favoritism, the rugged prophet of Tekoa flung the defiant challenge: "Are ye not as the Ethiopians unto me, O children of Israel? saith the Lord" (Am. 9:7). If Israel came to be the standard-bearer of religious truth, or—in the language of the Bible—"the chosen people," it should not make for a sense of superiority, but only for the consciousness of mission. Israel's choice means solely to serve God and to herald His truths to the nations. The concluding service for the Day of Atonement in the *Union Prayerbook* contains the following petition: "Grant that all the children of Israel may recognize the goal of their changeful career, so that they may exemplify by their zeal and love for mankind the truth of Israel's message: one humanity on earth even as there is but one God in heaven." The *Union Prayerbook* version of the Adoration (*Alenu*), which is used at the end of each public service, reads: "O may all created in Thine image recognize that they are brethren, so that, one in spirit and one in fellowship, they may be for ever united before Thee. Then shall Thy kingdom be established on earth and the word of Thine ancient seer be fulfilled: The Lord will reign for ever and ever. On that day the Lord shall be One and His name shall be One."

Jewish ethics is in a sense a history of Jewish life under the inspiration of the visions and ideals of Judaism. Life being unfinished, ethics, too, is not fully realized. It advances from the past and present to the distant horizons of the future, from history to eschatology. The *aharit hayamim*, to which Judaism has looked, represents the merging of the two lines of history and of morality. Human progress grows real when it moves toward an ethical end. Humanity advances to perfection by making God its goal and righteousness its path. An ideal social order need not forever remain a visionary Utopia. It may become an inspiring reality when men will venture to live by the ethical and religious ideals which they profess, and consecrate their skill and intelligence to the creation of proper instrumentalities and techniques for the establishment and preservation of conditions in which the noblest ideals and values of humanity may flourish. Faith in man as well as in God furnishes the ground for the belief in the ultimate realization of the Kingdom of God on earth.

# THE THREEFOLD WAY
# OF RELIGIOUS PRACTICE

# XIII. THE WAY OF TORAH

RELIGION does not content itself with the affirmation of the existence of God or with the recognition of the ethical principles that follow therefrom. It requires further that these verities and ideals be carried forward and developed in personal and social behavior. While religion may appear as a sudden inspiration in the mind of man, it grows into a power as a slowly and steadily unfolding way of life, as a continuous climb to the mountain of the Lord. The ascent is not achieved in one leap, but gradually, one step at a time. Spiritual-like intellectual and artistic perfection comes as a reward of rigid training, effort and exercise.

We analyzed some of the elements that enter into the ethical life of Judaism. But it is not merely with ethical obligations that Judaism is concerned. It sets before men a body of observances of purely ritual character. These in turn may possess ethical significance, but their chief value derives from the specific sphere of religion rather than from that of ethics. The wordly-minded may dismiss them as of little consequence. The religious soul welcomes them as means of "receiving the yoke of the kingdom of God in love."

Judaism recognizes the pedagogical necessity of singling out definite acts of devotion for the religious person to perform, certain forms to observe and particular days to hallow in order to give concrete expression to his faith. "Idle spirituality," accompanied by no effort or act, fails to nourish the hearts of men. Accordingly, in addition to its ethical path, Judaism —like every positive religion—has evolved a technique whereby it may render itself effective in the life of the individual and of the community. It may be viewed as a threefold way of (1) education and practice, (2) atonement, and (3) worship. The three are interrelated and organically connected with the ethical way. All three figure in other religions as well, but they assume distinctive characters in each.

THE IDEAL OF TALMUD TORAH. Rabbinic fancy extolled the Torah as the instrument wherewith God fashioned the universe. Whatever its role in the cosmic scheme, it has been the chief means of creating the world of Judaism. It has been the dynamic of Jewish living. Indeed, *Judaism is the religion of Torah*, not alone of the Written Law or the Pentateuch, nor even of the Oral Law, but of the progressive growth of the Jewish people in religious knowledge and culture. Therein lies the distinction of Judaism as a religion. In the words of Deut. 4:6, the Torah is our wisdom and understanding in the eyes of the nations. The Torah is also our source of life as a people. Perhaps nowhere except among the Brahmans in India has study of sacred literature been accorded so high a place as in Judaism. Touching and illuminating every phase of life, the Torah has welded religion and life into an indissoluble union. It not only presents a road map of life but makes the pursuit of its directions the very condition

of blessedness. Its scope is furthermore not only spiritual and moral but also intellectual. Instruction and
discipline are based on knowledge. As a religion
founded upon enlightened faith rather than upon credulity, that has sought the aid of the sciences and philosophies—to the limit of their powers—in the establishment of its creedal foundations, Judaism has ever
stressed knowledge as one of the chief duties which
man owes himself and God. Reason itself is a phase of
the spiritual life. To exercise his reason is part of man's
spirituality. If some phases of existence are beyond
reason, there are many others within its domain.
Among them are the ways of human conduct. To be
intelligent regarding the matters that most affect his
being is the religious obligation of man. "Thou shalt
know" and "lay it to thy heart"—knowledge and understanding—are the ever-recurrent motifs of Jewish
religious teaching. They are the steps which lead to
faith, appreciation, devotion and love.

Torah is the first of the three pillars which support
the Jewish world.[295] The other two, viz., worship and
benevolence, derive their inspiration and vitality from
the Torah. The Jewish houses of worship have functioned also as centers of learning. The Hebrew term
*Bet Hamidrash* and the Judeo-German *Schul* are
commonly used for synagogue. Expressive of the attitude of Judaism toward education is the judgment of
R. Joshua b. Levi that it is permissible to sell a synagogue in order to acquire a school.[296] The study of
Torah outweighs all other duties. The private devotion of the morning contains the petition that God

may "make pleasant the words of the Torah in our mouth and in the mouths of Thy people, the house of Israel." [297] The benediction preceding the *Shema* in the morning prays for "understanding and discernment to mark, learn and teach, to heed, to do and to fulfill in love all the words of instruction in Thy Law." The evening benediction before the Shema similarly voices the joy of the Jew in the Law and the commandments. They manifest God's love for Israel, "for they are our life and the length of our days." [298] Through the centuries the Jews found them to be the very source of their life and their gladness. Despoiled of human rights and of worldly position, they sought refuge in the cultivation of the Torah, and thereby recovered their dignity as men and achieved their cultural and spiritual aims as a people of God.

Legalists, mystics and rationalists united in the conviction that the way to commune with God was through the study of Torah and the observance of its commandments. A Mishnah, which is included in the private devotion for the morning, states that the study of Torah equals the fulfillment of all the commandments, "the fruits of which a man enjoys in this world, while the stock thereof remains for him in the world to come." [299] One opinion extravagantly claims that the study of Torah is more meritorious than saving a life, building the sanctuary and honoring parents. [300] Theory entertained different views regarding the relative importance of Torah and practice. Actuality rendered the two inseparable. Pedagogically R. Akiba was right in maintaining that Torah is greater inas-

much as it leads to practice.* The full significance of
learning in the scale of Jewish values is indicated by
the rabbinic opinion that a "learned bastard ranks
higher than an ignorant high priest." [301]

The various attitudes of the rabbis to this subject
may be gathered from the following comments. The
command of Exodus 19:5, "Ye shall be Mine own
treasure from among all peoples," was understood to
mean: you shall distinguish yourselves by your devotion to God and engage in the study of Torah rather
than in other matters. If a man cannot give the entire
day to study, let him study a couple of *halachahs* in
the morning and a couple in the evening. His study in
the morning does not exempt him from study in the
evening, any more than his morning prayer absolves
him from the obligation to pray in the evening.[302] The
opinion is voiced that if a man study only one chapter
of the Torah in the morning and one in the evening he
has fulfilled the command of Joshua 1:8, "This
book of the Law shall not depart out of thy mouth,
but thou shalt meditate therein day and night." The
view is further expressed that the command is fulfilled
even if one recites no more than the Shema in the
morning and in the evening. While some thought that
this fact should not be divulged to the ignorant so that
they should not be satisfied with the minimum, others
held the contrary view that it should be communi-

* Kid. 40b. The saying *Lo hamidrash ikkar ela hamaaseh* does
not disparage study in favor of action. It signifies that not
the interpretation of the law is of prime importance but the
fulfillment.

cated to them in order to encourage them to engage
in at least a minimum of study. The words of Joshua
1:8 appeared to one rabbi neither as a duty nor as a
command, but as a blessing. When God saw his great
devotion to study (cf. Ex. 33:11), He said: since the
words of the Torah are so precious to you, may not
the book of the Torah depart out of your mouth! It
is emphasized that the study of Torah must not be
reduced to a mere duty. Instead of a burdensome task
it should be considered as a blessed privilege.[303] Maimonides rules in his Code: "Every Jew is obligated to
study Torah whether he be poor or rich, in good physical health, or a sufferer, young or very old. Even if
he goes begging from door to door, and has a wife and
children to support, he must set aside time for the
study of the Torah. . . . And how long must he continue to study? Until his death." [304] The mind and
spirit must be kept active and awake by learning something every day.

A man's obligation does not end with his own study
of Torah. He must also teach it to his sons. The Law
reads: "Ye shall teach them [the commandments] dili-
gently unto your sons" (Deut. 6:7; also 11:19). The
father may delegate this task to a competent teacher,
but he must provide his sons and even his son's sons
with religious education. Even the poor made heavy
sacrifices for the sake of training their sons in Torah.
In case the father was too indigent, the community
considered itself obligated to secure religious instruction for every boy within its jurisdiction. The ideal of
Talmud Torah found expression in the universal edu-

cation of the male population and in the establishment
of schools in communities, no matter how small the
number of children of age to receive instruction. (The
education of daughters was a voluntary matter, and
was generally ignored. The Reform movement has
concerned itself with the religious education of girls
as well as of boys.)

Education ended neither with childhood nor adolescence, but continued through life. Popular education
was arranged for young and old. A considerable part
of public worship itself was turned over to instruction. The reading of the Shema holds the center in the
morning and evening services. On Sabbaths and on
holy days a section of the Pentateuch is read and is
supplemented with an appropriate reading from the
prophets. On Monday and Thursday mornings, too,
selections are read from the weekly section of the
Pentateuch. Each service includes a number of Psalms.
One of the five *Megillot* is read on Pesah, Shabuot,
Ninth of Ab, Sukkot, and Purim. The book of Job is
assigned for the afternoon [305] of the Ninth of Ab (a
practice still followed among the Sephardim) and is
recommended for houses of mourning. The tractate
Abot is studied on Sabbath afternoons between Pesah
and Shabuot in some communities and in others between Pesah and Rosh Hashanah. In some places the
tractate Derech Eretz Zutta was similarly read on Sabbath afternoons. Selections from the Mishnah were
studied on *Yahrzeits*. In addition, excerpts from the
three parts of the Bible Canon (Pentateuch, Prophets
and Hagiographa), Mishnah and Talmudic Haggadah

were arranged as supplements of the daily service and are known as *Maamadot*. Elaborate readings (*Tikkun*) were provided by Cabbalists for midnight meditation and for the nights of Shabuot and Hoshana Rabba. Where preaching took place on special occasions, the sermons were generally based upon the Biblical selections of the day and aimed to interpret them in the light of rabbinic teaching as guide for conduct.

Not alone through worship and pulpit preaching but also through study at home and in intimate circles was the Torah made the possession of the Jewish people. Every conscientious Jew considered it his duty to go over the weekly portion of the Pentateuch in the original and in its Aramaic translation and the rabbinic commentaries. Numerous Orthodox communities still contain faithful remnants of—what in older days formed a regular feature of synagogue life—men assembling at set hours for the purpose of reading together the Midrash on the weekly portion, Mishnah, Ein Yaakob, Talmud, Codes, Musar literature, or Cabbalah. These classes are conducted either by rabbis or by lay scholars for the sake of assisting those who might experience difficulty in studying by themselves and for promoting fellowship.

The ideal of Talmud Torah kept the Jewish people on a high plane of cultural and intellectual as well as of religious endeavor. It further provided an ideal occupation and interest for men in their leisure hours. The whole of Jewish life thus moved to the music of the Torah. Lilien well depicted the "Light of the Exile" in the form of a patriarchal Jew poring over a folio of Jewish lore. Israel's light has been Torah.

It is a sign of decadence of the Jewish religious fiber that Judaism has been reduced even by many of its devoted followers to occasional attendance at the synagogue for public worship and to philanthropic activities and that the study of Torah has been confined to professionals. Israel grew into a religious and cultural people, and richly contributed to the higher life of humanity only through love of Torah. Drawing strength and inspiration from it, Israel has weathered all storms. Israel has withstood exiles, persecution and misfortune, but will it withstand ignorance? Bereft of Torah, Israel is bereft of power. Our enemies can burn our books, but only we by our neglect can destroy their spirit.

THE FUNCTION OF TORAH. The study of Torah derived its incentive from the belief that the Torah represents the revealed will of God. To know its precepts and to learn how to practice them properly constituted the way of salvation both for this life and for the hereafter. It was believed that in the hour of judgment man will be questioned not only about his conduct but also regarding his study: "Didst thou deal honestly? Didst thou set aside regular hours for Torah?" [306] Obviously for moderns who have come to regard the Torah as Israel's upreaching to God rather than as God's recorded word, the compelling motives for study of Torah have been weakened. By the side of the supernatural authority of the Torah and the expectation of compensation in the hereafter, purely human considerations indeed pale. Nonetheless they alone remain for us. What, then, are our grounds for valuing the ideal of Talmud Torah? What needs does it supply and what satisfactions does it offer to men and women today?

The study of Torah does not signify for the Jew the mere acquisition of information but the illumination of the mind and the direction of the will and the emotions toward truth, goodness, righteousness and duty. It initiates the Jew into Judaism along the four lines which constitute religion. In the first place, it connects him with the *community* of Israel. The Torah has been compared to the Manna, which, according to Biblical legend, daily descended from heaven to sustain Israel while journeying in the desert. It has been the heavenly food whereon Israel has lived through the ages.[307] The Torah has been represented also as the tree of life. "As the days of the tree," says the prophet, "are the days of my people" (Is. 65:22). As long as the Torah will endure, the Jewish people will endure.[308] The Torah is not something extraneous but an inner force which keeps Israel alive as a people. Through its devout study, the individual Jew becomes naturalized in his spiritual fatherland, and comes into possession of his communal heritage. The classics of our three thousand-year-old literature, which have been the joy of the world, and the more recent creations of poets and thinkers are virtually non-existent for us unless they are permitted to take hold of our minds and hearts. It is not enough to have literary, cultural and spiritual traditions. The important thing is to let them have dominion over the soul. By growing conscious of his people's aspirations and strivings, the individual secures the means of an effective emotional and intellectual integration with his own and thereby grows to be at home with himself. Acquiring a communal memory, he comes to look with pride upon the past and to face the present with dignity and with confidence. He feels himself connected with fellow Jews of all lands by virtue of common participation in the heritage of Torah. Jewish unity is thus cemented with knowledge and conviction. The historic task or mission of the Jew to live his religion and to uphold it as a beacon to humanity grows in meaning and power. Cooperation with fellow Jews not alone in religious and cultural matters but also in the tasks that confront them as a historic community, whether of relief from distress or defense against hostility and danger, recommends itself as an expression of brotherhood.

Second, the study of Torah takes us to the living springs of our religion. It awakens our *sense of the holy* and carries it into the realm of clear thought. The inexhaustible resources of spiritual power stored up in our incomparable treasures of Bible and post-Biblical writings serve as vehicles of religious inspiration of the first order. God often comes to men in the words of the prophets and poets. The words and examples of the witnesses unto God kindle the Divine fire within our hearts and keep the eye of the soul open to the mysteries of life. The Bible confronts us with holy awe and reverence which are the essence of religion. The flaming words and the matchless records of the heroes of faith stir the deeps of our souls and lift our minds to the Divine. In the serene atmosphere of the Eternal, we secure freedom from bondage to the transient, the trivial and the commonplace. New visions unfold to the eye of faith and new joys. And new light is shed upon the fundamental beliefs and obligations of our faith.

Third, the study of Torah has ever been the chief means of fostering the *ethical consciousness*. In the words of the Mishnah: "He who masters Scripture, Mishnah and Derech Eretz (morals) will not be quick to sin . . . But he who has mastered neither Scripture nor Mishnah nor even morals is outside the pale of civilization." [309] We shall deal with the value of Torah for the building of character in the next chapter. Here we shall limit ourselves to the observation that the Bible has been the greatest moralizing and humanizing force not only in the life of the Jewish people, but also in the life of the entire Western world. It has stamped itself upon the mind and conscience of humanity by its spiritual power, moral earnestness, and poetic beauty. Through the characters of its leading figures, it holds up the mirror to life, and directs its blazing light upon the tangled web of good and evil in human relations. The prophetic ideals of right and justice, of mercy and compassion, of brotherhood and peace, have become the hope of aspiring humanity. Nowhere is greater attention directed upon the issues of life than in the utterances of the prophets, in the wisdom of the sages and the teachings of the rabbis. Jewish

sacred literature is a vast school for the training of
man in morality as well as in religion. No other body
of literature initiates him into such pure atmosphere of
godliness and moral health as the sacred writings of
Judaism. The study of Torah has helped build the
moral fiber of the Jewish people. Neither exile nor
persecution was permitted to rob them of their self-
esteem and of the hope in a brighter future.

Though we cannot consider the ethical any more
than the religious conceptions of the Bible and of rabbinic literature as authoritative and binding in all respects upon us, we feel the essential healthiness of the
Jewish ethical tradition. The lapses from the highest
standards are comparatively so few and its nobility
and naturalness so amazingly lofty that it represents a
matchless pedagogical instrument for man's achievement of his full stature as a moral and spiritual being.

Fourth, the study of Torah vitalizes the *practice of
religion*. Valuing knowledge as part of the religious
life, it places its accent upon action, both ritual and
moral. The goal of study and reflection is not mere
"sharpening the intellect" as it sometimes turns out to
be. "He who says that he is concerned only with
Torah does not possess even Torah." [310] One-sided in-
tellectualism is alien to Judaism. Knowledge and practice belong together in its conception of the spiritual
life. Religion is essentially an experience rather than
a gnosis. The practical side of the Torah is embodied
in the Halachah, which serves as a chart of life. It aims
to define in detail the requirements of religion, and to
show men concretely "the way wherein they shall go

and the work that they must do." These duties, dictated by faith, are viewed as *mitzvot*, commands of God. If piety requires intelligence, intelligence without piety is barren. "He who only studies Torah without applying its precepts to conduct is as if he were without God." [311] The rabbis interpret the words of Jeremiah 16:11, "They have forsaken Me, and have not kept My Law," to mean: "God says, Would that when they forsook Me, they had kept the Torah, for its leaven would have turned them toward the good." [312] They comment further that one who studies not for the sake of practice were better off had he never been born. [313]

The chief effort of the interpreters of the Bible and the Talmud was to render the Torah a practical guide to conduct. R. Solomon b. Isaac (Rashi), the foremost rabbinic commentator, strove to connect the Mosaic law with its rabbinic application to life. Maimonides composed his great Code for the purpose of rendering available the whole body of Jewish Law to young and old. R. Joseph Caro carried forward the process of simplification of the Halachah by arranging it as a "set table"—Shulhan Aruch—for ready consultation. Through these and similar aids, every Jew was able to acquaint himself with the rule of the Torah for every condition and circumstance. Prior to every sacred season of the year and for every occasion in his life, he was to familiarize himself with authoritative directions for the proper manner of observing them. Moderns who do not recognize the binding force of the Halachah in all its details can still derive from it much helpful guidance in their endeavor to make the practice of Judaism a reality.

Regard for specific acts of ritual or morals does not exhaust the total purpose of the study of Torah. R. Menahem bar Jose comments on Proverbs 6:23, "For the commandment is a lamp, and instruction is a light": Like a lamp, which offers help only for a brief hour, a command helps only in a definite situation. The Torah resembles light, which provides illumination steadily. It lights up the whole of life.[314]

For the modern Jew the Torah, while not a final deposit of truth, represents a continuous process of intellectual, moral and spiritual growth in religion. When approached not as the sum of all truth nor as an outlived body of archeology, but as the embodiment of the living and ever developing faith of the Jewish people, it grows into a creative force in our lives. In this way the modern Jew may still be taught, "Turn it and turn it over again, for everything is in it, and contemplate it; and wax grey and old over it, and stir not from it, for thou canst have no better rule than this." [315] By concentrating on the heritage of Torah, the Jewish people secured the unity of their spiritual growth. From the Torah as their starting point and center, they reached out after ever widening vistas of knowledge. The old faith disclosed new riches, new meanings for changed times, new applications to changing needs, and new insights into the unfolding realities of life. Progressive Judaism has no quarrel with science or with philosophy. In the measure in which they verify themselves, they do not oppose but supplement religion. Love of truth is part of man's love of God.

TORAH AND CHARACTER. The primary aim of the study and teaching of Torah, as we have pointed out, is not merely to secure and to impart information, but rather to integrate the individual in the religious experience of his people. Through it the individual Jew is initiated into the life, thought, convictions, and ideals of Israel. Religious education thus marks the socialization and spiritualization of the individual, the complete transformation of his personality after the pattern of his people.

*Training the Will and Character.* The object of the study of Torah as far as the individual is concerned is the training of his will and character. Free will is not a mere endowment of consciousness but also a moral goal to be achieved. At birth we are but helplessly dependent bundles of instincts and impulses. Gradually we grow into control of our bodies and acquire freedom of motion and direction. Most important of all, our minds are awakened—through parents, playmates, and teachers—to varied trains of thought. Our will ceases to be a matter of blind urge, and acts in response to the dictates of the mind. It gains the freedom to choose between the call of impulse and the voice of reason. Morality thus becomes a reality in our life. As rational and moral beings we come into possession of the ability to judge conflicting desires and ideas, and grow into power of vetoing certain inclinations in accordance with our acquired standards of right and duty. The measure of our life is no longer mere self-expression but also self-restraint.

The freedom thus acquired can be retained only through continuous vigilance. The impulses and passions are ever ready to revert to their unrestrained primitivity. Self-indulgence and self-centeredness are present obstacles in most lives. Jealousy, hatred, disregard for and exploitation of others are phases of man's self-centeredness. The lure of the flesh, the seduction of pleasure and the siren call of ease enslave us to the lower self. The narcotic addict, the drunkard, the gambler, the libertine, and the social parasite have paid for their habits with their freedom. They are held in the clutches of their desires more firmly than in fetters of steel. Complete self-possession and perfect self-mastery are conditions of freedom.

The art of life consists in so training the will as to ever retain the power of self-determination in the choice of the good and in the avoidance of evil, to build up resistance against temptation and to habituate oneself in upright conduct. The feelings, thoughts and volitions must be coordinated and given firm and consistent character. The chief danger to man is lack of harmony between his emotions, his mind and his will. Where the self is not properly integrated there can be no real morality. Subject to no law and governed by no definite attitude or principle, the self is vacillating and anarchic. Good becomes indistinguishable from evil, for the motives behind the deeds are blurred. In the absence of central moral gravity, waywardness and excess are natural consequences.

The object of all education and culture is, therefore, not so much the acquisition of information or developing mental efficiency and social graces as of the cultivation of the inward grace of character. The generally recognized purposes of education, of training in health habits, in proper use of leisure time, in homemaking, in social adjustment, in vocations, and in arts and sciences can be only subsidiary to character building. The main business of life is to secure rational control over oneself so that conduct may prove satisfying to oneself and contributing to social welfare.

From the social standpoint, character represents the community's estimate of the individual as a basis for prediction of his behavior. From the viewpoint of the individual himself, character is a thorough integration of emotion, mind and will, a well-organized combination of distinctive traits, which manifests itself unmistakably in all acts and thoughts. The stamp of character is neither a biological endowment, with which we came into the world, nor is it something extraneous to ourselves which may be imparted to us in a course of study. It is rather "a tissue of habits and attitudes which we, in part, weave." [316] While some traits may be hereditary and some built into the child by the environment, others are acquired by the growing person's response to the social patterns and values and by organizing his experience in accordance with them. We grow from within, and, in a measure, shape our characters in the pattern of our ideals. In the final analysis, "a character," as T. H. Green teaches, "is only formed through a man's conscious presentation to himself of objects as his good, as that in which his self-satisfaction is to be found." [317]

No less than mental qualities, traits of character require careful nurture. Left to themselves they may go to weed. Frequently it becomes necessary to extirpate dangerous and anti-social habits which are entrenched in the feelings, desires and hungers before the character can be directed toward the sunlight. The process of character formation does not terminate with youth. Modern psychology supports the claim of religion that it is continuous. While mental fixity is greater in middle and in old age than in youth and in adolescence, it does not exclude the possibility of intellectual growth, though the process becomes more difficult with the passing years. R. Akiba began his education at forty. The acquisition of new standards of behavior as of knowledge is the prerogative of persons of all ages. Indeed, experience shows that religious interest and moral responsibility generally increase rather than decline with age. Men of advanced years have been known to break away from their old grooves and to rebuild their lives upon new foundations. They mastered the art of keeping open "the soul's east window of Divine surprise." Welcoming new truths and revising their old opinions and ideals, they have steadily progressed intellectually and spiritually. The task of self-culture can only end with death.

*Conditions of Character Training.* The welfare of humanity is bound up with the belief that men may mend their ways and effect wholesome changes in their characters. This belief forms the foundation of all religious and ethical aspirations. This belief, in turn, is predicated upon faith in human nature. Notions of human depravity, as held by Paulinian Christianity, and of mechanistic determinism, as professed by dogmatic science, are doubtful aids to the free growth of character. If a person of normal health and mentality acquires tendencies that are injurious to himself and others, it is not because of an ineradicable taint in human nature, derived from the mythical fall of Adam, nor because of physical or social conditioning, but because of his failure to apply intelligence to his will, to respond to the higher standards of his environment, and to guide himself by proper moral and spiritual influences. The good at the heart of every human being requires training to become a directing force in life.

Faith in human nature must form part of the larger faith in the goodness, orderliness and majesty which lies at the heart of all existence, i.e., of faith in God. As the light of the sun calls forth the color of the flower, so religious faith evokes the beauty and nobility of the soul. Character training reaches its climax in the consciousness of the sacred, in reverence for spiritual values, in living in the conscious presence of God. Morality ceases to be something remote, still to be attained; it becomes part of the very process of living. Amid the continuous change in social standards, ideals and modes of behavior, religion acts as a steadying and compelling purpose and thus serves as a life preserver. Hugh Hartshorne writes: "The great problem in the formation of character is not how to cultivate certain specific qualities, such as courage, nor certain specific habits, such as honesty, but how to make all one's acts and attitudes the expression of some self-chosen purpose to which all else in life is subordinate. The essence of character is the organization of purposes and plans." [318] Such a life purpose is presented by the idea of God, which, from the moral standpoint, represents the summation of all personal and social striving after truth, goodness, righteousness, and love. "Let all thy works be for God's sake," is the precept of Judaism. "Make thy will conform to God's will." [319] Do not drag the Divine down to your level; rather seek to rise to the Divine. Be a servant of the All-Highest. There must be no conflict between our desires and the highest good. By making God's purpose our own, by surrendering ourselves to Him, we come into possession of a transforming motive. We no longer live selfishly and aimlessly, but for the sake of all that we consider part of godliness. We attach ourselves to the spring of reality, and sense something of the wonder, awe and mystery which haunt the physical universe. The idea of the holy thus exercises a purifying effect upon us, and helps to combine our loose moral ends into a consistent character.

The upbuilding of character calls not only for the application of intelligence to the power of will, but also for the play of imagination. The Chronicler places in the mouth of David this striking prayer: "O Lord, the God of Abraham, of Isaac, and of Israel, our fathers, keep this for ever, even the imagination of the thoughts of the heart of Thy people, and direct their heart unto Thee" (1 Chr. 29:18). The creative power of imagination, which gives life to the plastic, literary, and musical arts and which enters deeply into philosophy and science is essential also to the art of life. Neither religion nor morality are possible without this constructive force. To attain to the highest reaches of the spirit it is necessary to have keen insight into one's own life and the lives of others, and keen vision to recognize whither the moves on life's chessboard lead. Without vision men perish. What appears as wickedness and immorality may sometimes be the result of deficient imagination rather than of viciousness or wantonness. Ability to estimate the consequences of our deeds might change our course of action. Likewise, placing ourselves in the position of our neighbor, we may judge him more charitably. Constructive imagination as distinguished from idle fancy helps to awaken the sense of generosity, which makes for readiness to sacrifice personal advantage upon the altar of public welfare, and to create foresight to forgo the joys of the hour for the sake of lasting good. Instead of living in the appetites and satisfactions of the moment, man secures a larger perspective for the full realization of his life.

*Methods of Character Training: Ritual Deed and Thought.* The history of Judaism discloses a twofold method whereby faith has been turned into a dynamic of character building. Josephus, in his spirited defense against Apion, correctly evaluates its nature and effectiveness. There are two types of education and moral training. One teaches by precept, the other by example. The legislators of the other nations used one or the other of these methods. The Lacedaemonians and Cretans preferred practical to verbal training. The Athenians and nearly all the rest of the Greeks formulated laws of conduct, but neglected to familiarize the people with them by putting them into practice. Moses went beyond them by carefully combining both systems of instruction. He did not leave practice without teaching, nor teaching without its application into practice. He left nothing in the life of the individual to his own caprice or discretion, regulating his diet, social relations, and the days for labor and for rest. "For all this our leader made the Law the standard and rule, that we might live under it as under a father and a master, and be guilty of no sin through wilfulness or ignorance." He concludes: "religion governs all our actions and occupations and speech." [320]

Josephus adds that whereas among others not even those who held the highest offices knew the Law, among the Jews knowledge of the laws of the Torah is universal, and obedience to them quite general. Mastery of the Torah, of the admonitions of the prophets and of the precepts of the sages and rabbis constituted the ideal of the People of the Book. However, religious knowledge was not a purely theoretical affair. The Written and the Oral laws figured as socially approved norms and patterns of behavior. The Halachah was not meant to be a mere subject for mental gymnastics, but rather the authoritative guide to conduct. The direct method of character training was thus combined with the indirect one. Knowledge alone cannot metamorphose a man into a moral and religious being. To knowledge must be added practice. Moral perfection is not attained in a vacuum. Character is best trained in the school of experience, through reactions to different situations. Pure-mindedness is secured not by keeping oneself ignorant of the ugly and the unseemly, but by developing in oneself the power of resistance to their lure, through centering the mind upon wholesome thoughts and engaging in socially beneficial interests and activities. Good is produced by the constant doing of good things; justice by being just, under all conditions, to all men, whether they are our friends or enemies; mercy by the steady exercise of kindness; religion itself by engaging in religious deeds.

Morality and religion are ineffective when left as abstractions. They grow into power when they are particularized and translated into definite ways of behavior. Judaism provided specific tasks for daily performance as a means of keeping alive the spirit of faith. Rabbi Aaron Halevi of Barcelona observes acutely that "man is affected by all his actions; and his heart and all his thoughts follow the deeds which he does, whether good or bad. Though one be altogether wicked at heart and all his inclinations be always evil, if he makes a valiant effort to continually study the Torah and follow its commandments, even if not out of pure motives, he will in course of time incline toward the good, and, despite his engaging in religious pursuits out of impure motives, he will come to follow them for their own sake . . . On the other hand, a perfectly righteous person, whose heart is upright and sincere, who takes delight in the Torah and its commandments, but engages in offensive matters—say, for example, that the king compelled him to pursue an evil occupation—if he devotes himself to that business all the time, he will ultimately turn from his righteousness and become wicked; for it is well established that, as we have stated above, every man is affected by his actions. Hence our sages said: 'The Holy One, desiring to endow the people of Israel with merit, gave them an abundant Torah and commandments.'[321] This thought is further conveyed by their saying that 'whoever has a *mezuzah* upon his doorpost, show-threads (*tzitzit*) upon his garments and phylacteries (*tephillin*) upon his head is assured that he will never sin';[322] for these commandments are of a continuous nature, and man is steadily influenced by them."[323]

Hence the unquestioning observance of ritual requirements has recommended itself to the rabbis as of the highest value. The ceremonies at home and at the synagogue, the observance of the Sabbath and the festivals by abstaining from labor and joining the community in worship and kindred activities, offer the individual so many opportunities for practicing his religion and for identification with his people, and thus vitally influence his character.[324] "Ritual" has been described as "poetry addressed to the eye."[325] Ceremonies represent the poetry and the drama of religion translated in forms that are universally understandable. They speak to the emotions, and invest life with holiness.[326] In the view of tradition, they are to be kept not because of their attractiveness, but rather because they were commanded by God. *Mitzvot lo lehanot nitnu*—"the commandments were not given for the purpose of affording pleasure." [327]

On the other hand, the rationalists would find moral grounds even in those ceremonial laws, which the rabbis ascribed to the will of God and which historical criticism traces to ancient tabus. Maimonides, for example, holds that all commandments serve a useful object. For only a few of the six hundred thirteen Pentateuchal laws, Maimonides confesses his inability to give adequate reasons, but he is certain that even these have reasons which may some day be discovered. "The general object of the Law," he maintains, "is twofold: the well-being of the soul, and the well-being of the body." [328]

As a rationalist, Moritz Lazarus objects to the view of Aaron Halevi on the ground that the "relation between deed and thought, act and conviction, is literally turned upside down." [329] But the religious history of the Jewish people as well as modern psychology support Rabbi Aaron's position. While men who lead an intellectual life may proceed from thought to deed, the generality of men learn by doing. The visible symbol and the concrete act are the most potent means of leading to communion with God.[330] There is profound truth in the order of words in Israel's acceptance of the covenant: *Na'aseh v'nishma*, "we shall *do* and *hear*" (Ex. 24:7).

To be sure, excessive concern with details, in forgetfulness of the underlying intention, runs the danger of degenerating into bare formalism. Nonetheless, from the standpoint of character training, specific objects—especially if they possess distinctiveness—are of supreme value. In this realm the rule is: "Precept by precept, precept by precept; line by line, line by line; here a little, there a little" (Is. 28:10). When true to itself, Judaism has endeavored to unite conduct with conviction, to keep the underlying motive fresh in the minds of the people while encouraging them to perform definite religious deeds. The Cabbalists provided special meditations before the performance of ceremonial acts expressive of their purpose. All wings of Judaism stressed the inwardness of ritual observances.

In the development of man's character, Judaism has followed both the direct and the indirect method. The direct method of teaching morals appears in Jewish ethical writings and figures, to some degree, in popular Jewish education. At the same time, as our analysis has shown, dissatisfaction has manifested itself with the barrenness of teaching without practice. Dwelling upon the virtues in themselves, however valuable as a phase of ethical knowledge, may prove sterile as a pedagogical means of developing virtue. Memorizing abstract moral precepts—aside from rendering them trite and, to some people, irritating and odious as a form of lip service—is at best a poor substitute for practicing them in concrete situations. *Haggadah* must be completed by *Halachah*. It is through proper responses to definite situations that man builds up a set of habits that makes for an attitude of true manliness, honesty, responsibility, service, and loyalty toward his associates, family, community and nation as well as to the highest interests of humanity.

Character training, in the view of the Torah, reaches its consummation in man's total development as a spiritual personality. In the daily round of duty, whether at school or the house of worship, at home or in the market-place, in business, in manual or intellectual labor, man must express the faith that is in him. Every endeavor must be charged with moral earnestness and sincerity of purpose.

*Note on Character Building Agencies.* While character is formed through all phases of personal and social life, certain agencies are particularly adapted to that end. Foremost of these is home life. The home is, indeed, the nursery of religion and of morality as well as of culture. In the intimacy of its atmosphere the child reacts to every influence, whether good or evil. Here its habits are formed, its attitudes to all kinds of conditions trained, and its early notions of right and wrong developed. Together with the language which it learns and with the religious or irreligious attitudes and ideas which it imbibes with the mother's milk, it is fitted as a useful or parasitic member of society. No other influence may compare with the home for the lasting and far-reaching effects upon the child's development. Hence the great responsibility of the parents for the child's moral and spiritual character.

Educational agencies can only supplement the influence of the home. They help to develop the mind and, in part, to cultivate the moral qualities of the child. The study of language, literature, art, science, civics, etc., tends to socialize the child and makes it conscious of its relation to the rest of the world. Cooperation with teachers and fellow pupils translates the social consciousness into actuality.

The religious school and house of worship, by reaching the child for comparatively brief periods of time, at best make a limited contribution to direct character training. Their influence is exerted more indirectly through the agencies of the home and the school as well as of the press, literature and amusements. Though the American public schools do not teach religion formally, they build considerably on the moral principles fostered by the religious bodies of the country. The same is true of the theater, the daily paper, the magazine, the novel and the poem. Both directly and indirectly they often reflect the moral ideals of religion.

Of great influence in the child's life is the atmosphere of the street and the playground. Here the child meets other children and freely exchanges modes of behavior. In the give and take of the general atmosphere there is much evil as well as good. Though the home, school and house of worship stress moral values, the moral laxity of the environment, the general disregard of the rights of others, and the craze for emotional excitement often make for delinquency.

Character training must, therefore, be reinforced from other directions. First there is the power of example set by distinguished men. Their lives, full of heroic effort, of struggle and of victory, serve as incentives to young and old. Their very heartaches, sufferings and martyrdom open moral possibilities to the rest of us. Their flaming ideals set our hearts aglow. The faith that was in them becomes a light to us.

"Just as courage is so often a reflex of another's courage, so our faith is apt to be," as Max Müller somewhere says, "a faith in someone else's faith. We draw new life from the heroic example. The prophet has drunk more deeply than anyone of the cup of bitterness, but his countenance is so unshaken and he speaks such mighty words of cheer that his will becomes our will, and our life is kindled at his own" (cf. Is. 32:2; 25:4).[331] Hence the sage announces the purpose of all moral instruction:

> That thou mayest walk in the way of good men,
> And keep the path of the righteous.—PROV. 2:20.

Not only the histories of great men but the history of nations and of humanity at large presents the richest form of teaching by example. History is the great laboratory of character. Here effects of human welfare or misery are traced to their causes in the ideas and deeds of men; the growth and the decay of empires are revealed as the resultants of certain moral and religious conditions. The tangled web of human relations is disclosed in its orderly sequence. The fruits of human behavior, of national policies and ideals are presented, not in the abstract but concretely, as incorporated in human happiness or misery.

Through the study of history the individual is further trained to regard himself not as an isolated unit but as a link in a long chain, going back to distant times, connected and interlinked with others in the society of the present. A sense of reverence is thus awakened for one's own people, for its strivings and achievements; a loyalty to its goals and ideals and above all a feeling of identification with its present and future.

The ministry of art effectively serves the ends of character. The soul can be moved by beauty when all other means fail. Beauty in line and color, translated into daily surroundings, into cheerful homes, shops, offices, and countrysides uplift the spirits of young and old. The same is true of music, of imaginative literature, of drama, and of poetry. When set to a high key of idealism, they are potent means of building character.

# XIV. THE WAY OF SELF-RENEWAL

THE MEANING OF SIN. We have dealt with the nature of evil which befalls man from the outside, independent of his will and determination, and we have considered some ways in which religion helps him face its onslaughts. Let us now analyze the nature of the evil which originates within man himself, which religion designates as sin and which mars and blights personal and social life. While religion prepares man to combat external evil, its primary concern is to stimulate him to overcome his inner discords, the conflicts which arise within his consciousness between warring impulses, desires and motives, which disintegrate personality, and to bring him the peace and the harmony essential to creative living. The birth of the religious sense in man is marked by the urge to self-mastery, to the subordination of the cravings of the flesh to the demands of the spirit, and to the subjection of self-love and self-interest to the religious and ethical ideal. The sacred grows real when the passional elements are put in the service of the divine goal of life.

The concept of sin often frightens liberals as much as the sense of sin used to terrify the old-fashioned believers. This is part of the modern reaction to the excessive preoccupation with sin in Jewish as in Christian orthodoxy. The pall of sin burdened the consciences of men. How to avert the impending punishment of sin constituted much of the practical life of the past. In contrast, large numbers of modern men and women seldom give a thought to the subject. Some thinkers deny its very reality. The new cosmic perspective and the newer interpretation of the Bible, we are told, rule sin out of civilized nomenclature. We may admit the reality of immorality and crime, but scarcely of sin, which is technically "a wilful and direct affront to God," a violation of His will. With the difficulty of proving the existence of God or of showing any direct solicitude of God for our ephemeral lives on this petty planet, and with the abandonment of the dogma regarding the Bible as the revealed will of God, the nature of God's commands concerning human behavior grows indefinite. Sin thus becomes "indefinable and unknowable." *

The notion of sin is not so easily disposed of as this exercise in semantics would suggest. Under different names its hideous reality manifests itself in the life of the individual and of society. The claim that from the standpoint of modern science sin is untenable holds if we limit ourselves to the physical sciences or even to biology, physiology and medicine, but not if we include the study of the human mind. Sigmund Freud, for example, though not an exponent of religion and avoiding theological terminology, considers the feeling of guilt as one of the permanent elements of human nature. It may be that the sense of guilt like that

---

* H. E. Barnes, *The Nation*, January 16, 1929; compare E. A. Burtt's criticism of the Humanist movement for failing to recognize properly the nature of sin in two trenchant papers in the Humanist, 1945, pp. 108–114 ("Does Humanism Understand Human Nature?"), and 1946, pp. 173–180 ("Humanism and the Doctrine of Sin").

of shame is transmitted to children by their parents and teachers, and forms no inborn part of their characters. The fact remains that a person devoid of either is hardly conceivable. Though some persons claim to be free from the consciousness of guilt, a careful examination may show it operative in their unconscious, if not conscious, selves. One of Freud's interpreters concludes that "total lack of a sense of guilt is a disease which would necessarily make man a beast." If found in actual experience, such a person could hardly form the ideal for our emulation. Furthermore, the widespread delinquency among men and women of varying ages and stations and the frightful irruption of human passion, which culminated in the Second World War and filled the whole world with grief and with sorrow, show the woeful superficiality of the view of human nature that ignores the grim fact of sin.

Allowing for certain aberrations in the conventional ideas of sin, the notion itself, coming as it does as *a criticism of human conduct*, is of great value to the religious life. It has been well observed that as soon as religion rises from the magical to the ethical plane, and strives to improve conduct and to inculcate reverence for the Divine which is latent in every human being, "it becomes at once the expression and instrument of man's ennobling discontent with himself, or the sense of the evils in his actual nature which thwart his self-fulfillment. It becomes the influence, individual and social, which summons the deeper resources of our being to the evolutionary effort (for all evolution is by effort) which gradually raises men above their given selves." [332]

What is a mere element of behavior for psychology and for ethics is a central fact in religion. As Solomon Schechter observes: "Consciousness of sin and the assurance of grace are the great motive powers in the working of religion. Without them, religion sinks to the level of a mere cult or a kind of ethico-aesthetico-spiritual sport in which there is no room for devotion and submission." [333]

Like all other religious conceptions so that of sin has undergone much change. Many an act or practice condemned as sinful in the past may no longer appear so to the conscience of religious men today. In modern usage the evils which proceed from men are grouped into different classes. Atrocities against the social order and grave violations of public law are classed as crimes. Lesser offenses are designated as misdemeanors. Habitual deviation from moral rectitude and especially the habitual gratification of a debasing appetite or passion constitute vice.[334] Offenses against the Divine in nature or in human nature are termed sin. No such differentiation of the subject is to be discovered in the Bible and in rabbinic literature. Indeed, the Hebrew vocabulary has no special terms for crime and vice.[335] Deriving its sanctions from the Divine, Judaism includes all man-made evils in the category of sin. Offenses against the law or against society or even against one's own self are considered an affront to God. Something of the same spirit is reflected in the English usage of the term, despite its clear distinctions between different types and forms of misbehavior.*

Despite its wide latitude of usage, sin belongs essentially to the vocabulary of religion. It represents the opprobrium which religion attaches to unworthy forms of human behavior. Its primary meaning is the negation of religious values and standards, the violation of the sanctities of life. The synonyms which come closest to it are: ungodliness, unholiness, profanity, and impiety. Through the fusion of religion with morality, sin came to connote, as Fernald states, "any lack of holiness, any defect of moral purity and truth, whether in heart or in life, whether of commission or omission." [336] However, we miss its true meaning if we confine it to purely moral offenses. It grows not from the soil of rational ethics, but from that of the non-rational or "numinous." Mere morality, as Rudolf Otto has shown, produces neither the sense of sin nor the desire for purification, forgiveness, and deliverance, nor the "need for that other unique good which is likewise altogether and specifically numinous in character, 'covering' and atonement." [337]

---

* James Fernald informs us that "sin in the generic sense, as denoting a state of heart, is synonymous with *depravity*; in the specific sense, as in the possession of a sin, the term may be synonymous with *transgression*, *crime*, *offense*, *misdeed*, etc., or may denote some moral activity that could not be characterized by terms so positive. *Immorality* denotes outward violation of the moral law. *Sin* is thus the broadest word, and *immorality* next in scope; all crimes, properly so called, and all *immoralities*, are sins; but there may be *sin*, as ingratitude, which is neither *crime*, *transgression* nor *immorality*; and there may be *immorality* which is not a *crime*, as falsehood. *English Synonyms*, p. 333.

*Development of the Idea of Sin.* Though the term *aberah* does not appear in the Bible, its root meaning of transgression or disregard of God's will may be taken to express the permanent conception of sin in Judaism. The variations in this conception derive from the changes that took place in the idea of God and of His will. The earliest notions of the will of God were bound up with tribal mores and tabus. Breaking them constituted an offense against God. This idea underlies numerous Hebrew words for sin.* The most characteristic word for sin in the Bible and in post-Biblical literature, *het,* is derived from a verb expressing the idea of "missing the mark," as when a bowman misses his aim (Judges 20:16; cf. Greek *Amartía*). The word is often linked with terms denoting "error," "folly" and "want of skill." It was borrowed from ordinary human relations, where it was applied to "any act that put a man in the wrong with those who had the power to make him rue it" (II Kings 18:14;

---

* *Pesha,* the most common word for transgression, literally means rebellion against God, defection from His authority. *Mered* conveys the same sense (Joshua 22:24). *Zadon* denotes insolence or presumptuousness as exhibited toward God or His representatives. (Its opposite is *shegagah,* the sin of error or inadvertence. *Shegiah* and *Mishgeh* denote unwilful error or mistake.) *Aven,* which is often coupled with *'avlah,* means wickedness, iniquity, unrighteousness, wrong. It sometimes stands for idolatry, the arch sin of monotheism (Hosea 12:12; Isaiah 41:29). *Resha* and *ra'ah* similarly express the idea of wickedness and evil. *Asham* and *ashmah* carry the meaning of guilt, offense or wrongdoing. *'Avon,* from the root *'avah,* to err from the right way, iniquity, suggests wilful perversion or rendering crooked that which was straight (Hosea 12:9).

1 Sam. 21:1). Its religious significance was accentuated by the belief that God as the supreme Judge and
King in Israel was offended by each act that ran
counter to His will. A sin against one's fellow men
thus figured as a sin against God (Exod. 22:20–6).*

Sin, incurring the anger of the deity, is fraught with
danger for man. Moral and ceremonial offenses are
placed on a par. The criterion of sin in early times was
not the consciousness of wrong-doing. Sins were committed also "unwittingly" and in error. Punishment
followed just the same, unless proper means of expiation of the guilt were taken. Not the subjective intention, but the objective act formed the sole ground of
judgment. Jonathan did not hear when his father
placed a tabu upon the honey in the forest, but inasmuch as he tasted of it he incurred the death penalty,
which he escaped only through the intervention of his
grateful people (1 Sam. 14:27). Only later were distinctions made between wilful and inadvertent sins,
and between acts of omission and acts of commission.

Common to the ancient conceptions of sin is its defiling character. It contaminates both the land and the
people (cf. Deut. 21:1 ff.; and see Ezek. 14:11; 22:3
ff.). The pollution was removable by proper acts of

---

* W. R. Smith writes: "In by far the greatest proportion of
passages in the older parts of the Bible where sins are spoken
of, the reference is to religious offenses, to the worship of
false gods, or of Jehovah Himself in ways not acceptable to
Him, to disobedience to some particular injunction—as in the
case of Saul's failure to fulfill his commission against Amalek
—or neglect to discharge a vow." (1 Sam. 14:38; Judges
21: 22.) *Prophets of Israel*, p. 103.

purification, such as lustrations, sacrifices, the scapegoat ceremonial, and by personal confession of sin,
whether known or unknown, in order to purge oneself of dire consequences.

Sin though committed by an individual involved the
entire community in the wrath of God. Achan broke
the *herem* (ban) and thereby brought disaster upon
the entire people (Josh. 7). Farnell writes: "Both
(Greece and Babylon) reveal the phenomenon that
marks the early stage of social morality: as the tribe of
the family are of one flesh, one corporate unit of life,
so the members are collectively responsible, and the
sins of the fathers are visited on the children. This was
the familiar law of old Hellas, and we may say of the
ancient Mediterranean society; the first to make the
momentous protest against it, and to proclaim the responsibility of the individual conscience, was Theog-
nis (b. 540) for the Greeks and Ezekiel for the
Hebrews." [338] Ezekiel's teaching was not altogether
unknown in Israel long before his day. In ii Samuel
24:17, David pleads with God: "Lo, I have sinned and
I have done iniquitously; but these sheep, what have
they done? Let Thy hand, I pray Thee, be against
me, and against my father's house." It forms part of
the higher religion of the prophets in general and particularly of Jeremiah. Ezekiel carried these ideas to
their logical conclusion, and he made them the basis of
his new morality. However, the community's share in
the sins of the individual has persisted in Judaism.

With the prophetic advance in religion the conception of sin was ethicized and deepened. God mani-

fested Himself to the conscience of the prophets as the Eternal who wills justice and mercy, integrity and truth. Social morality loomed foremost in their preaching. The primary interest of the pre-Exilic prophets was not the cult but right human relations befitting the people consecrated to the service of God. Consequently sin appears in their teaching as the negation of moral as well as of specifically religious values. *Sin for them is the obverse of both holiness and righteousness.* They are conscious of a distinction between sins growing out of ignorance of the requirements of the cult and sins due to the ignorance of God's character and His moral demands. Hosea 6:6 declares that God is concerned with justice and not with sacrifice. Isaiah, while considering mortal men impure in the presence of the Holy One and calling for cleansing from sin, deals particularly with moral offenses as acts of rebellion against God (1:2–4). The depravity of Israel, denounced in the preaching of Jeremiah, consists in apostasy and in disregard of the laws of morality (Jer. 4:1–4, 22; 5:1–5; 7).

In Ezekiel ritual offenses figure by the side of the moral (8; 16, etc.). His view is shared by the post-Exilic prophets (Hag. 1:2; Zech. 6:12; 14:16–21; Joel 1:9; Mal. 1:8; 3:8–10) and by the Priestly and Holiness Codes. The prophetic belief that God searches the heart resulted in the recognition of a distinction between "secret errors" and "presumptuous sins" (Ps. 19:13f.) or sins committed "with a high hand" (Num. 15:30; individual responsibility is stressed in Num. 16:20–22). The Priestly Code limited the atoning ef-

ficacy of the sin and guilt offerings to offenses committed unconsciously and without deliberation. The
post-Exilic prophets, too, tremble at the thought of
the consequences of sin. "Your iniquities," says the
prophet, "have separated between you and your God,
and your sins have hid His face from you, that He
will not hear" (Is. 59:2). And again: "And we are all
become as one that is unclean, and all our righteous-
nesses are as a polluted garment; and we all do fade as
a leaf, and our iniquities, like the wind, takes us away.
. . . Thou hast hid Thy face from us, and hast consumed us by means of our iniquities" (ibid, 64:5–6).
Sin is a stain upon the soul of man. Hence the idea of
cleansing, of washing away the impurity (Ps. 51:
4–5, 10).[339]

Conscience plagues the sinner, and gives him no rest
by day or by night.* The relation between sin and
suffering continually tortures his soul. With the growing refinement of religion, the sense of guilt is more
feared than the danger of physical disaster. It marks
the estrangement from God, who is the source of all
happiness (Ps. 38:3ff.). Confession in this stage seeks
to secure God's pardon and to remove the guilt rather
than the consequences of sin.[340] The primary aim is to
restore the interrupted communion with God and to
draw near to His presence.

It has been noted that "in the history of religious

* Smend writes: "For the Jews sin is a power which brings
ruin to sinners, because it is fundamentally identical with
punishment." *Lehrbuch der A. T. Religionsgeschichte,* p.
431; cf. p. 196 and W. R. Smith, *Religion of the Semites,*
p. 423.

ideas each new development does not cancel or repeal all that went before. Custom, with the force of an almost religious sanction (cf. II Sam. 13:12) is nowhere more powerful than here. The old and the new tend to persist side by side, each acting and reacting upon the other." [341] A revolutionary conception of sin is sounded by Elihu:

> Look into the heavens, and see;
> And behold the skies, which are higher than thou.
> If thou hast sinned, what doest thou against Him?
> If thou be righteous, what givest thou Him?
> Or what receiveth He of thy hand?
> Thy wickedness concerneth a man as thou art;
> And Thy righteousness a son of man.—JOB 35:5–8.

Sin, from this standpoint, is not an affront to God, but rather an offense to one's own true humanity. Correlating it with the religious conception of man, we may conclude with Kaufmann Kohler that sin is "the desecration of the Divine image in man, the violation of his heavenly pattern of nobility." [342] However, the older viewpoint was preserved by the side of the new. Sin continued to be treated as a rebellion against God's holiness and righteousness. Post-Exilic times are marked by a deepened sense of the burden of sin upon the soul of man. Fearing sin came to figure as the criterion of the religious man (cf. Ps. 19:13–14).

A modified idea of sin emerged with the acceptance of the Pentateuch as the revealed will of God. The essence of piety now came to be conformity to the written word of the Pentateuch. Any deviation from

it represented sin. Thus in a new sense all sin came
under the category of *aberah*, transgression or rebellion
against God's will as expressed in the Torah. The dis-
covery on the part of the rabbis of 248 positive and
of 365 negative commandments in the Torah gave
them a concrete approach to sin as a violation of a
specific command or prohibition. This formal conception of sin did not obscure the difference between sins
against God and sins against man—between sins of
presumption and sins of error, and between light and
grave sins. During the Hadrianic persecutions, the
rabbis decreed that when life is at stake a person may
break all the commands of the Torah, excepting idolatry, incest, and bloodshed. The violation of these robs
life itself of all worth. Man must, indeed, be cautious
with light offenses as well as with grave ones, for by
falling victim of a seemingly minor offense his resistance to grave offenses is weakened. Sin may appear at
first as thin as a spider's web and ultimately grows into
a strong cable. "An *aberah* dulls the mind of man." [343]
It removes the sense of distinction between right and
wrong. It defiles the spirit and leads to perdition. Sin
causes the Shechinah to depart from Israel.[344] It is the
root of all suffering and of all death.[345]

The recognition of offenses committed uninten-
tionally and ignorantly as sins creates difficulties for
the modern conscience, which inclines to regard the
very nature of sin as implying conscious choice. The
rabbis dealt not only with the intentions which lead to
sin, but also with sin's consequences. Ignorant and un-
intentional non-compliance with or transgression of

the Law or tradition may not indicate active rebellion, but they definitely involve the sinner in guilt, which he must seek to expiate. A distinction between the two is preserved.[346] A minor or a mental defective does not transgress. Nor is a person of another faith considered a sinner when acting contrary to the laws of the Torah. Not having received the yoke of the Divine Kingdom, he is not obligated to bear the burden of its *mitzvot*. Only citizens of the Kingdom of God share in the responsibilities imposed by this spiritual citizenship, and are deemed sinners when falling short of fulfilling them. Ignorance of the law is no complete excuse only for those who submit to the rule of the Torah. The sinner is like a man who incurred a debt—*hobah*. The sin remains until he has remitted the debt or expiated the offense. The fulfillment of a *mitzvah* is an act of merit—*zechut*, which is accounted to one's credit.

What Judaism conceived as sin is best evidenced by the Yom Kippur confessional. The *Al Het* mentions the sins committed publicly and secretly, presumptuously or ignorantly, by compulsion and voluntarily, through stubbornness and faintness of heart; sins committed through evil imagination and cogitation of the heart, foolish and malicious words of mouth, slander, calumny, scoffing, hatred, talebearing, false swearing, immodest discourse; sins of haughtiness, arrogance, shamelessness, lawlessness, envy, levity, treachery, violence, bribery, usury, embezzlement, fornication, dishonesty in business, disregard of parents and teachers, intemperance, and ritual impropriety in meats and drinks. The list includes the sins of profanation of God's name, *hillul hashem*, as well as the sins against humanity in oneself and in one's fellow men. The *Ashamnu* refers also to blasphemy, perversity, presumption, scorn, iniquity, wickedness, theft, robbery, oppression, corruption, etc.

Sin as the desecration of the holy means first, disregard of God, and, second, setting up the self in His place as the Absolute. The idolatry of the self takes on many forms: self-glorification, self-righteousness, pride, arrogance, conceit, and hardness. The self and its extensions, the tribe, state, nation, race, and class receive the homage due to God. Not God's will but our own becomes the standard of conduct. The creature defies the Creator.

*The Root of Sin.* Pascal remarked that society consists of two classes: of saints who confess to be sinners and of sinners who profess to be saints. While for the irreligious sin is non-existent, religious souls are weighted down by its burdens. Instead of applauding their own self-righteousness, they probe their hearts in continuous self-criticism. The universality of sin is an ever-present reality to them. The prayer of Solomon states: "There is no man that sinneth not" (1 Kings 8:46). Ecclesiastes 7:20 elaborates: "There is not a righteous man upon earth, that doeth good, and sinneth not." Proverbs 20:9 exclaims: "Who can say: 'I have made my heart clean, and I am pure from my sin'?" The sense of sin oppresses the saintly psalmists. They feel themselves alienated from God, and, in regret and penitence, seek His grace and forgiveness.

Whence comes sin? Why does man rebel against
holiness, goodness and righteousness contrary to the
better counsel of his reason? The Biblical story of
Adam's disobedience and expulsion from Eden was
utilized by Paul for his Christological solution of the
problem. From this standpoint, all sin derives from the
original infection of the race through Adam (Rom.
5:12–21). Normative Judaism rejects the doctrine of
original sin, i.e., of evil cleaving to man from his very
birth as a sort of hereditary disease. The Paradise story
of Genesis 3 was not intended to convey the idea that
the infraction of a tabu by the first parents of the race
altered the moral character of any one beside themselves. Neither does it suggest the imputation of their
guilt to their descendants as an inherited taint of the
soul. Like the etiological myths of other peoples, it
merely seeks to account for the sad facts of physical
hardship, pain and mortality, which the first couple
brought upon themselves and upon their posterity.
During Biblical times no conclusions were drawn from
this story. Only in Apocryphal and Pseudepigraphic
writings—and under Parsi and Greek influence—ideas
of a fall and of original sin began to shape themselves.
These appear in 1Enoch, the Secrets of Enoch, the
Wisdom of Solomon and 4Ezra. Paul drew upon them
for his conception of the moral depravity and corruption of the human race as the ground for his doctrine
of salvation through the death and resurrection of
Jesus, modelled after the mythology of the mystery
religions. The rabbis (also 2Baruch) interpreted the
Genesis story to mean that the transgression of Adam

and Eve introduced into the world death and physical suffering, but not the corruption of man's inner nature. While dwelling upon the striking changes that came upon them in consequence of their transgression, they avoid the thought that Adam and Eve lost their Divine image and mental capacities or that they forfeited their freedom of choice between good and evil. Even the mystics who believed that "the pollution of the serpent" infected humanity, refused to regard human nature as hopelessly corrupt. The "broken channels" of Divine grace can be repaired by human effort. Spiritually every person enjoys complete autonomy. Against the despairing view of the vitiated nature of man, Judaism has consistently upheld his Divine capacities and endowments. Goodness inheres in him as a bearer of the Divine image. In the light of modern anthropology, man's decline from a pristine state of untarnished virtue appears to be a pure myth. Ethical judgment rules out the possibility of all generations suffering for the infraction of an imaginary tabu by a legendary progenitor of the race. The empirical fact of the universality of anti-social behavior, of immorality and sin cannot be accounted for by a mythical fall of Adam. It must be noted that within Christianity itself strong opposition to this doctrine has prevailed through the centuries. Some newer Christian teaching is frankly abandoning this doctrine.[347]

A related explanation of the root of sin is offered by the rabbinic doctrine of the *Yetzer Hara*, or the evil impulse. However, its evil nature is by no means absolute. The Men of the Great Synagogue, according to rabbinic legend, wished to banish it, but found that without passion life could not continue. They, therefore, stopped the war on the Yetzer Hara in general and concentrated their attacks on idolatry, i.e., on the illegitimate use of the passions, on the glorification of the senses.[348] The impulses, desires, hungers, appetites, instincts, and feelings constitute the raw materials out of which life is fashioned. They belong to man by virtue of his citizenship in the biological realm. Where they are absent life is at a low ebb. Without passion, there is little excellence in the artist, poet, singer, composer, prophet, thinker, statesman or social leader. "The greater the man," so runs a rabbinic saying, "the greater is his Yetzer." [349] Our instinctual responses are neither moral nor immoral, neither sinful nor virtuous, but neutral and may be turned into good or evil. They become evil, when, in disregard of moral and religious standards, they are permitted to run unbridled and to grow into wild lusts. Our lives turn into sources of danger to ourselves and to society when they are driven by passions for power, for pleasure, for wealth, or for sex.

Thus sin appears to be the product of folly, ignorance and weakness. It represents the yielding of our spirit to the primitive within our natures, the relaxing of the reins that control our consciousness and the releasing of the tiger, the ape, and the peacock within us. It is a reversion to the archaic, to the pre-human, the preponderance of self-love over social well-being as symbolized by law and authority. It expresses our usurpation of God's sovereignty and setting up our will against His. Virtue, on the other hand, consists in the victory of the forces of reason and of conscience within us, of the emerging soul over the buried Titan, and the enthronement of God in our lives.

Thus sin and virtue are predicated upon human freedom. We sin when we fail to exercise properly our freedom of choice, when either wittingly or unwittingly we pursue the path of self-indulgence in place of following the road of self-discipline, of duty and of right. A man sins not because he is endowed with physical hungers, but because he surrenders himself to them despite his awareness of the higher good. Where choice is excluded there is no responsibility and consequently no sin in the proper sense of the word. The gravity of the sin is proportionate to the extent to which it is conscious and deliberate. The root of sin reduces itself to wrong choice and wrong motivation, due to straying after one's own heart and one's own eyes. The rabbis observe that "a man does not sin except when the spirit of folly possesses him." [350]

Sin is essentially negative in character. It is the absence of holiness, of reverence, of thoughtfulness, of probity, of goodness, of truth, of mercy, of humanity, etc. It is a form of moral and spiritual defectiveness, of blindness, and of turpitude. It is not a hereditary and ineradicable taint of the soul, but a form of dereliction or blunder, of failure to aspire after the higher aims of life. It may be the product of the selfish or rebellious spirit, of the lack of sufficient self-mastery, or it may be stimulated by certain environmental factors, which entice and allure to evil. While it is the affair of the individual, it is also the concern of society. Wrong social standards are responsible for much of the sin which fills the world with woe. Its removal, too, calls for the application of intelligence to social as well as to personal relations and for the guiding of human affairs by high standards of ethical religion. Consequently, it is the conviction of Judaism that man may achieve his moral and spiritual regeneration directly through his own effort and requires no intermediary to save him. In the conscious self-consecration to God and in obedience to His will, man is given the means and the power to overcome sin and to shape his life in the pattern of His divinity.

DEVELOPMENT OF THE IDEA OF ATONEMENT. The recognition of the reality of sin forms one phase of the religious consciousness. The desire to overcome it constitutes the chief goal of religious striving. The Jewish idea of atonement has kept pace with the development of the idea of sin. Through all the stages of its growth, it has derived its vitality from the essential character of Judaism as a religion which expresses itself in the consciousness of communion with and consecration to the holy and righteous Sovereign and loving Father. By his misbehavior man often impairs this relationship and thereby endangers his well-being, both physical and spiritual. He, therefore, stands in need of proper means for the restoration of the interrupted relationship, i.e., of *at-one-ment* with God. What constituted the right means, whereby the individual and the community sought to reconcile themselves to God and to win His favor, varied at different times. In the evolution of the idea of atonement, as of Judaism in general, the destruction of the Temple in 70 C.E. marks a sharp dividing line. Prior to that event the chief means of atonement were sacrificial. With the cessation of the sacrificial cult the emphasis shifted to its accessory forms of worship. In the first period itself we may distinguish three stages in the development of the idea: (1) the pre-prophetic, (2) the prophetic, and (3) that of the priestly Torah.

*Biblical Phase.* The earliest notions of sin as dereliction or blunder, whether conscious or unconscious, suggested mechanical means for its removal, as is indicated by the Hebrew term *kipper*, cover, remove, wash away. The Babylonian *kuppuru* expresses the notion of *ritual purgation*. By certain magical ceremonies a priest "purges" or "purifies" a king, a sick person, or a house. The act of atonement removes disease, which is believed to be the consequence of sin, and expels the demons who were regarded as the cause of sickness and other troubles in those whom they possessed. The Hebrew term seems to have had a similar primary meaning of ritual purgation, and came to express the more definite idea of expiation, purification from sin, propitiation, and reconciliation.[351]

Blood-guilt required expiation with blood. In the case of an untraced and unavenged murder, the blood was "covered" or "wiped away" by means of a symbolic rite of expiation (Deut. 21:1–9). Deuteronomy 32:43 announces that the defilement of the land, caused by the slaughter of Israelites, will be removed by God's avenging their blood upon their enemies, thus making expiation for the land of His people. Numbers 35:33 lays down the principle that "no expiation can be made for the land for the blood that is shed therein, but the blood of him who shed it." Consequently money compensation was ruled out in cases of murder.[352] Offenses other than manslaughter could be propitiated by means of a gift, whether in the form of a sacrifice or of "forfeit money" (*asham*) and of "sin-money" (*hattat*) which were given to the priests in order to satisfy the offended God (II Kings 12:17; Amos 2:8).

The act of atonement appears to have sought to restore the interrupted relationship with God, to counteract the evil consequence of the offense committed, to prevent the offense from being seen by God, and to have God close His eyes to the offense of the people. As the ultimate subject of atonement was God, the notion of to "atone" came to be equivalent of to "forgive." Forgiveness represented the result of the covering, wiping out or atoning the sin.[353]

In line with universal ancient practice, the rites of atonement assumed sacrificial form. Indeed, the entire institution of sacrifice may be considered as aiming at the atonement of men with God. It is based upon primitive notions regarding the sacrosanct nature of blood as the vehicle of life (cf. Lev. 17:11; Gen. 9:4; Deut. 12:16). Sacrificial blood is covenantal in character. It restores the bond of fellowship with God, and is, therefore, effective in ritual purgation.[354]

The deepened prophetic idea of sin as the obverse

of holiness and of righteousness challenged the popular
notion that ritual exactness was sufficient to cover up
moral obloquy and wrong. Some iniquities, like those
of the house of Eli, were not to be "expiated with
sacrifice nor offering for ever" (1 Samuel 3:14). In the
view of Amos, the wickedness of Israel requires more
than holocausts to be expiated. The sole way of securing God's salvation from the overhanging doom that
threatened the nation was by seeking God, by practicing justice and righteousness. Hosea similarly announces that God desires mercy rather than sacrifice.
Isaiah stresses that the sin of Jacob can be wiped away
only through the extermination of all idolatry and the
whole-hearted return to God, by ceasing to do evil
and learning to do good. In the same spirit, Micah
argues that God requires neither human nor animal
sacrifices, but only doing justice, loving mercy and
walking humbly with Him. Jeremiah is equally firm in
repudiating the efficacy of oblations and in insisting
that righteousness alone can save the nation.

Though the words of the prophets sound as if they
were unconditionally opposed to every form of ritual,
Jewish tradition has understood them as merely pro-
testing against all ritual that is intended to wipe away
outraged righteousness. "The sacrifice of the wicked
is an abomination to the Lord," the sage admonishes
(Prov. 15:8). This seems to be also the view of Psalms
50:8–13 and 51:18–21. While denying that communion with God is effectively mediated by sacrifice, these
—possibly emended verses—point to the sacrificial
worship that will be acceptable to God.

The prophets of the Exile and after unite in their high valuation of a sacrificial ritual that is based on an ethical foundation. Ezekiel is particularly emphatic on this point. With his predecessors he recognized the doom that was to befall his people in consequence of their evil doing, and going beyond them, he repudiated the popular belief that men suffer in expiation of the sins of their forebears, and taught that men are personally responsible for their own misdeeds. The only way to salvation, in Ezekiel's view, is to cast off sin and fall back in sincere repentance upon the mercy of God. Atonement consists in complete spiritual regeneration, in true penitence, and in the amendment of the sinner's ways. It is wrought by man and is aided by God as an act of grace. God will effect atonement for the guilt-laden exiles not for their own sake, but rather on account of His own self, His holy name, in order to prevent its profanation among the nations. He combines the hope in God's redeeming power with the purified ritual of the future, which shall reconcile the people to God.

Deutero-Isaiah stresses the same note. Not the people's holocausts, but God Himself blots out their transgressions for His own name's sake (43:22–25). The afflicted nation is bidden to take comfort in God's unfailing love. The author of Isaiah 56:7 combines his universalistic outlook, which places Jew and non-Jew on terms of absolute equality before God, with the belief in the efficacy of sacrificial worship. "Their burnt-offerings and their sacrifices shall be acceptable upon Mine altar; for My house shall be a house of prayer for all peoples." Malachi 3:4 summarized the attitude of the post-Exilic prophets regarding the purified worship: "Then shall the offerings of Judah and Jerusalem be pleasant unto the Lord as in the days of old, and as in ancient days."

The Jews who survived the Exile no longer limited piety to sacrificial worship. Under the influence of prophetic teaching and in consequence of the nation's suffering, they learned to appreciate the moral foundations of religion as well as its ceremonial forms. Accordingly the restored ritual of the Second Temple, as reflected in the Priestly Code, combines the prophetic view of religion as righteousness with rites of distinctly primitive character, whose origin in some instances may be traced to pre-historic Semitic antiquity.

The Priestly Code takes on the form of an elaborate apparatus for expiation of sin in order to preserve the holiness of the community and to retain the necessary union with God. The intensified consciousness of sin in post-Exilic times accentuated the propitiatory functions of the burnt-offering and oblations, and gave new prominence to the sin-offering (*hattat*) and guilt-offering (*asham*). Whereas in pre-Exilic times the sin and guilt-offerings figured as occasional fines, paid to the priests at the sanctuary, they now appear as regular parts of the ritual, and assume a commanding position in the religious life of the people.

A wrong done to one's fellow man at the same time constituted an offense against God. Concealing testimony in a trial under oath, contact with an unclean animal or other defilement and failure to carry out an oath, uttered rashly or thoughtlessly, alike incurred guilt. In such instances *confession* of the sin had to be made in connection with the guilt-offering. In case of misappropriation of things belonging to the sanctuary, the trespass or guilt-offering did not suffice. In addition, *restitution* had to be made to the priesthood together with a fine of a fifth of the value of the object. In the case of a misappropriation of a neighbor's property, infringement upon his rights in the matter of a deposit or pledge, or a robbery, or of any fraud perpetrated against him (e.g., in case one found a lost article and denies it on oath), full reparation had to be made to the rightful owner plus a fine of a fifth of the value involved, before bringing the "forfeit unto the Lord" to have the priest make atonement for him (Lev. 5).

The growing prominence of the moral element in the rites of atonement is further indicated in the limitation of the power of atonement to sins and injuries committed inadvertently, i.e., stemming out of human frailty, ignorance or passion. Offenses perpetrated high-handedly, presumptuously or with malice aforethought, in defiance of the will of God, do not obtain forgiveness, but are punished with excision (*karet*). They disqualify the offender from remaining in the sacred community and expose him to the wrath of God (Num. 13:22–31). Sometimes the community itself, in order to preserve its favorable relations with God, exterminated such offenders from its midst (Num. 25:1–15).

By the side of the moral elements, the purely me-

chanical and ceremonial rites of atonement are retained
in the Priestly Code. Not only persons, but houses,
the altar and sanctuary require atonement or ritual
cleansing (Ex. 29:36–37; Lev. 8:15; 16:16–20; cf.
Ezek. 43:20–27). A certain defilement, possibly con-
tracted from the presence of unclean or sinful people,
clings to them and requires atonement. The process
of atoning consists of ritual purgation. To atone (*kipper*) means to "un-sin" (*hitta*), to cleanse (*tihar*), and
to sanctify (*kiddash*), i.e., to restore to holiness.

The various rites of atonement reached their climax
on the Day of Atonement (*Yom Hakippurim*), observed annually as a fast on the tenth day of the
seventh month (*Tishri*), four days prior to the Feast
of Tabernacles. The institution probably dates back
to early times, though the first reference to it appears
in Ezekiel 45:18–20, where it is proposed that two
days of atonement be set aside, in the first and in the
seventh months, in order to remove the defilements of
the sanctuary and of the people, growing out of the
neglect of the cult. The ritual of the day, as set forth
in Leviticus 16, aims to atone for the sanctuary and
the altar, for the priests and for the entire community.
The ceremonies centered in the person of the high
priest. In addition to the sin and burnt-offerings of the
day, the high priest burnt frankincense and made confession of sin on behalf of the people. The unusual part
in the order of the day consisted in his laying the sins
of Israel upon the head of a goat and dispatching the
animal into the wilderness, thus to carry away the sins
of the people from the land to Azazel, probably a

demon of the waste.* The day was observed by the people as a "Sabbath of solemn rest," upon which every Israelite, home-born slave and resident alien alike were required to "afflict their souls" by abstaining from all food and labor. Yom Kippur is the only fast prescribed in the Pentateuch.

As a comparison of Leviticus 16 and its interpretation in the Sifra and in the Mishnah Yoma shows, the Day of Atonement underwent significant modifications in the last centuries of the existence of the Temple. It steadily grew not only in ceremonial impressiveness, but also in spiritual value.[355] From a mere day of cleansing the sanctuary in preparation for the great pilgrim Feast of Tabernacles, it developed into the most sacred day of the Jewish religious year.

Non-sacrificial means of atonement were likewise available to the people. According to the prophets these mainly consisted in whole-hearted loyalty to God and in moral uprightness. They also included certain ritual elements, which evolved from sacrifice.

First among them is *prayer*, which since earliest times seems to have been associated with sacrificial

---

* Driver, *Leviticus*, p. 81. The LXX renders *la'azazel* with *to apopompaio*. Accordingly the B.D.B. Lexicon translates *'azazel* as "entire removal." A. W. Mair writes that "the Greek *farmakos* is led 'beyond the borders,' and just this is the lot of the Hebrew scapegoat." By this ceremony the impurities are removed from the land. Compare Lev. 14:4ff.; art. Sin, *H. E. R. E.*, XI, p. 548; and commentaries of Ibn Ezra, Nahmanides and Bahia to Lev. 16:8. Cf. the later Jewish ceremonies of *Tashlich* and *Kapparot*, which seem to be substitutes for the atonement ritual.

worship. In prayer both priests and prophets partici-
pated. Prayer is spoken of as incense and the evening
sacrifice (Ps. 141:2). Intercessory prayer figures as a
means of securing God's grace. Abraham prays on behalf of sinful Sodom. Moses, Samuel, Amos, Jeremiah,
etc., implore God's forgiveness on behalf of Israel.
Solomon's dedicatory prayer asks that in case of war,
drouth, famine, pestilence, and sickness, when people
will "come to pray and make supplication unto Thee
in this house, then hear Thou in heaven and forgive"
(1 Kings 8:30).

*Fasting* is connected with both sacrifice and prayer
(Jer. 14:11–12). It is often linked with mourning
customs. It may have originated as a mere preparation
for the participation in a sacrificial meal, but came to
possess independent value.[356] It appears to have fitted
a person for communion with God as in the case of
Moses, Elijah and Daniel.[357] It also served to give
emphasis and reinforcement to prayer. As a means of
humbling oneself before God, fasting was deemed
sufficiently meritorious to avert punishment (1 Kings
21:29). It came to be regarded also as a form of *penitence*, and was associated with *confession of sin* (1
Sam. 7:6; Neh. 9:1–2; Joel 2:12–13). The Psalmist
dwells upon the comforts of confession and upon the
relief which it brings to the burdened heart (32:1–8).
With the increased frequency of fasting in post-Exilic
times, the prophets sought to keep it from becoming a
mechanical performance. Fasting was to be associated
with righteous conduct and with benevolence (Zech.
7–8; Isaiah 58).[358]

The prophetic doctrine of the atoning power of righteousness and mercy was extended to *benevolence*. Prov. 10:2, "Righteousness delivereth from death," was understood to mean almsgiving. Daniel 4:24 definitely counsels: "break off thy sin by almsgiving, and thine iniquities by showing mercy to the poor." Sirach teaches similarly that as water quenches fire "so doth almsgiving atone for sin" (3:30).[359]

From earliest times the belief was current that expiation by means of *suffering* or enduring full punishment for the offense forms a condition of pardon for both the individual and the nation. Under a system of strict social responsibility, the nation was believed to suffer for the sins of the individual even as the individual bore the sin of his kinsfolk and nation. Popular belief assumed further that "the wicked is a ransom for the righteous" (Prov. 21:18). Deeper religious reflection showed to the contrary that the righteous sometimes suffer for the wicked. According to Isaiah 53, the servant of the Lord—probably a personification of ideal Israel—bears the penalty of the sinful nations and thus atones for them.[360]

The idea of *vicarious atonement* underlies the remarkable episode in the life of Moses, when, in consequence of Israel's apostasy, God said unto him: "Let Me alone . . . that I may consume them; and I will make of thee a great nation" (Ex. 32:10). In reply, Moses pleaded with God to pardon the people's sin, or else to erase his name from the book (of life). Though God responded: "Whosoever hath sinned against Me, him will I blot out of My book," Moses persisted in imploring forgiveness. Finally, in answer to his entreaty, God revealed Himself to Moses in the thirteen attributes of mercy, which form the basis of His forgiving grace (Ex. 34:6–7; Num. 14:18). The self-abnegation of Moses made him appear to Rabbi Simlai as the suffering servant of Isaiah 53, who "bore the sin of many" that he might expiate the sin of the golden calf. His burial near Bet Peor was intended to atone for Israel's licentious worship of Baal Peor (Num. 25:3; Deut. 34:6).[361]

The atoning power of the suffering and death of the righteous is preached in IV Maccabees (6:28; 9:24; 12:18; 17:20–23; cf. Ps. 116:15). It forms the traditional basis of Paul's doctrine of atonement through the death of Jesus, which, in its full form embodies conceptions of the dying savior derived from the mystery religions, and clashes with the pure ethical monotheism of Judaism.

*Rabbinic Phase.* The fall of the Temple in 70 C.E. produced a radical change in the conception of atonement. The Jewish people were now compelled to look for effective substitutes for the extinct sacrificial ritual. These they found ready to hand in the non-sacrificial elements of worship. The sacrificial cult itself was now idealized all out of proportion to its actual significance. A halo of sanctity now surrounded everything that pertained to its forms. The rabbis devoted themselves with loving care to the preservation of all the details of the Temple worship and to investing them with meaning. The very study of the laws of the sacrifices came to be considered an effective substitute for their performance. In the opinion of Rabbi Simeon, the words of the Torah are more precious to God than burnt-offerings and sacrifices.[362]

Prayer, which steadily grew in importance by the side of sacrificial cult, now appeared as its main substitute. Praying three times a day, which came to be the practice of the pious during Temple times (Ps. 55: 17; Dan. 6:10), was now turned into a standing institution for both private and public devotion. The time and the form of these services (*shaharit, minhah* and *maarib*) on week-days and the additional (*musaph*) service on the Sabbath, New Moon, and Holy Days, as well as the fifth service (*neilah*) on Yom Kippur, were made to correspond to the public sacrifices at the Temple. In the words of the rabbis: One who in proper state of bodily cleanliness lays tephillin, recites the Shema and offers prayer is considered as having built an altar and sacrificed upon it.[363]

Torah and prayer have atoning power because they direct the heart to God. Their effectiveness in reality consists in their leading men to repentance. The high valuation of repentance in the thought of the rabbis is indicated by their observation that whereas the gates of prayer are sometimes open and sometimes closed, the gates of repentance are ever open.[364]

An essential part of repentance, according to the rabbis, is confession of sin. Public worship came to include general confessions, but in case of a particular offense special confession was required. This was to be no perfunctory verbal exercise. Confession and repentance have to be from the heart and definitely lead away from sin if they are to effect atonement. "If a man is guilty of a sin and confesses it, but does not change his way, unto what is he like? He is like one who holds a defiling reptile in his hand. Though he should immerse himself in all the waters of the world it will not avail him; but as soon as he throws away the reptile, an immersion in forty *seah* of water serves him as a cleansing bath, as Proverbs 28:13 states: 'He who confesses and forsakes (his sins) shall obtain mercy.'" [365]

Where a sin was committed by offending a fellow man, repentance and confession cannot atone without propitiating the offended party. Where the guilt involved money matters the first duty is proper restitution. The scrupulous care of the rabbis regarding restitution is illustrated by the following controversy between the schools of Hillel and of Shammai. "If a man robbed another of a beam and used it in the erection of a building, the Shammaites held that he was to pull down the structure and restore the original beam to its owner, but the Hillelites maintained that it was sufficient for him to pay the value of the beam." The more lenient view of the Hillelites was adopted in order to encourage sinners to repent. [366] Before one thinks of atonement he must do justice.

In addition to justice a life of atonement with God calls for lovingkindness. When Rabbi Joshua, upon seeing the Temple ruins, exclaimed: "Woe to us that this is destroyed, the place where the sins of Israel were atoned!" R. Johanan replied: "Grieve not, my son, we have a means of atonement similar to it, for it is said: 'I desire mercy and not sacrifice' " (Hosea 6:6).[367] "When the Temple was in existence," we are told, "the altar atoned for man; now a man's table atones for him," i.e., by giving of his food to the needy.[368] R. Eleazar ranks charity above offering all the sacrifices.[369] During the existence of the Temple a person secured atonement by paying his shekel, but now he may secure it through charity. In the opinion of R. Johanan b. Zakkai charity atones for the nations as the sin offering atones for Israel.

"Prayer, charity and repentance annul the evil decree" [370] came to be a cardinal doctrine of Judaism. R. Eleazar valued fasting more than charity, for it is a sacrifice of oneself and not merely of one's substance.[371] The fast which acquired ever greater spiritual value for the Jewish people is the Day of Atonement. With the discontinuance of the atoning rites at the Temple, the day itself was vested with atoning efficacy. "The scapegoat atones, but in the absence of the scapegoat the Day atones." [372]

The authoritative doctrine of the rabbis regarding atonement reads: "The sin and guilt-offerings atone. Death and the Day of Atonement expiate if accompanied by repentance. Repentance (by itself) atones for light transgressions, whether of omission or commission. In the case of grave transgressions repentance suspends the punishment until the Day of Atonement comes around and atones. If a man says: 'I shall sin and repent, and shall sin again and repent,' no opportunity is afforded him for effectual atonement. If he says: 'I shall sin and the Day of Atonement will atone for me,' the Day effects no atonement for him. Transgressions of man against God the Day of Atonement removes, but transgressions of man against his fellow man the Day does not remove until he has appeased his fellow man."

In what appears to be direct opposition to the doctrine of vicarious atonement as taught in the early Church, R. Akiba exclaimed: "Happy are ye, O People of Israel! Before whom do you purify yourselves, and who purifies you? [No mediator, but] your Father in Heaven, as the prophet says: 'And I will sprinkle clean water upon you, and ye shall be clean' (Ezek. 36:25). Similarly [God is referred to as], *Mikveh* (literally, 'hope,' but by a word play, construed as a 'ritual bath') of Israel (Jer. 14:8). As the ritual bath purifies the unclean so the Holy One blessed be He cleanses Israel." [272] The Jewish doctrine of ethical monotheism is here applied to personal morality. Living in a world governed by a righteous and loving God, man is given the initiative in atonement, of cleansing himself and of resuming his union with God.

The tribulations of the Jewish people in the centuries following the fall of Jerusalem gave special prominence to suffering as a means of expiating the guilt of the people preparatory to the advent of the Messiah. Personal suffering and death likewise appeared as punishments which satisfy the Divine claims of justice and restore the bonds of union with God. Accordingly, R. Nehemiah considered suffering a more effective means of atonement than sacrifice. Men were taught to rejoice in their afflictions, for through

them they obtain forgiveness. The righteous are purified by their chastisements in this world in order to
enjoy unmarred bliss in the hereafter.[374]

Self-inflicted suffering assumed the nature of an
atoning sacrifice. Despite the discouragement of asceticism on the part of normative Judaism, the medieval temper, especially under the influence of the
Cabbalah, delighted in ascetic rites, prolonged fasts,
and various penances as effective ways of gaining
God's favor. In the writings of R. Eliezer of Worms
and of R. Samuel and his son R. Jehudah Hasid, a
technique of penitence of extravagant and bizarre
character was evolved. Ascetic exercises were under-
taken as restitution for offenses against God in order
to be freed from His wrath in the hereafter. A veri-
table "tariff of penitence" was established, specifying
the forms of self-torture wherewith the sinner might
offer satisfaction to the angry God.[375] Some of these
mortifications were of an obsessive kind, prompted by
perversions of physical sensibility so that the self-
inflicted pain was felt as pleasure. The five general
steps in repentance, stressed by Isaac Luria, were suggested by the letters of the Hebrew word for repentance (Teshubah): taanit—fasting, sak—sackcloth,
vaepher—ashes, bechiyah—weeping, and hesped—
lamentation.[376] Various other forms of self-torture
were resorted to. One of the supreme acts of penance
was voluntary exile (galut). In the process of purging
life of sin, life itself was crushed. A wholesome reaction to this morbid trend did not fail to appear in
Judaism, as we shall note later.

PERMANENT ELEMENTS OF ATONEMENT. While the rabbinic doctrine of atonement still forms the basis of present-day Orthodoxy, the progressive trends in modern Judaism have departed from it in many vital points. Reform Judaism, for example, attaches no special efficacy to the sacrificial cult and does not bemoan its passing. Ascribing no particular potency to the Day of Atonement, and prizing it only as a great day dedicated, by thousands of years of Jewish usage, to the soul's communion with God, Reform does not regard it capable of automatically removing men's sins. Nor does Reform ascribe any value to substitutionary atonement. In line with the ethical tradition of historical Judaism, it stresses: "No man can by any means redeem his brother, nor give to God a ransom for him" (Ps. 49:8). Man's ethical progress requires that each soul recognize its own burden of guilt and responsibility before God and society. Reform Judaism lays less stress upon expiation and more upon *at-one-ment* or reconciliation with God by means of moral and spiritual regeneration. In its view the purpose of atonement is to achieve harmony with God, with one's fellow men, and with oneself.

Despite the many changes that have taken place in the development of the doctrine of atonement, certain permanent elements remain. Our survey of the growth of the doctrine has brought to light the combination of moral elements with purely religious ones. The concept itself derives from the distinctly religious sphere and cannot be grasped through rationalization or through transference to the exclusive sphere of ethics. The moral element while in the forefront is of secondary character. Sin represents the pathology of religion; atonement its therapy. The process of atonement discloses three steps: (1) the recognition of sin and the consequent estrangement from God, (2) the sense of remorse and abandonment or removal of the causes that led to the estrangement, and (3) the consciousness of the restored unity with God, i.e., of forgiveness.

From the moral standpoint, the idea of atonement is predicated upon the conviction that despite the corruption and the degradation of men and despite the moral leprosy which so often erupts in the social body, human nature possesses an element of incorruptibility. There is in it, as Felix Adler observed, an inmost core which corruption cannot attack. "And starting from this core, this deathless seed, the process of self-renewal is always possible. Even in the worst cases we have no right to exclude the expectation that regeneration shall start from within the man or the woman, but we are always to look for it." [377] Sin forms the shadow rather than the substance of character. Though man fall to the level of the beast, it is given him to rise to the angel's height. There is something Divine in his nature. The lowliest mortal is endowed with a deathless soul. He is a child of God.

*Confession.* Self-examination is of the essence of religion as a catharsis of the soul, a purification of heart and mind as well as of hands before God and one's own conscience. The Psalmist prays: "Examine me, O Lord, and try me; test my reins and my heart.

. . . I will wash my hands in innocency; so will I compass Thine altar, O Lord"(26:2, 6). The recognition of the sin which has stained the soul forms the basis of self-criticism and self-judgment. To cleanse himself, man must acknowledge his error and seek to rid himself of it. By exteriorizing his rottenness, he frees himself of the hypocritical show of virtue, and strives to attain a level of purity and veracity.

In Judaism this phase of the religious life has assumed wholly different forms from those of either Catholicism or Protestantism. Having taken the common sense view of sin as the product of human frailty and folly rather than an ineradicable taint of the soul, Judaism avoided the panicky manner of removing its effects. It has fostered none of the sudden and spectacular conversions which are typical of Evangelical piety. While invoking God's grace in showing sinners the way, Judaism stresses the normal development of character.

Psychologically, as we pointed out in our discussion of psychotherapy, we may explain the efficacy of the practice of confession on the ground that the breaking of the shell of secrecy and permitting the pent-in abscess to burst affords relief to the troubled spirit. This accounts for the craving experienced by most human beings to talk to some one of their troubles. This natural desire has led to the establishment of Auricular Confession in the Catholic Church, which has become its chief means of moral and pastoral work. The service that it has rendered to countless folk is beyond question. That it fails of its purpose in the case of some morally obtuse persons furnishes ground for the opposition to the practice on the part of Protestants. Psychoanalysts, on grounds antithetical of religion, have grasped the confessional with avidity as a means of making over "the harsh conscience" and the rigid standards which contribute to the inner conflicts. Sick souls are freed of the sense of guilt by confessing their difficulties to someone who stands for them as the prototype of authority, who may hear the worst that they have to say without condemnation. Psychological counselling, if it is not to secure physical benefits at the expense of the moral and religious, calls for rare spiritual insight and sympathy.

Judaism does not require confessions before a mediator. No person, whatever his position, may atone for us. We ourselves must effect our own atonement. It is sufficient for every individual to turn his heart to God in sincere repentance to secure His pardoning grace. A petition for Divine pardon is included in the daily worship. In the ritual of the Day of Atonement, a prominent place is assigned to the confessional. As an acknowledgment of the sins of the entire people of Israel, it names the violation of every precept of the Torah. It is recited by both saints and sinners. It is impersonal in so far as the conscience is clear of the avowed sin; and it is personal only where the conscience is burdened with the guilt of a particular offense.[378] The public recital serves to emphasize the communal accountability for the sins of the individual, and thereby to strengthen the sense of social responsibility. The Talmud further prescribes that on his

death-bed man should make confession, without specifying a definite form. The text now in use was handed
down by Nahmanides. It, too, was designed for the
individual's own use. Only in case he is unable to offer
the prayer himself is he aided by another.[379]

An attempt was made by the Hasidim to encourage
confessions before the Tzaddik. R. Nahman of Bratzlav
counselled that "whoever wishes to follow the path
of holiness must break his bad habits, and confess them
before a scholar, who shall explain and point out to
him a path in accordance with the roots of his soul." [380]
However, its purpose was spiritual guidance rather
than an official act of religious practice for the re-
mission of sin.

*Repentance.* Confession of sin is part of the larger
program of spiritual rehabilitation which goes under
the name of *repentance.* Some moderns are not kindly
disposed to this phase of religious expression. Even
William James permits himself to damn it with faint
praise. He writes: "Evil is a disease; and worry over
disease is itself an additional form of disease, which
only adds to the original complaint. Even repentance
and remorse, affections which come in the character
of ministers of good, may be but sickly and relaxing
impulses. The best repentance is to be up and act for
righteousness, and forget that you ever had relations
with sin." He cites Spinoza's condemnation of repentance as deleterious and of worry of conscience and
remorse as evil passions, "inasmuch as they form a
particular kind of sadness." [381] Such a view is quite
understandable in Spinoza who tried to treat the

"actions and appetites of men as if it were a question of lines, of planes, and of solids." In such a mechanical system of psychology there really is no room for either remorse or conscience. These expressions notwithstanding, repentance not as "a groaning and a writhing" over the commission of sin but rather as *a determined and decisive turning away from evil* is an effective way of keeping up one's spiritual health. Religion works its miracles of personal regeneration by urging the wicked to "forsake his way, and the man of iniquity his thoughts; and let him return unto the Lord" (Is. 55:7).

It is an emancipating thought that man as a free agent is not sold as an eternal bondman to his evil habits or to follies into which he may have fallen either wittingly or unwittingly. While man's actions at any given moment grow out of previous acts, his resolution and effort to discard his old ways are often crowned with success. Even alcoholics and drug addicts have been known to have been cured. Though we are enchained in our past deeds, we still enjoy a certain degree of freedom to extricate ourselves from their meshes. It is the firm conviction of Judaism that "whoever seeks to purify himself is aided from above." [382] He may cast off the shackles imposed upon him by evil habit and regain his moral liberty. Kaufmann Kohler rightly spoke of repentance as "the brightest gem among the teachings of Judaism" and one of its most unique and precious contributions to religious thought. It holds out to man the hope of "restoration of the Divine image which has been disfigured and corrupted by sin." [383] According to the rabbis, repentance is one of the things which antedate creation.[384] Without it no spiritual regeneration would be possible for erring humanity.

In the teaching of the synagogue, as we have pointed out, repentance can be of no spiritual value if it leaves moral wrongs unrighted. Repentance is effective only in matters relating to purely moral and spiritual things, as they affect one's conscience. If it cannot undo the sin, it undoes the state of mind which brought it about. Hence the emphasis upon *Haratah* or regret over the sin as preparatory to the forsaking of sin. A change of heart when man errs is the first step toward spiritual rehabilitation. "Great is repentance," the rabbis teach, "for it reaches the throne of Glory," and "brings near the redemption." [385] It restores man to his better self and to God. Far from considering the sinner lost, religion holds out to him the possibility of rising to heights which he had not occupied before. The opinion is voiced that "where repentant sinners stand wholly righteous men cannot stand." [386] They made greater sacrifices to return to virtue. By removing the infection of the soul and subduing the evil inclination, the good emerges with new promise and power.

*Sacrifice*. Self-criticism, a turn of heart and confession lead to an inner transformation of man. Something more is needed to free him from the burden of sin and guilt. We have referred to restitution as the prime requirement where the offense was committed against a fellow man. The next requisite is some concrete deeds whereby one may place himself and his substance upon the altar of God and of righteousness.*

Of the various means whereby man seeks to enter into right relations with the Divine, sacrifice has been the most persistent. Even after the institution of animal sacrifice was eliminated by the force of historical circumstances, it continued to figure as the supreme symbol of religious idealism. By a homiletical play upon Lev. 6:2, *zot torat ha'olah hi ha'olah*, the rabbis express the great truth: "This is the law of the burnt-offering; it leads upward." [387] Only sacrifice lifts man to the highlands of the spirit. "Religion rightly understood," Rudolf Eucken writes, "is, in its direct affirmation of life, very far removed from all eudemonism, and, indeed, frees itself fundamentally from the narrowness of such an easy-going affirmation. Inseparable from religion is the idea of sacrifice—the idea not of a sacrifice happening but once, but a continuous sacrifice." [388] The author of the *Song of Unity* exclaims:

> Sin and burnt offering Thou demandest not.
> An altar I shall build out of my broken heart,
> And shall break my spirit within me.
> The haughtiness of the heart I shall lower and
>     the haughtiness of the eye,
> And shall rend my heart for the sake of God.
> The fragments of my spirit are thy sacrifices.
> May they be offered acceptably upon Thine altars. [389]

---

* Albo writes: "Since a sin is committed in thought, in speech and in act, or in all of them combined, repentance must express itself in all three of them: in thought—regret, in speech —confession, and in act—it is not sufficient that the sin be abandoned, but deeds must be done to offset the sin committed." Ikkarim, IV:26.

He who would keep his vision of the Holy One pure and undefiled must be ready to make heavy sacrifices of his pleasant vices, his cynicism, smartness, arrogance, his vain pride, crudity and sensuality, and every form of self-indulgence, self-seeking and self-importance.

The religious ideal becomes the opposing force not only to the evils of the external world but also to the evils that proceed from us. The struggle against one-self is not without rewards. If it entails heavy sacrifices, it also "shapes life into a heroic deed," and the "constant struggle becomes an incessant conquest. In the great works of music we often observe the fundamental theme develop and maintain itself through a seeming chaos of tone and conflicting discords, and also, in the very conquest the conflict does not altogether vanish, but sounds on and on, yet now as something overcome, until at last the harmony finally triumphs." [390]

Sacrifice offers the key to the treasures of the spirit. Self-sacrifice and self-realization represent the two phases of the religious life. Alexander the Great asked the sages of the South: "What shall man do that he may live?" Their reply was: "Let him die unto himself." To the further inquiry, "What shall he do that he may die?" they answered: "Let him live unto himself." [391] This paradox expresses a truth which in various forms most great spirits of humanity persistently have stressed. In the alphabet of religion, selfishness spells spiritual death, sacrifice eternal life. The religious man is expected to offer himself upon the altar of his faith, to exemplify through his deeds the ideals he professes. He is asked not only to abandon his self-centeredness, but above all to invest his strength and his substance in the service of his ideals of goodness and truth, and in the relief of the poor and the sorrowing, the suffering and the downcast. The soul that sacrifices little knows little of the true quality of religion.

*Fasting.* The most striking act of atonement in Judaism is fasting. As we noted above, this rite was associated with both sacrifice and prayer. On Yom Kippur the fast consists of total abstinence from food for twenty-four hours at a time.* The Hebrew terms *innuy nephesh* and *taanit* indicate that fasting has figured as a form of self-humiliation and self-mortification. In addition to Yom Kippur, Orthodox Jewry observes the four national fasts, commemorative of the fall of Jerusalem in 586 (Fast of Gedaliah, Tenth of Tebet, Seventeenth of Tammuz, and Ninth of Ab (see Zech. 8:19) and the Fast of Esther, preceding Purim. Pious individuals keep the three fasts of Monday, Thursday and Monday in the months of Iyar and Heshvan, following the festive seasons of Passover

---

* In Bible times the fast lasted from sunrise to sunset, e.g., Judg. 20:26; I Sam. 14:24; II Sam. 1:12; 3:35. This is the practice with all fasts other than Yom Kippur and the Ninth of Ab. Palestinian Jewry observed more fast days than the Babylonian. Even the three fasts mentioned in Zechariah 8:19, besides the Ninth of Ab, were not regarded obligatory by the Jews of Babylonia. Rosh Hashanah 18b; Taanit 11b. See Mordecai Margolis, Moadim V'tzomot B'eretz Yisrael, *Areshet*, 1944, pp. 213ff.

and Tabernacles (cf. Job 1:5), Yom Kippur Katon (the day preceding the New Moon, introduced by the Cabbalist Moses Cordovero in the sixteenth century), and numerous other fasts on occasions of public calamity and of private character, like Yahrzeit, etc.[392]

While ascetics indulged in fasting to the extent of endangering their lives, the leaders of Hasidism discouraged excessive fasting and self-mortification as being contrary to the spirit of Judaism, which bids man to worship God in joy. The Conservative wing in American Judaism honors only the Ninth of Ab besides Yom Kippur. Reform Judaism disregards the Ninth of Ab as well as all the other national fasts. Secularistic influence in Jewish life threatens to do away with fasting on Yom Kippur as well. To abandon this hallowed practice would inflict irreparable loss to the already attenuated religious life of Jewry. A pampered generation like ours can ill afford to dispense with this sobering institution, which subjects the gratification of bodily appetites and cravings to the needs of the spirit, which forcibly brings home the truth that not by bread alone does man live, and which rouses the community to the fact that while some are sated with plenty, others are continually subjected to hunger and want. The fasting on Yom Kippur takes on the character of intense devotion and consecration to God. Coupled with repentance, prayer and charity, it vitally affects the currents of man's life and works miracles of spiritual regeneration.

*Self-Discipline*. Fasting, like sacrifice, forms part of the rule of self-restraint and self-discipline, which, in one form or another, enter into every system of morality and religion. Even the athlete, as part of his preparation for the ring or the race, submits himself to strict regulations in matters of rest, play, diet and sex. Organic hardihood often leads people to disgust with too much ease and with pampering of the body. Moral refinement generally expresses itself in temperate habits and in avoidance of sensuality. To a more exalting degree religious mindedness prompts men to restrain their passions and appetites in accordance with the standards of their faith. In consequence, they gain a freedom which the libertine can never know. They conquer their desires and become masters of themselves. They grow capable of foregoing a temporary for a lasting good. Their apparent sacrifices in reality may be distinct gains. They are ever strict with themselves even in matters that are quite proper, following the rabbinic rule to which we referred in an earlier part: *Kaddesh atzmecha bemuttar lach*—"sanctify thyself in what is permitted to thee." They never relax in their effort to live on the heights.

# XV. THE WAY OF WORSHIP

ALL THE ELEMENTS of religion, considered above, are embodied in worship. Personal piety, ethical values and standards, and the elements of reflection, repentance and atonement culminate in and gain power through their articulation in prayer, meditation and song. The way of holiness, therefore, is the way of devotion or worship. While religion is much more than worship, it is nothing without worship. Where men do not lift their hearts and minds toward God and where the voice of prayer is silenced, religion is not merely mute, but dead. It is a function of worship to impress upon young and old the traditions of the religious community, to evoke a feeling of reverence and solemnity, and to enhance and elevate the religious way of life. We cannot rely upon reason alone nor upon the emotions to keep religion alive within our hearts and minds. To come to power over our lives, the religious spirit must find adequate expression. Ritual serves as the sign language of religion, translating in word, act and song the faith that wells up within the soul. Hence our sages recognized worship as the central pillar upon which the religious world of Judaism rests.

THE NATURE OF PRAYER. We have noted the role of Torah in Jewish worship and have considered prayer as a means of atonement. Let us now examine the nature of prayer, its underlying logic and some of its

forms. Though not explicitly commanded in the Torah
—since the customary form of ancient worship was
sacrificial—prayer has ever figured as a means of communion with God. While the prophets occasionally
inveighed against the sacrificial cult, they lived lives
of aspiration and prayer. Jeremiah, for example, repeatedly sought refuge from life's hardships in confessions before God and in supplications. He counselled the exiles in Babylonia to practice the presence
of God by means of prayer (Jer. 29:12–13). The
psalmists and the early Hasidim continued the prophetic traditions of prayer. Their piety provided the
materials and fashioned the forms for Jewish private
and public prayer.

The rabbis, endeavoring to discover a basis for
prayer in the Torah, found it implied in the Deuteronomic monition: "To love the Lord your God,
and to serve Him with all your heart and with all
your soul" (10:12). They asked: "What is the service
of the heart?" and replied: "It is prayer." [393] Though
the worship of prayer did not come into its own until
the sacrificial worship ceased, attempts were made to
trace the institution of prayer to the patriarchs themselves. R. Elazar ranked prayer above sacrifice. [394] R.
Joshua b. Levi believed it to be so efficacious that it
breaks even an iron wall which separates Israel from
the Heavenly Father. [395] Prayer removes all obstacles
and dangers to the spiritual life. Maimonides treats
prayer in his Code under the section *Ahabah*. Love is,
indeed, the life breath of prayer, love in the sense of
longing and yearning for God and of the direction of

the spirit and self-dedication to Him. It is the placing of oneself at the disposal of God, offering heart and mind, soul and being upon His altar. R. Nahman of Bratzlav considered prayer a category of faith, of spiritual creativeness which fills the emptiness of the heart with the consciousness of the Divine. Through prayer God's holiness increases. True spiritual vitality is derived only through prayer.[396]

The nature of Jewish prayer is partly disclosed by the terms employed in Hebrew for prayer. The most general word is *Tephillah*, from the root *palal* (Ps. 106:30), to intervene, to interpose, connoting also the idea of arbitration and judgment as well as of intercession and prayer. Goldziher accordingly took the original meaning of Tephillah to be "invocation of God as judge." [397] It is a form of judgment to which a person subjects himself in the presence of God. This meaning may be accounted for by the circumstance that the earliest prayers of Israel were offered in conjunction with the sacrifices, the acceptance of which was deemed conditional, depending upon the worthiness, purity, and guiltlessness of the worshipper. Cain's sacrifice was rejected (Gen. 4:5). Manoah interprets the acceptance of his sacrifice as an indication of Divine favor (Judg. 13:23). The Psalmist testifies to what God had done unto his soul:

> I cried unto Him with my mouth,
> And He was extolled with my tongue.
> If I had regarded iniquity in my heart,
> The Lord would not hear;
> But verily God hath heard;

He hath attended to the voice of my prayer.
—66: 16–19.

Each offering appeared as a test of man's righteousness. Hence the Psalmist's frequent appeals to God to be judged when seeking a favorable response to the particular supplication. The prophetic teaching intensified this ethical aspect of worship. While at first the people may have remained passive in worship, in course of time they began to take an active part. They themselves laid their cause before the Heavenly Judge, King and Father. The term *tephillah* thus acquired the meaning of prayer in our sense of the term as devout turning to God with reverent petition for His blessing, grace and favor. The idea of request, entreaty or beseeching is expressed also by the words *bakashah, sheelah, tehinah* and *tahanun* (supplication for favor). Most of the other words for prayer express the outpouring of the heart before God, self-justification before Him, confession, meditation, thanksgiving and praise.*

* The verbal form *'atar*, from which the post-Biblical *'atirah* is derived, denoting "to pray, supplicate," was originally connected with sacrifice. Its Arabic equivalent designates "slaughter for sacrifice." See B. D. B. Lexicon, under *'Atar.* The words *sihah, hagigah, higgayon* (complaint, musing, meditation), *tze'akah, shav'ah* derive from the manner in which the prayer was articulated. *Berachah* (from *barach*, to kneel, bless) and the post-Biblical *'Amidah* (standing) for the Eighteen Benedictions, indicated in the first place the bodily position in worship, and subsequently came to indicate a form of prayer. The term *selihah* denotes supplication for God's pardoning grace, *todah* and the post-Biblical *hodaah*—thanksgiving. The Hitpael form *hitvadah* signifies to confess. The

Great is the range of Biblical and rabbinic prayer. It is as varied as the needs and strivings of man. There is the spontaneous cry in distress and the silent meditation of the joyous heart. A lonely pilgrim searches his way on life's darkening road and a festive assembly sings jubilant hallelujahs. Earnest pleas for life, health and prosperity often alternate within the same liturgy with stereotyped formulas. Grateful praise appears by the side of lamentations over personal and national misfortunes, confessions of sin and pleas for pardoning grace. One prayer requests daily bread, and another the nearness of God. One asks imprecations and curses upon an enemy, whether real or imaginary, and another prays in utter self-renunciation for the welfare of others. There is prayer which sounds the depths of human pain and despondency, and the prayer of adoration of God and of exultation in life. Some prayers dwell upon the formal aspect of institutional religion and ceremonial observance, and others touch the eternal spirit of faith. One seeks to appease the anger of God, and another basks in His love. There are humble petitions of simple hearts, and profound meditations of sages. In some prayers the language is direct and plain, while in others it is intricate and ornate. Simple prose may be used in one, and lofty poetry in another. But whatever its contents and form, prayer marks the direction of the human spirit toward its heavenly source. It represents the offering of the verb *halal* is employed for praise of God from which stem the forms *hallel* and *tehillah*, a song of praise, often appearing as a parallel of *todah*. Of related character is *mizmor*, psalm or hymn of praise.

heart upon the altar of faith, and serves as the means of communion of finite men with the infinite Creator and Father. At one end is the recognition of creaturely dependence upon God and confidence in His abounding mercy and readiness to aid those who call upon Him, and, at the other, rapturous joy in God and the abandonment of the soul in Him. Prayer is a venture of faith in which the aspiring soul seeks to establish communion with God.

TYPES OF PRAYER. In any classification of prayer *petition* ranks foremost. It may be regarded as the characteristic manifestation of religion as a feeling of dependence upon God, as the first stirring of the soul toward the source of all life and of all good (cf. Pss. 123:2; 131:2). Evelyn Underhill writes: "The open beak and expectant trust of the baby bird are a tribute to the mother's faithfulness and love; an acknowledgment of fact. So, in this ever-renewed moment of supplication, this waiting on God, we express that deep sense of the infinite Generosity on which we depend and our own poverty and need over against it, which is the very heart of man's religion: tempering the awe-struck worship of the Holy by a confident appeal to the Father and Shepherd of souls." [398] Man voices his needs before God in the belief that from Him comes help. Brinton quotes this definition of prayer from an old theological dictionary: It is "a petition for spiritual or physical benefits which (we believe) we cannot obtain without Divine cooperation." [399] An even more felicitous definition states: "Prayer is the soul's sincere

desire uttered or unexpressed." It is not always articulated in words. It is a cry of the heart for life, health
and happiness, for help in trouble and guidance in
perplexity, for sustenance, success and victory.

Prayer might never have arisen were man free from
all wants and desires, if he had not agonized in grief
and distress, if he had not sought deliverance from
peril and from evil. Out of the depths of despair men
have lifted their eyes and hearts unto the heights.
Man's first needs obviously were physical. With the
rising level of his life, his needs grew more complex,
and he became aware of ethical and spiritual wants.
The satisfaction of his personal wants was not enough.
He craved also for the welfare of others, his family,
fellow tribesmen, etc. His own deliverance seemed
incomplete without the redemption of his people. Thus
man's social nature rendered prayer an instrument of
group life and of group cohesion. The tribe or community, facing hardships, trials, diseases, floods, drouth,
famine, war, and panic, united in addressing its petitions to its spirits or deities. In advanced society the
whole nation joins, on special occasions, in fast and in
humiliation before God or in joyful thanksgiving for
its prosperity, plenty or triumph. It brings its arts and
skills to its worship and renders its prayers in the
form of dignified and stately liturgies.

By means of lifting the heart heavenward a unique
relationship is established with God. In the words of
Amiel: "We dream, we suffer alone, we die alone;
but nothing prevents us from opening our solitude to
God and turning the dreary monologue into a dia-

logue." Prayer of this sort may spring from the heart not when we are in the midst of a festive assembly nor at stated occasions, but when we are most alone with ourselves and with our God, in hours of soul-trying anguish or of earnest self-searching, when "deep calleth unto deep." We then seem to contact the Source of our being and of our strength.

Petitionary prayer concerns itself not only with material goods. Besides asking for *bane, hayye, ume-zone*—"children, life and food"—men ask for the soul's redemption from evil, for the liberation of the spirit from bondage to material things, for insight into life's true ways, for the realization of moral values, for the adjustment of the human will to the will of God. (See the middle benedictions of the 'Amidah.) It is of such prayer that Kant wrote: "A heartfelt wish to be pleasing to God in all our action, that is, a disposition to transact all our business as though done in God's service, is the spirit of prayer which 'without ceasing' can and ought to be in us." [400]

The petitional element enters into every phase of prayer. Even prayers of *thanksgiving* and *adoration* are at bottom petitional. They express man's gratitude and appreciation for the things that matter most to him and upon which he depends. The classic prayer of thanksgiving in Jewish liturgy reads: "We gratefully acknowledge, O Lord our God, that Thou art our Creator and Preserver, the Rock of our life and the Shield of our help. We render thanks unto Thee for our lives which are in Thy hand, for our souls which are ever in Thy keeping, for Thy wondrous providence and for Thy continuous goodness, which Thou bestowest upon us day by day. Truly Thy mercies never fail and Thy lovingkindness never ceases. Therefore in Thee do we put our trust." [401] The interconnection between petition, thanksgiving and adoration may be illustrated by the traditional *Birkat Hagomel*. A person who escaped grave peril offers the following benediction: "Blessed be Thou, O Lord our God, King of the universe, who vouchsafest benefits unto the undeserving, who hast also vouchsafed all good unto me." To this the congregation responds: "He who hath vouchsafed all good unto thee, may he vouchsafe all good unto thee forever." [402] Thanksgiving for past favors turns into a petition for future benefits. [403] So essential is thanksgiving to the religious life that, according to the rabbis, in the Messianic era all sacrifices will be abolished (since there will be no more sin for which to atone) except the sacrifice of thanksgiving, and all prayers will cease except the prayer of thanksgiving. [404]

Of similar nature are the adorations of our liturgy. The classic Adoration (*Alenu*), glorifying God as the Lord of all, expresses the hope in the speedy establishment of His sovereignty throughout the world and in the banishment of all idolatry and wickedness. In the *Kaddish* (Sanctification), too, the exaltation of God serves as the ground of human confidence that the souls of the dead as of the living are safe under His sovereign rule. The attributes of God are detailed by way of bringing home to the worshipper the true ground for faith and trust. This is the underlying mo-

tive of the formulae for the opening and the closing
of prayer and of the benedictions in the presence of
phenomena expressive of Divine majesty. Praise is
predicated upon the recognition of worth. Hence the
emphasis in prayer on the aspects of God's character
which are of supreme value to the individual and to
the community.* Prayer in this sense represents a
characteristic attitude of the religious consciousness,
an attitude of contemplative adoration and an act of
reverence for God.

*Didactic* prayer stems from man's intellectual life.
Man seeks to know the source of things and their whys
and wherefores. To the source of truth he turns in

---

* C. P. Tiele sought to find in adoration the essence of piety,
which, in his view, constitutes the core of religion. (See
above, Piety and Spirituality.) The spirit of adoration draws
God and man into a union. We look up to God and seek to
establish a kinship with Him. Tiele writes: "For adoration necessarily involves the elements of holy awe, humble reverence,
grateful acknowledgement of every token of love, hopeful
confidence, lowly self-abasement, a deep sense of one's own
unworthiness and shortcomings, total self-abnegation, and un-
conditional consecration of one's whole life and one's whole
faculties. To adore is to love 'with all one's heart and soul
and mind and strength.' To adore is to give oneself, with all
that one has and holds dearest. But at the same time—and
herein consists its other phase—adoration includes a desire to
possess the adored object, to call it entirely one's own, and
conversely a longing on the part of the adored to feel that
he belongs to the adored one forever, in joy and in sorrow,
in life and in death. He gives himself, in order to attain perfect union with the object of his adoration. He cannot feel
happy except in the presence of that object." (*Elements of
the Science of Religion*, II, pp. 197ff.) Adoration thus forms
the basis of human hope of redemption and deliverance.

his devotions for enlightenment concerning life's dark spots and for guidance on its devious and confusing ways. Sometimes through word and argument and sometimes in the silence of inner thought and intuition, the spirit that slumbered within him is evoked. "Recognizing God as He emerges from the depths of his soul, he calls upon His light and His truth for this life and for the next." This type of prayer in reality expresses "an intuition of Divine wonder, by means of which man, as he prays, enters the realm of the prime source of intellectual light." * He steeps himself in God's mysteries and inexhaustible fountains of wisdom, and feels himself sustained by His everlasting arms. It is this phase of worship that led Emerson to define prayer as "the contemplation of the facts of life from the highest point of view. It is the soliloquy of a beholding and jubilant soul. It is the spirit of God pronouncing His works good." [405] The perplexing and confusing facts of experience are envisioned in their relation to the source of all life. The key-notes in didactic prayer are: "Teach me Thy way," "Show me Thy path," "Illumine my darkness," "Make me know Thy truth," "Send forth Thy light."

The doctrinal element, as we noted in our discussion of Torah, pervades all Jewish worship. The cognitive

---

* Puglisi, *Prayer*, pp. 181–82. In his Hymn to the Unknown God, Nietzsche exclaims:

> "Ich will dich kennen, Unbekannten,
> du tief in meine Seele greifender,
> mein Leben wie ein Sturm Durchschweifender,
> du Unfassbarer mir Verwandter!
> Ich will dich kennen, selbst dir dienen."

function of religion merges with the ethical, coloring every utterance which man makes before God. The longings of the heart, its wants and its aspirations are all shaped by the ideas of God which the ruling theology presents. Similarly ethical standards serve as sanctions and measuring rods for every wish, desire and hope. Selfish petitions are rejected as unworthy of the spirit of faith. Not all things that the untamed instincts crave are fit to be offered upon the altar before God. "Prayer is a halter to the lustful soul." [406] The Divine throne rests upon holiness and goodness, upon truth, justice, and love. Worship divested of these is blasphemy. Hence the emphasis upon moral preparation for worship. "Man must purify his heart before he prays. Thus Job says (16:17): 'Since there is no violence in my hands, my prayer is pure.' R. Joshua the priest, the son of R. Nehemiah, comments: Is there turbid prayer? What is meant (by this verse) is this: Any one whose hands are stained with robbery calls unto God, but is not answered. Wherefore? Because he prays in transgression." [407] R. Elazar used to give alms before praying. A rabbinic saying declares that the prayer of one who does not distribute his tithes liberally does not ascend to God.[408]

This type of prayer may be characterized also as *ethical* or *prophetic*, since its finest forms appear in the Prophets (and in the Psalms).* The standards of

---

* Heiler's distinction between prophetic and mystical prayer is far from absolute. Some of the characteristics of mystical prayer appear in the prophetic type, and avowedly prophetic elements are prominent in mystical prayers.

faith and of righteousness are applied to human life. In their light the troubled heart pours out its complaints and vexations, and generates renewed confidence and trust in the abiding goodness of God and of His purposes. Worship on the prophetic plane is not a flight from reality but rather a deep view of its nature, of its shadows as well as its lights, the contemplation of actuality *sub specie aeternitatis*. When truly fruitful, such worship opens up new vistas for the human spirit and strengthens it for new adventures and new tasks.

In the prophetic prayer the element of *recollection* plays a prominent role. Out of the past the most significant experiences are brought to light as aids for the new problems with which the worshippers are confronted as individuals and as communities. To generations burdened with oppression, the story of the Exodus speaks not only of an event that occurred thousands of years ago, but also of the undying ideal of freedom which ever carries hope to struggling men. It is utilized as an extra motive for the observance of the Sabbath; it is dramatized in the feast of *Pesah*, and is combined with the idea of Law in the celebration of *Shabuot* and with the spirit of thanksgiving of *Sukkot*. The solemn days of *Rosh Hashanah* and *Yom Kippur* echo with voices of Sinai, of the high priest's service at the Temple of Jerusalem, and of the priestly service of Israel through the ages. The great historic events, enshrined in the memory of the Jewish people—the Maccabean struggle, the deliverance from Haman, Jewish survival despite the fall of the Temple and the

state and centuries of persecution—serve to buoy the
spirit as it faces the uncertain future and strengthen
our will to live as a religious community. Such recol-
lections revive our attenuated sense of religious values,
which give meaning to Jewish life. Here historical experience merges with the ethical.[409] The situation of
the moment is confronted with ideals that stem from
days of old.

The ethical element often forms the special theme
of prayers.[410] Human life and destiny are tested in the
light of these ideals. The interest centers on what God
demands of man and on man's weakness and inability
to carry out all that is demanded of him. This makes
also for the penitential note in prayer, for probing of
heart and mind, and for the confession of sin (e.g.,
Ps. 51).

In prophetic prayer the feelings and memory are
enriched by reflection and thought. The mind medi-
tates on God's works, on His relation to ourselves
and to the world around us. It thinks of the ways of
Providence, of the revelation of God in nature and in
the human heart, of His majesty and grandeur. Im-
pressive examples of this type of prayer outside the
Bible appear in parts of the benedictions before and
after the Shema, the 'Amidah, the Tahanun, and the
Vidduy, and in the Malchuyot, Zichronot and Shofarot of the New Year service.

While all prayer takes on the form of an outreach-
ing after God, *mystical prayer* represents the rarest
and most striking manifestation of inward communion
or converse with God. Here we have not pleas for

aid or judgment, but rather contemplation of God, rest in Him, delight in His love and joy in His presence. Here the nobler emotions rather than reason hold sway. The nearness of God appears as the supreme good and the glowing light in which the soul basks.* The Psalmist sings:

> How precious is Thy lovingkindness, O God!
> And the children of men take refuge in the
>     shadow of Thy wings.
> They are abundantly satisfied with the
>     fatness of Thy house;
> And Thou makest them drink of the rivers
>     of Thy pleasures.
> For with Thee is the fountain of life;
> In Thy light do we see light.—36:8–10.

In mystical prayer the soul seeks to unite itself with God and even to lose itself in Him. Its atmosphere is that of love. Eliezer Azkari exemplifies it in his prayer which appears in the Sephardic ritual:

> Beloved of the soul, merciful Father, draw Thy
>     servant unto Thy will,
> That swift as a hart he may run to prostrate
>     himself before Thy glory.
> Sweeter is Thy love to him than the honey comb
>     and every tempting savor.
>
> Majestic, beautiful is the splendor of the world;
>     yet it is for Thy love that my soul pineth.

* Abelson writes: "Nowhere in Jewish literature is the idea of prayer raised to such a pitch of sublimity as in the lives and writings of the Jewish mystics." *Jewish Mysticism*, p. 12.

O God, heal it, I pray Thee, by showing unto it
the delight of Thy splendor.

Then will it grow strong and be restored and
rejoice everlastingly.

O mighty One, manifest Thy mercies, and have
compassion upon Thy beloved child.

For, oh, how long have I been consumed with
yearning to behold the triumph of Thy might!

My God, desire of my heart, take pity and turn
not away.

Reveal Thyself, O adored One, and spread over me
the canopy of Thy peace.

Let the earth shine with Thy glory, and we shall
be glad and rejoice in Thee.

Hasten to show Thy love, for the hour of tryst-
ing is nigh; and be gracious unto us as in the
days of yore.[411]

As in mysticism generally so in mystical prayer the inwardness of the religious experience is the all in all.
The still small voice of faith commands the heart.
Where words fail devout silence and symbolism effectively express the inner feelings.* Under the influence
of both speculative and practical Cabbalah, mystic
prayer grew into an exaggerated symbolism that over-
taxed the spirit of devotion. But in its pure form expressing inward perception of God's nearness and
grace, it remains the noblest form of devotion. It

* Bergson writes: "In the religion which we shall call dynamic (i.e., mysticism), prayer is independent of its verbal
expression: it is an elevation of the soul that can dispense with
speech." (The Two Sources of Morality and Religion, p.
191.) Among the Hasidim pure melody sometimes took the
place of words.

reaches its highest expression in *Kavvanah*, the union of thought and word, of idea and deed, whereby the soul is directed to its heavenly source.[412]

The various forms of prayer often appear combined in the Psalms and in the traditional Tephillah. The 'Amidah or Eighteen Benedictions presents every type of prayer. The prophetic and mystical elements lend dignity and depth to the simple cries of the soul. They assume the nature of "a prayer of the afflicted, when he fainteth and poureth out his complaint before God" (Ps. 102:1), and also of "a song of thanksgiving unto God." Through this union, Jewish prayer transcends ordinary suppliancy and becomes an expression of longing for the nearness of God and of self-dedication to His service.

THE LOGIC OF PRAYER. "We hear," William James remarks, "in these days of scientific enlightenment, a great deal of discussion about the efficacy of prayer; and many reasons why we should not pray, while others are given us why we should. But in all this very little is said of the reason why we do pray, which is simply that we cannot *help* praying. It seems probable that, in spite of all that 'science' may do to the contrary, men will continue to pray to the end of time unless their mental nature changes in a manner which nothing we know should lead us to expect." *

* *Psychology*, Vol. I, p. 317. "Any one thing in the creation," says Epictetus, "is sufficient to demonstrate a providence to a modest and grateful mind . . . And what words can proportionately express our applause and praise? For, if

James seems to refer to petitional prayer. It is this type of prayer that has drawn the severest criticism from the rationalistic elements in both Christendom and Jewry. An added indictment of petitionary prayer is the crass and materialistic nature of the things often asked for. The Infinite is approached with so many insignificant trifles that one would hesitate to mention to a human being. However, it is precisely this condition that makes prayer a matter of such intimate nature and consequently of such great help to the troubled heart. The heart has its hungers, and it cries out instinctively for help. In the dark night of sorrow, grief, or peril, a hope for light, deliverance or salvation is born in the heart of normally conditioned human beings. That

we had any understanding, ought we not both, in public and in private, incessantly to sing hymns and speak well of the Deity, and rehearse His benefits? Ought we not, whether we are digging, ploughing, or eating, to sing the hymns to God? Great is God, who has supplied us with these instruments to till the ground: great is God, who has given us hands, a power of swallowing, a stomach: who has given us to grow insensibly, to breathe in sleep. Even these things we ought upon every occasion to celebrate; but to make it the object of the greatest and most divine hymn, that he has given us the faculty of apprehending them, and using them in a proper way. Well then: because the most of you are blind and insensible, was it not necessary that there should be someone to fill this station, and give out, for all men, the hymn to God? For what else can I, a lame old man, do but sing hymns to God? If I was a nightingale, I would act the part of a nightingale: if a swan, the part of a swan. But since I am a reasonable creature, it is my duty to praise God. This is my business. I do it. Nor will I ever desert this post as long as it is vouchsafed me; and I exhort you to join in the same song." Moral Discourses, transl. by Elizabeth Carter, Book I, ch. XVI.

hope, "uttered or unexpressed" is the substance of
prayer, a hope which is fed on faith. Indeed, faith itself is born of inner need and is stimulated by constructive imagination and reason. "I have faith in my
future," G. B. Foster writes. "I cannot prove that I
have a future that is worth while, but without that
conviction I could not live. Madness lies that way." [413]
This type of faith cannot be validated by proofs, and
requires no proofs, for life cannot go on without it.
On this account the soul generates it. Prayer, expressing the deep yearnings of the heart, charges this life-
giving faith with power. "Seek Me and live" (Amos
5:4). Prayer is the eternal hunger and thirst of the soul
for God.

As the reflection of man's inner cravings, hopes and
strivings, prayer will be high or low, refined or common, thoughtful or stupid in accordance with the
character and spiritual endowments of the person
praying. But who will despise the cry of anguish that
comes from a foolish heart? The farmer who needs
rain will most naturally call for it. The city shop-
keeper with a logic no less natural may possibly at the
very same time be asking for dry weather. Similarly in
times of war, both sides petition for victory. While
the moral sense of neutrals is shocked by such a performance, the combatants feel nothing incongruous
about the proceeding. In their distress they naturally
look unto the height whence they derive help. This
may be explained by the non-rational and subjective
elements which underlie religion and which make it so
valuable. As the people advance morally and intel-

lectually, their prayers take on a profounder character. Their petitions avoid all that is crass and vulgar, revengeful and brutal; they no longer are importunings and beggings but only earnest outreachings toward God. The rabbis admonish us to avoid petitions of an irrational nature—*tephillah shel tiphlah*. When expressions of personal need are made, they should be of a character worthy of being offered before God, and with the hope that not man's but God's will be done. "It is proper for you to know, my brother," says Bahia ibn Pakkudah, "that the aim of our devotion in prayer consists in naught save the soul's longing for God, humbling itself before Him, and extolling the Creator with praise and gratitude unto His name, and casting of all burdens upon Him." [414]

While need is the driving force of religion in general and prayer in particular, not every need brings forth a prayerful sentiment. Things that man has learned to obtain by his own efforts he no longer includes among the objects of his prayers. He also learns to exclude things recognized as being under fixed laws, such as the rising and the setting of the sun, the ocean tides, eclipses, floods, thunder and lightning, the weather, etc. The human heart, terrorized or transported by them, may react to them in one way or another, but under the influence of advancing science, it will not ask for their alteration to suit its individual need. What it may pray for when periled by nature's forces is strength of will and courage to face the danger and overcome it.

Petitionary prayer, though prompted by personal

and social need, transcends material self-interest. Predicated upon the sense of dependence upon God and trust in His power, it stimulates the higher religious feelings of reverence and adoration, resignation and humility, self-searching and penitence, gratitude and love. The selfish thought of converting God to the worshipper's desire gives way to the longing to be worthy of enjoying His grace and protective care. Heiler writes: "Yet it is true that this expression of trust stands in intimate connection with the naive request, and grows out of it with self-evident naturalness. Hope and confidence, which are already at work as a motive of prayer, banish all anxiety and fear, and rise to joyful assurance. The wish and the yearning yield to a sense of an inner appropriation and possession. In the midst of the prayer the pious man discovers that a profound psychological change has taken place within him. When he has poured out his need and uttered his desires, he finds himself filled with such confidence that he is indubitably certain that his prayer has been answered." [415]

The efficacy of the petition is believed to depend upon the free will or grace of God rather than upon the potency of the words and formulas uttered. Where prayer is conceived as possessing unfailing power which binds God, it represents a reversion to magic. The essential difference between a magic spell and a formula of prayer even of the most primitive kind may be said to consist in this: whereas the first seeks to *coerce* the supernatural to do its bidding, the other *appeals* for aid. The magic spell operates automatically; prayer expresses man's submission to God's will. Prayer is always conditional, depending upon the disposition of the deity and the merits of the worshipper. Man lays his need before God, and asks God to do what seems best to Him.* Its motto is: "Not my will, but Thine, O Lord!" "We cannot know whether what we ask is really for our good. Thou alone knowest and orderest all things well, whether Thou grantest our petitions or deniest them." † Josephus counsels: "Let our prayers and supplications be made to God, not (so much) that He would give us what is good . . . as that we may duly receive it, and when we have received it, may preserve it." [416]

As a substitute for sacrifice, prayer represents a self-dedication to God and to His service. Even when repeated mechanically, it is a form of lifting of the heart to God. When entered into with heart and mind, it becomes the most potent force in the upbuilding of the religious life. Through it the worshipper gives sol-

---

* Ber. 29a; Mt. 6:9–13; Epictetus prayed: "Do with me as thou wilt; my will is thy will; I appeal not against thy judgments," cited by Farnell, op. cit., p. 245. See Albo, op. cit., IV:24.

† Union Prayerbook (newly revised), I, p. 20. Sentiments of this order appear in the prayers of peoples of various stages of culture. Brinton cites the following prayer of the Khonds, a Dravidian tribe in Northern India: "O Lord, we know not what is good for us. Thou knowest what it is. For it we pray." Religions of Primitive Peoples, p. 105. Among the Greeks we find an anonymous poet petitioning: "King Zeus, give what is good, even if not prayed for, but keep far from us evil, though we ask for it." Socrates prayed to the gods "to give whatever is good, since they know best what is good." Heiler, op. cit., pp. 82, 91.

emn expression before God and man to what he ought to be.[417]

By efficacy of prayer, people often mean producing a change in the physical environment, such as bringing rain to break the drought, success in warlike or in peaceful pursuits, health in sickness, etc. And while the accumulated testimony of humanity should make us hesitant to deny the effectiveness of prayer even in cases of this sort, we need not gauge the value of prayer by the external changes which it may bring about.

"The answer to the prayer," C. G. Montefiore writes, "may be in the prayer; the effect upon the man who prays may, in one sense, be produced by the man; but if so, that is only because the man himself is not 'alone,' or because (in other words) prayer may make him receptive to mysterious influences, or strengthen and make vivid within him a part of him which is Divine." [418]

The efficacy that is looked for in prayer is, primarily, of a subjective character, falling mainly in the moral and spiritual realm. From there it may extend, secondarily, into the outer realm of external nature. It gives man creative power to modify nature in accordance with his needs.

"The mental consequences of a prayerful condition of mind," Brinton writes, "are to inspire patience under afflictions, hope in adversity, courage in the presence of danger and a calm confidence in the face of death itself. How mightily such influences have worked in history is shown in every religious war, and in the lives of martyrs of all faiths. It matters not what they believe, so long as they believed it thoroughly, and the gates of Hades could not prevail against them." [419]

Inasmuch as prayer stems from religious conviction, it does matter as to what to believe and to whom to pray. Judaism, for example, forbids praying to angels or souls of saints. It knows of God alone as "the hearer of prayer." In the words of the Maimonidean Creed: "to Him alone it is proper to pray, and it is not proper to pray to any being beside Him."

Prayer vindicates itself by its effect upon the human soul. It has proven to be a formidable weapon in man's struggle for existence, a weapon tested in myriads of battles. [420] Men in fox-holes, on stormy seas and in pest-ridden jungles have tapped a deep source of power through lifting their spirits in prayer. They threw off their crushing burden of anxiety and care; and their troubled spirits experienced a measure of freedom and renewed hope.

It has been observed that "we do not pray because we believe in God—we believe in God because we pray." Through the exercise of prayer we bring God nearer to our consciousness. The Lord of all whose reign we may discern in rare moments of reflection becomes—through prayer—an intimate companion and friend, and ever-present guide and help. Dean Sperry similarly remarks that we do not set first to "draw up a speculative account of God and then adore Him; the act of worship is itself the process by which we first define God." [421] Prayer is the language of faith, the living voice of religion. To pray means to make religion real. By verbalizing the spirit of religion, prayer endows it with vitality. The idea of God conceived through reflection and speculation is obviously abstract and seemingly unrelated to the lives of ordinary men. Hence, despite advanced views of God in philosophical circles, the masses continue to present Him in concrete images and likenesses of familiar things. Partly on account of their ingrained polytheistic notions and partly because of psychic needs, the common man continues to lower God to the level of natural objects and forces. Judaism, without yielding to the idol-making proclivities of the masses, has sought to overcome the vagueness of its spiritual idea of God through prayer. Utilizing poetry in the service of faith, it brings God close to the heart of the worshipper. While preserving some anthropomorphic expressions, it endeavors to keep before the mind of the worshipper the idea that these expressions are mere symbols of God, whose true nature transcends the human mind. It steadily strives to translate the cosmic character of God in terms of human relationship. The source of all existence and the fountain of life is invoked as father and shepherd, as friend and as lover of the soul. As the indwelling Presence (*Shechinah*) and as transcendent sovereign, He evokes the sense of reverence, awe and solemnity in the human mind. As the merciful one He is related to the gentler emotions of kindliness, sympathy, charity, etc. Through these and similar attributes the mind grasps the idea of God as the overarching Providence.

Here the mystical and the didactic types of prayer meet. Both of them consider the concentration of all thought upon God as the real purpose of worship. Maimonides speaks of this object of worship as "peculiar to those who have acquired a knowledge of the highest truths; and the more they reflect on Him, and think of Him, the more they are engaged in His worship. . . . All such religious acts as reading the Law, praying, and the performance of other precepts, serve exclusively as the means of causing us to occupy and fill our mind with the precepts of God, and free it from worldly business; for we are thus, as it were, in communication with God, and undisturbed by other things." [422]

Thus prayer enlarges our vision of God and of the world, and opens to us new goals of endeavor. It makes our shadowy ideals shine forth like radiant stars upon our horizon, and shows us the role that we are to play in life. We learn to judge ourselves in the light of these ideals. Here the confessional comes into play, summoning before the mind's eye the behavior that has grown repulsive to our better selves, and awakens the desire to be restored to divine sonship. Its spirit is expressed in the Psalmist's prayer: "Create in me a clean heart, O God; and renew a steadfast spirit within me" (51:12). We are helped to reintegrate our warring inclinations into a united bond of purpose. We link our whole lives—not merely the fragments of our will—to God and to His law.

Thus, too, prayer gets us out of ourselves, of our self-centeredness and self-love, and unites us with high purposes that make for the well-being of our fellow men. We are stimulated to appreciate the lives and efforts of others. We think of our kindred, our friends, our compatriots, our co-believers, our nation and humanity. Thus the hour of prayer may become the truest and most creative in our spiritual life, making holiness the very atmosphere of our souls. As we pray for the things whereby men truly live, and as we voice our fervent hope for the well-being of others, we ascend as on an invisible ladder to the life of faith and ideal values. The answer to our prayers comes in a quickening of the spirit and in an enrichment of life. From anxiety and fear, from perplexity and grief we rise to peace and serenity, from weakness to moral courage. We can face darkness, because we have wrestled with it and have prevailed.

While self-analysis is a preliminary phase of self-purification, excessive introspection and subjectivity lead to the exaltation of self rather than to the worship of God. In true prayer all occupation with self, all forms of self-regard and self-pity, all self-centered ambition and longing for esteem and position are laid aside. The altar of God must be approached in complete humility, self-oblivion and surrender, with hearts full of love for and devotion to Him and to the values which we associate with Him. "To do Thy will is my desire"—represents the true attitude of devotion. Behind every prayer is the conviction that man is not alone in the world and that in some way he is related to the all-controlling mysterious Reality. Relinquishing his own self-sufficiency and self-righteousness, man humbly recognizes his dependence upon God. There is an eye that sees and an ear that hears. By endeavoring to contact the Divine does prayer become spiritually fruitful. Where this effort is lacking, the voice of prayer is reduced to empty sound.

In prayer the two factors of the religious life are brought into relation: the Divine influence and the human initiative. As the Life of our lives and the Mind of our minds, His light kindles our vision and illuminates our paths. Prayer seeks to communicate this sense of Divine nearness and to connect our spirits with the source of Divine power and of light. Thereby, too, the appeal to human initiative is raised above auto-suggestion. The spirit of man is not separated from the Divine, for in Him it lives and has its being. Appealing to man's initiative and courage, prayer reaches out after the Divine endowment in man's spiritual life, and summons man to act as co-worker of God. Plotinus teaches: "We must not think of ourselves as cut off from the source of Life; rather we breathe and consist in It, for It does not give Itself to us and then withdraw Itself, but *ever* lifts and bears." [423]

It is the conviction of men of piety that God not only hears prayer, but also initiates it. The Psalmist prays: "O Lord, open Thou my lips; and my mouth shall declare Thy praise" (51:17). He sets in motion the direction of the soul toward Him. Prayer thus appears as the response of the soul to the Divine urge. Therein lies the meaning of grace or the movement of God's love toward man (Ps. 13:6). It draws us to Him

as the sun draws out the pigment of the flower. Our
lights and aspirations are kindled by His eternal fire
(Ps. 18:29). Yet He lifts us to Himself only as we
direct our hearts toward Him. We must place our un-
developed spirits at the disposal of "His molding
spirit." There is, then, a passive as well as an active
element in prayer, a receptiveness of the Divine and
a cooperation with Him. Man can hope to secure the
Divine favor only as he purifies himself from iniquity
and unworthiness. God's presence may be seen
through righteousness (Ps. 17:15). The clean of hand
and the pure of heart may ascend unto His mountain
and dwell in His tabernacle (Pss. 24:4; 15).

While man seeks the nearness of God and endeavors
to commune with Him, he must "keep his heart
watchful and open to the working of God." As we
strain to find Him, we may be found by Him (cf.
Jer. 29:13–14; II Chr. 15:2). Felix Adler expressed
gratefulness for the idea that used him. Religious spirits regard themselves as mere instruments of God.
Men and nations are chosen by Him to further His
ends (Jer. 18:1–12). Robert Browning sang:

> There is that in me
> Which turns to Thee, which loves,
>     or which should love. . . .
> Is it not in my nature to adore,
> And e'en for all my reason do I not
> Feel him and thank him, and pray to
>     him—now? [424]

The devout soul feels that "God is nigh to all that call
upon Him, unto all that call upon Him in truth" (Ps.

145:18). The mere turn of the heart in sincerity
brings God near. The Sufi poet Jalal ud-din Rumi's
Masnavi tells of a man who cried aloud to God. Satan
mocked him: "No answer comes to thee from nigh to
the throne, how long wilt thou cry 'Allah' with harsh
face?" The man feared that he had been repulsed by
God. But Khixr was sent to him by God and said to
him:

God has given me this command:
Go to him and say, O much-tried one,
Did I not engage thee to call upon Me?
That calling "Allah" of thine was My "Here am I,"
And that pain and longing and ardor are thy messenger;
Thy struggles and strivings for assistance
Were My attraction and originated thy prayer,
Thy fear and thy love are the covert of My mercy
Each "O Lord" of thine contains many "Here am I's." [425]

Similarly St. Gregory said: "When a soul truly desires
God, it already possesses Him." [426] Pascal, crying out
in the anguish of his soul, in the silence of the night,
heard this reply: "Be comforted, thou wouldst not
have sought Me, unless thou hadst possessed Me." [427]

PRIVATE AND PUBLIC PRAYER—*Synagogue*. The two
phases of religion as personal experience and as a social
phenomenon are reflected in prayer. *Tephillah belahash* represents the one; *tephillah betzibbur*—the
other. A Hannah pours out her heart before God in
silence. Modesty bade her shield her heart's petition
even from the priestly ear of the aged Eli. "Only her
lips moved, but her voice was not heard" (1 Sam.

1:13). To articulate in public one's innermost wants seems indelicate to some minds, and amounts to a profanation of the holy. Men live their truest spiritual life in solitude. There they wrestle with the forces of darkness, and there, too, they catch glimpses of light. An Elijah flees from the madding crowd to the desert to be alone with his God and to catch the whisperings of the still small voice. However, "out of the abundance of my complaint and my vexation have I spoken," says Hannah. The pent-up emotions break out into cries, whether subdued or loud. A Jeremiah, overpowered by the inner spiritual struggle, gives vent to soliloquies, confessions and petitions. Impressed upon the hearts of his auditors, his expressions of faith were preserved for future use as fitting utterances for the inarticulate longings of others. Embodied into his book of prophecies and reechoed in a number of Psalms, these prayers became the vehicle of popular piety.

Furthermore, the individual does not live his own life in solitude. As a social being, his needs are not exclusively his own. Most of them are shared by the entire group or people. These are reflected in prayer. Though he prays as an individual, he reflects the community. The Psalms are believed to be the songs and petitions of all Israel, despite their use of the first person singular. They represent all Israel in the act of adoration of God. The transition from personal to corporate devotion may be seen in the practice of the people to turn to the priests to offer the sacrifices for them and to recite the ritual formulas, and in the similar practice of asking men of piety to voice their petitions. Moses is introduced in the role of intercessor for the people. Other prophets figure in a similar role. To the ancient Hasidim, who lived a life of prayer, people went to voice their heart's desires. Honi Hameagal, Abba Hilkiah, Hanina b. Dosa, etc., interceded in behalf of the sick and the suffering and in behalf of the entire people. In such cases the listeners identified themselves with the prayers of their representatives and made brief responses in the form of *Amen, Hallelujah, Hoshia na, Ki leolam hasdo,* and doxologies. To these practices at the Temple and the early synagogue the antiphonal responses in worship owe their origin. The spontaneous element of prayer came to be subordinated to the fixed and conventionalized forms, and personal petition merged with the liturgy of the congregation. The Eighteen Benedictions strikingly illustrate this tendency. Developing gradually by the process of accretion as the ritual formulas of the priests at the sanctuary and as the prayers of saintly individuals, they were at last codified, under the auspices of Gamaliel II, and made the center of the three daily services. The private and public phases of these benedictions are preserved in the mode of their recitation in Orthodox worship. First they are spoken silently by each worshipper and then repeated by the reader or Hazzan for the entire congregation (*belahash* and *bekol ram*).

Public prayer aims to answer the needs not of one type of man only but of all types, the ignorant and the learned, the introvert and the extravert. The untaught promptings of the simple heart find expression by the side of those of the precious traditions of the community, the simple words of thanksgiving by the side of the great outpouring of poetic genius, purely personal petitions by the side of social aspirations.

The conscious attempt to compose prayers, hymns, and meditations for public use has led to the creation of liturgic art forms. Thereby public worship has gained in impressiveness. While something of the original spontaneity of personal devotion is retained in some, others became formal, rigid and artificial. The Bible itself exhibits this tendency, which appears more fully in the standardized Tephillah, the acrostic Psalms, the tedious refrains (e.g., Ps. 136), the mosaics of Bible verses, and the repetitious litanies, producing a monotony which is sometimes overcome only by their deep religious fervor. The spirit of devotion gives way to pedantry in the *piyyutim*, especially of the Ashkenazic rite. In the Selihot and Tehinot genuine religious sentiment is often obscured by wearisome verbosity. Artificiality is by no means limited to the ancient liturgies. To an even greater degree it abounds in modern prayer books. Many compositions of recent origin are little more than homilies on diverse personal and social problems addressed to God, with hardly a trace of true prayer.

With the transformation of prayer from a spontaneous outpouring of emotion to a fixed ritual of worship for set occasions, the personal element, if not wholly eliminated, is very much submerged. The original fervor of the prayers, coming from devout hearts, evaporates, and the prayer texts come to be valued for their antiquity and tradition. Surrounded by a halo of sanctity, they exercise a rare influence upon the minds of men. Meticulous care distinguishes their mode of recitation. Like the sacrifices, with which prayer was connected in the beginning, its formulas came to be regarded sacrosanct. The least change in the transmitted text and form of presentation—as in the case of a magic formula—was believed to impair its efficacy, and hence invalidated the ritual.[428] The rabbinical Codes devote much attention to the minutest details of worship. So commanding and so effective have these traditional forms become in Jewish religious life that worship without them seems barren and unsatisfying. Even in Reform circles when new prayers are added they are generally adapted to traditional patterns, thus lending an archaic character to the newest liturgic creations.

While the individual may pray in the privacy of his home, in the shop or factory, or in the open field, the community requires a set place for worship. The collective aspect of worship comes to full expression in the synagogue, the unique creation of the democratic spirit of Judaism. Each synagogue constitutes an independent institution, formed and maintained by a voluntary association. Free from ecclesiastical domination, it is governed by its own members and officers. The rabbi functions purely as teacher and guide, and enjoys only such authority as the congregation vests in him. However, while autonomous in its government, each synagogue is united with the *Keneset*

*Yisrael* (Congregation of Israel) by its dedication to
the common heritage of faith and duty. As a communal center and school, and, above all, as a house of
worship, the synagogue serves as the power-house of
Jewish religious life. It represents the prime historic
agency whereby Judaism is fostered and preserved
within the Jewish community. As a spiritual center
and rallying point, each synagogue unites the individual Jews of its vicinity into a community with common ideals and purposes and thereby binds them to all
Israel. In its worship the individual associates himself
with his people. His personal needs are integrated
with those of the collective community. He shares in
its beliefs and ideals, its memories and hopes, its sympathies and enthusiasms. Hillel's counsel, "Separate not
thyself from the community," [429] applies with special
force to communal worship. R. Simeon b. Lakish remarks that "whoever has a synagogue in his city and
does not enter into it to worship is called 'an evil neighbor.' " [430] "In a synagogue at worship," R. Isaac
teaches, "God is found. Indeed, wherever ten men
unite in prayer, the Shechinah (God's Presence) is
with them." The hour of congregational worship is
considered a time of God's favor. The Holy One
says: "Whoever engages in Torah and benevolent
works and joins in public worship is accounted as if
he has redeemed Me and My children from among the
heathens." [431] Personal Jewish piety is considered incomplete without identification with the local congregation and without sharing in the fellowship of the
entire congregation of Israel.

LANGUAGE OF PRAYER. Few things preserve the religious consciousness of a community and link the generations of worshippers into a bond of unity as a historic liturgy. The prayers of the fathers mold the spiritual life of their children. The Psalms and the basic elements of the Tephillah, which have remained unaltered for many centuries, have provided the thought patterns of the passing generations of Jews. Worship generally excludes novelties and clings to time-honored forms and texts, investing their language itself with sanctity. Heiler comments about the continuation of traditional formulas of prayer long after a complete change had taken place in the religious conceptions of a people, and even though their language has ceased to be understood. "In the time of the Roman Empire old Latin prayers were still spoken which were completely unintelligible even to the priests. Sometimes such ancient formulas were transplanted to countries where a foreign tongue was spoken. In the Hellenistic mysteries of Isis, the priest in the holiest act, that of opening the tabernacle, made use of the Egyptian language. The verbal persistence of the ancient formulas, in spite of the developments of the language of their adoption by peoples speaking other tongues, brings about the rise of languages wholly ritual in character. The most ancient ceremonial speech is the Sumerian which was always regarded as sacred by the Semitic Assyrians and Babylonians." [432] Sanskrit is employed in the Buddhist mass in China and Japan. Arabic constitutes the language of the *salat*, prayer, five times daily in Islam. (Recently Turkey introduced the vernacular.) Latin is the medium of the Roman Catholic Church. Even in the worship of Protestant churches special emotional value is attached to certain liturgic formulas derived from the Hebrew, such as Amen, Hallelujah, Selah, etc. The very fact that these half intelligible or wholly unintelligible words are removed from ordinary usage enhances their worth as vehicles of religious awe. Of such character is Hebrew in Jewish worship. For the mind an idea expressed in one language is as good as when expressed in another. Not so for the emotions. Here the association and usage and even sound are paramount. And religion is more of the heart than of the brain. The distinguished ethnic psychologist Steinthal writes: "In the Hebrew sound religion is revealed, created." [433]

While stressing the formal side of prayer, the masters of Judaism sought to guard it against the dangers of formalism. "Be heedful in the reciting of the Shema and the 'Amidah; and when thou prayest, regard not thy prayer as a fixed routine, but as an appeal for mercy and supplication before the Omnipresent." [434] Worship must not degenerate into a mechanical affair, dry, cold, lifeless and external. It must ever be an act of inward adoration, the outpouring of the spirit of faith and reverence, of joy and of love of God. It must express the inmost longings of the heart, true devotion, and self-consecration. "God demands the heart." [435] Unless the heart is directed to Him, the prayer is but a rhetorical exercise. "Man must ever test himself," the Talmud teaches, "if he can direct his heart to God, let him pray; but if not, let him not pray." [436]

Accordingly while public worship was to be conducted in Hebrew, private devotion was limited to no one language. The command, "Shema" (hear), was construed in the sense of understand, i.e., in any language which one understands—*Shema bechol lashon sheatta shomea*. Prayer is a petition of grace, and may be spoken in whatever tongue one pleases. The Mishnah rules that the Shema, Tephillah, and Grace may be recited in any language. [437] In personal prayer only the language of the heart matters. Jehudah Hasid counsels those who do not know Hebrew to use a translation of the prayer book in the vernacular, "for prayer depends upon the understanding of the heart, but if the heart does not know what the mouth speaks of what value is it to man?" [438] To satisfy such a need, translations of the prayer book were prepared in most languages spoken by the Jewish people. Books for private devotion written in the vernaculars of the Jews have appeared in considerable number since the sixteenth century. R. Nahman of Bratzlav advised all men to pray extemporaneously in Yiddish in addition to reciting the stated daily prayers in Hebrew. [439] The Reform movement, endeavoring to render worship intelligible, has made large—sometimes exclusive—use of the vernacular.

While providing German and English translations as well as original prayers to enrich the synagogue worship, Isaac M. Wise wrote in the introduction to the last volume of his *Minhag America*: "The Hebrew language in our public worship is the medium of our synagogual union. Dispersed as the house of Israel is in all lands, we must have a vehicle to understand each other in the house of God, so that no brother be a stranger therein; and this vehicle is the Hebrew. Aside from this consideration, however, the Hebrew sounds are sacred to the Israelite; they are holy reminiscences of his youth, which can as little be replaced to him in another language, as the Psalms of David can be reproduced in another tongue. Those who are not at all conversant with the Hebrew . . . can resort to translated prayerbooks which will always enable them to follow the minister in the public worship. In the house of the Lord, let us always remain a unit, as our sires have been." * Where the Hebrew has practically been eliminated from the service there has been a decided impoverishment of the historical character of Jewish devotion.

FIXED LITURGIES. Though public worship has come to hold the center of religious life, it has not dispensed with the need of private devotion. The human heart

* *Hymns, Psalms and Prayers,* pp. 3–4.
  Morris Joseph writes in similar spirit: "Among the bulwarks of the religious consciousness in Israel there was none more powerful" than Hebrew. Should it be expelled from public worship, "with it would vanish much of the Jewish spirit." And again: "You will get rid of Hebrew, but with it of the synagogue too, of the synagogue as a living organism, as the well spring of Jewish feeling and the inspiration of the Jewish life." Sermon on "Hebrew and the Synagogue," *Message of Israel,* pp. 31, 37. The truth of this statement is illustrated by the history of the Jews of K'aifeng Fu. While

experiences ever new needs which are not expressed in standardized rituals. Provision, therefore, has been made for personal petitions to be inserted in the Tephillah. As the average person is tongue-tied when it comes to verbalizing the longings of his heart, he has been supplied with aids. The private prayers of men of deep piety have been included in the books of prayer or in special collections. Thus in private devotion, too, spontaneous prayer is the exception. Traditional usage has rendered certain Psalms and prayers appropriate for the various occasions of the heart's communion with God. Of such character are the devotions at rising and retiring, the prayers in sickness and in sorrow, and the thanksgivings at recovery from illness and deliverance from danger, confession on a death-bed, prayers in time of mourning, and at visiting the grave of a dear one, etc. Of public character are services at circumcision, marriage, and burial, and dedication of a tombstone. The family aspect of religion is accentuated by the ceremonies of kindling the lights and the recitation of the Kiddush on the eve of Sabbath and the Holy Days, and of grace at meals.

economic and political factors played their part in bringing about the ruin of their community, the disappearance of all knowledge of Hebrew and of Jewish tradition among them led to the decay of their religious life. Following the death of their last rabbi (about 1800), public worship and all religious observance ceased, the venerable synagogue was disposed of, and all spiritual light went out of their lives. See William Charles White, *Chinese Jews, A Compilation of Matters Relating to the Jews of K'aifeng Fu, 1942,* I, pp. 17, 101, 187, etc.

The Passover is graced with a special ritual for the home, the *Seder Haggadah*. It is only in deference to those who have no such service in their homes that congregational Sedarim have been held in recent years in numerous communities. However, in order not to interfere with the home character of the Seder, the congregational Sedarim, in many instances, are conducted on the second night of the festival. The standardized services themselves may be used in private devotion. The introductory parts of the various services were intended for private use. Furthermore, in the absence of a quorum (*Minyan*), the ritual is recited by the individual worshipper, with the omission of the specifically public parts (like the *Borchu*, *Kedushah* and the *Kaddish*.)

The personal element of the ritual is accentuated by the provision for silent devotion in the public service. Here we must distinguish between the Quaker type of worship without words and the Jewish type of *tephillah belahash*. The first may be suited for introverts and for virtuosi in prayer. R. Nahman of Bratzlav writes: "Before prayer it is necessary to attach one's spirit to God, and through this union with Him the words of prayer will find expression." [440] In reality few people can think connectedly without verbalizing their feelings and thoughts. The mental concentration required for such exercise to be fruitful overtaxes the capacities of the ordinary individual. Instead of meditating in silence, he may easily slip into a mental stupor, a kind of somnolence, or uncontrolled brooding. The fact that a modification of this practice has been made in some Quaker churches indicates the difficulties inherent in this type of worship. In order to preserve its good effects, the Jewish form of *tephillah belahash* provides the worshipper with prayers of personal nature, which he may read and take to heart. With this as a basis he may be aided to further reflections that are close to his heart.

While spontaneity is desirable in prayer, experience teaches that the prayer mood and habit are best cultivated by a set liturgy and by regular occasions of worship. Through regularity and frequent repetition prayer becomes the atmosphere of our lives. To be sure, there is danger in this procedure of turning prayer into a mechanical affair. However, the remedy does not lie in breaking away from set prayer and in reliance upon extempore devotions or improvisations by the rabbi. The experience of Protestantism on this point is instructive. W. A. Brown observes that the minister's "spontaneous prayer tends to harden into an unofficial liturgy without the protection which the antiquity and the dignity of the older prayers furnish us." [441] Dean Sperry testifies that the free prayer lies open to the play of the minister's idiosyncrasies and private hobbies. Unless rigidly censored, it tends to become either informational or an "exercise in self-analysis." Its ideas are often random or irrelevant. Its informality robs the service of beauty and impressiveness, which is not compensated even by its directness and freshness. Its language generally becomes either stereotyped or haphazard and commonplace. "The present fact is that the original truth of the free service

has become in practice a rather uninspired and unin-
spiring platitude. . . . Every minister who has conducted free worship for a period of years has unconsciously developed and in the end has consciously
adopted certain forms of speech and action which
have become habitual with him. Simply because his
prayers have not been printed in a book or his usages
dignified by rubrics, he is not a 'non-liturgical' minister." [442] Furthermore, such worship is divorced from
tradition,* and lacks the authority and the appeal
which ancient usage bestows. In consequence, a return
to the older liturgical practice of the church is the
order of the day in a number of Christian denomina-
tions.

While some experience great difficulties in the way
of prayer, devout souls derive strength, joy and peace
from both public and private devotion. Indeed, there
is a hunger among many people for devotion as distinct from instruction and exhortation, for prayer and
ritual apart from preaching and teaching. This is
partly witnessed by the Anglo-Catholic movement,
by the endeavor to restore to the Lutheran churches
the liturgical usages of the Lutheran church in the
sixteenth century, by the faith cults in Christianity

* W. A. Brown writes of the churches of the non-liturgical
tradition, like the Congregational, Methodist, and Baptist,
that their flexibility of service is controlled by a certain tradition. The order of their services follows models of the past,
"and the effectiveness of the service depends in no small part
upon the participant's consciousness that he is sharing in the
fellowship of prayer which unites worshippers of many different traditions." (*Op. cit.*, pp. 78–79.)

and by their Jewish imitations. Much of the effectiveness of traditional liturgies comes from the consciousness of the worshippers that they are sharing in a faith that is from of old and in rites which link them with the generations of the past and with their brethren of other lands. The preaching may evoke criticism and tend to divide the worshippers, but the liturgy unites them into one religious community.

CEREMONIES AND MUSIC. The deep psychic experiences, which are at the core of prayer, naturally affect the mood of its expression. The stirring of the heart as it is directed to God, the overflow of the emotions, passions, and desires translate themselves into bodily gestures and vocal sounds. The feelings of anxiety and fear, of anguish and grief, of trouble and vexation, of awe and reverence, of adoration and rapture, of longing and resignation, of confidence and hope manifest themselves in bodily attitudes, posture, gesture, and song. The rhythm, with which the pent-up emotions express themselves, is marked among primitive peoples by clapping of hands, striking the breast, stamping the feet, dancing, ejaculations, cries, shouts, and bursts of song. With the cultural advance of the people, these accompaniments of prayer are refined and molded into artistic forms. In public rituals hushed silences are retained by the side of the vocal utterances on the part of the leader and congregation.

Traditional Jewish worship is marked by the separation of the sexes, by the covering of the head, bowing, standing during certain prayers, taking three steps backward at the end of the 'Amidah and the Kaddish, and kneeling on Rosh Hashanah and Yom Kippur (during the *Alenu* and *Vehakohanim* in the *'Abodah*).[443] During the morning devotions on week-days, whether public or private, phylacteries (*tephillin*) and prayer-shawls (*tallit*) are worn by males generally above the age of thirteen. The prayer-shawls are used on the Sabbath and Holy Days as well. On fast days men remove their shoes during worship. On Yom Kippur they also wear a *kittel* (a white linen gown, which serves them ultimately as a shroud).

Reform Judaism, with its emphasis on the aesthetic, restrained still more the spontaneous bodily responses in worship, and has abandoned the use of special galleries for women as well as the practice of covering the head and of wearing the tallit. The fact that Reform practically limited public services to the Sabbath and Holy Days automatically did away with the use of tephillin. The postures, which it has reserved, are limited to rising during certain parts of the service, to silence during private meditations, and to bowing the head during the adoration and the closing benediction.

Of greatest prominence in religious worship is the musical accompaniment. Orthodox Jewish worship derives its special character from the chant in prayer and in reading of Scripture. The mood of each occasion and prayer is expressed by an appropriate melody. Each festive day has its special melodic character, so that the common prayers used during the entire year are invested with distinctive festivity. As the song of the synagogue voices the Jewish soul in its struggle for life, for hope, and for sanctity through ages of trial and hardship, it fittingly interprets and enriches the devotions of the Jewish people. Reform Judaism, in its endeavor to beautify the service, introduced classical harmony and instrumental accompaniment. As the music and choir directors for the most part have been non-Jews, they neglected the distinctive character of Jewish song. Not even the great masters, like Sulzer, Lewandowski, Weintraub, Stark, Idelsohn, etc., have been able to check this neglect and the consequent impoverishment of the Reform service. Much of the mischief is due to the desire on the part of the music leaders to provide the congregations with musical entertainment instead of aiding them in devotion. Orthodoxy is often as guilty of this sin as Reform. Amusement is the antithesis of the spirit of worship. The service assumes the character of a concert for the exhibition of the virtuosity of its performers. True Jewish worship is not the exclusive domain of either cantor or rabbi, but of the entire congregation. They are to lead it in devotion rather than entertain it with eloquence or with music. The fact that Judaism recognizes no distinction between laity and priesthood and that any Jew may conduct the public service at the synagogue has checked the tendency to render it the affair of a professional, whether cantor or rabbi. The congregation must not be reduced to a mere audience, but must participate actively in both prayer and song. While congregational participation does not permit the singing to assume ornate art forms, it serves as a true channel of devotion, which is the sole aim of worship.[444]

The conduct of the service, the bearing and the artistry of its leader, and the decorum and responsiveness of the congregation must be expressive of deep reverence and solemn joy. While men are enjoined to serve the Lord with gladness, the atmosphere of their worship must not be too informal or cheaply familiar. It must be marked with the awe that comes from the awareness of the presence of the Holy One, akin to that which a Jacob felt on awakening to the realization that he faced the gates of heaven, a Moses on beholding the burning bush, or an Isaiah on hearing in the Temple the angel choir singing: "Holy." "When you pray," an ancient master taught, "know before Whom you stand." [445] The worshipper must enter the sanctuary eager to seek the Lord and His strength, and to worship Him in the beauty of holiness.

# EPILOGUE

OUR PRESENT NEED. The expression of the full
character of Judaism as a way of life requires not
merely knowledge of Torah and ethical discipline, but
also worship, enriched by appropriate art-forms and
symbols and the use of Hebrew by the side of the vernacular. Ceremonies voice more eloquently than words
man's spiritual yearnings. As "testimonies" and "me-
morials" they also preserve our historical consciousness
and enrich our lives with sanctity. The poetic and
symbolic elements make religion a power and a joy for
young and old. They serve as effective aids in our religious development by their appeal to our emotions as
well as to our minds. They invest worship with dra-
matic power and beauty.

To guard the spiritual health of our people, special
effort must be made to revive the habit of private and
public worship. Prayer constitutes the life-breath of
religion, the very essence and concrete expression of
piety and faith. It is the mystic ladder upon which the
devout soul mounts to the throne of God, enters into
communion with Him, and enlists in His service. Vital
religion is born in the heart of the individual as it is
lifted to God in prayer. As an affirmation of belief, as
a cry for help, as a petition for grace and for guidance
and as an exultation in the Divine, it discloses the characteristic elements of religion. Prayer lays bare the
soul before God, its fears and hopes, its griefs and
joys, its worries and satisfactions, its anguish and bliss,

362

its defeats and triumphs, its vexations and enthusiasms. It solemnizes life's festivities and soothes its sorrows. It invests the high moments of personal and group experience with significance and sanctity.

The human spirit stands eternally in need of self-renewal and self-purification. Prayer has served as a regenerating force in the lives of men, turning their visions and aspirations into means of self-discipline. Out of the broken fragments of character it molds harmonious personalities. Prayer is socially as well as personally fruitful. Through prayer we get out of our self-centeredness and are drawn toward our kindred and friends. We think not only of ourselves but also of our brethren far and near, and concern ourselves with the well-being of all our fellow men. Prayer comes to serve as the collective voice of the religious community, as the mighty pulsation of its invisible soul, strengthening the links that unite it despite the barriers of geography, language and politics.

Public worship accentuates the values and ideals which have preserved it through stormy centuries, re-awakens them in wavering hearts and plants them in the minds of the young as the undying possession of Israel. No Jew can spend an hour in true worship, whether private or public, without feeling himself enriched spiritually. He cannot but feel invigorated in faith and purified in outlook by a Sabbath hour of devotion in the midst of his people, or uplifted and regenerated by the joyous services of the festivals and by the solemn worship of the High Holy Days. Prayer is, indeed, the life nerve of religion.

To be effective, prayer must not be a mere mumbling of words, nor an indifferent and careless repetition of routine formulas, but an earnest upreaching of the whole being Godward. The supreme imperative of Jewish faith is: "Thou shalt love the Lord thy God with all thy heart, and with all thy soul and with all thy might." The worshipper should divest himself of all selfish thoughts and of all unworthy desires and ambitions and give himself unreservedly to God and His service. Concentrating his mind upon God he must resolve above all so to live as to merit God's approval.

The habit of conscious prayer, which has fallen out of many lives, must be restored if the spiritual health of the Jewish people is to be preserved. People who abandon prayer in large measure cut themselves off from the rich reservoirs of religion and impoverish their spiritual life. Possibly the greatest menace to Jewish welfare today is the neglect of religious devotion in all its forms, of study of Torah, self-discipline and prayer. We shall know of no peace of mind as Jews nor shall we recover our inner strength and soundness until we shall restore religious faith, observance and worship to their proper place in personal and public life, in our homes and in our synagogues.

Fortunately, by the side of much that is disconcerting and alarming in our religious life, there are some signs of health. It is encouraging to note signs of hunger for living faith. Sensitive spirits in Jewry as in Christendom now and then voice their longing for devotion as distinct from amusement in Divine service.

They crave more poetry and traditional song, more symbolism and ceremonial. In addition to the emphasis on social justice they call for personal religion. They also seek in the modern synagogue stronger bonds of union with past forms of Jewish religious striving and effort. Though their voices are still few, they hold the promise of our religious future. Their faith and devotion may serve as the foundation of the synagogue and of Jewish life tomorrow.

NOTES

GLOSSARY

BIBLIOGRAPHY

QUESTIONS

INDEX

# NOTES

## NOTES TO CHAPTERS I–IV

1 Genesis Rabba 1:1.
2 Makkot 23b–24b.
3 *Sermons on the Old Testament*, pp. 131–132.
4 Tanhuma, Old, Shelah, 15.
5 *Introduction to Philosophy*, pp. 218–219.
6 Yoma 67b.
7 Gen. R. 44:1.
8 Rosh Hashanah 28b; Berachot 13a; Sanhedrin 106b; cf. Nazir 23ab.
9 Cf. Hobot Halebabot, Introduction.
10 *English Synonyms*, p. 307.
11 Hullin 69a; S. Schechter, Saints and Saintliness in *Studies of Judaism*, II, p. 151.

12 See Kuzari, III: 1–5, and below the section on Righteousness and Justice.
13 Baba Kamma 30a.
14 Abot 6:1.
15 Sotah 9:15. See Fragment of an Unknown Midrash, ed. Louis Finkelstein, *Hebrew Union College Annual*, XII–XIII, p. 543; A. Buechler, *Types of Jewish Palestinian Piety*.
16 Abot 2:5.
17 Mesilat Yesharim, ch. 26.
18 Menahot 13:11.
19 Sukkah 45b.
20 Ber. 33b.
21 Yoma 38b.

## NOTES TO CHAPTERS V–VIII

22 *Varieties of Rel. Exp.*, pp. 47–48.
23 *The Religious Consciousness*, pp. 35–36.
24 *The Life of the Spirit*, p. 30.
25 Worcester, McComb and Coriat, *Religion and Medicine*, p. 268.
26 *Ibid.*
27 *Amer. Journal of Psychology*, Vol. VIII, p. 242; cited *ibid.*, p. 269. See John Dillard and Neal E. Miller, *Fear in Battle*, 1944.
28 Dr. Beard, *American Nervousness*, p. 202; cited *ibid.*, p. 278.
29 *Talks with Teachers on Psychology*, cited *ibid.*, p. 280.

30 *Op. cit.*, p. 289.
31 Art. Materialism, *H.E.R.E.*, VIII, p. 490.
32 *In Harmony with Nature.*
33 Hab. 1:3–4; Jer. 12:1–3; Pss. 49; 73.
34 Erub. 13b.
35 Ps. 92:13–16; Is. 2:12–22; Mal. 2:18–20.
36 Gen. R. 9:5–13.
37 Gen. R. 51:3; Tanhuma, Buber, Vayera 18.
38 Taanit 21a.
39 Ber. 60b.
40 Sab. 55a.
41 Kid. 40a, b; also Ber. 5b; Sifre, Dt. 307.
42 On the Yetzer and Original Sin, see S. Schechter, *As-

*pects of Rabbinic Theology*, pp. 242ff.; K. Kohler, *Jewish Theology*, pp. 215, 218–225; A. Cohen, *Everyman's Talmud*, pp. 98–99.

[43] Midr. Psalms 5:7.

[44] Gen. R. 3:5; Tanh. Tazria, 9; Lament. R. 2:1. See L. Ginzberg, *Legends of the Jews*, V, p. 5.

[45] *De Opificio Mundi*, ch. v.

[46] C. G. Montefiore, *Florilegium Philoni*, J.Q.R. (Old Series) VII, p. 489; see Neumark, *Essays in Jewish Philosophy*, p. 61.

[47] Schürer, *Hist. of Jewish People*, Vol. III, pp. 376ff.

[48] M. Waxman, *Mishle Yisrael*, 5364.

[49] Tzavaat R. Israel Baal Shem Tob, in Zweifel's *Shalom al Yisrael*, I, part 2, p. 7; *Keter Shem Tob*, ibid., p. 9; Teitelbaum, *Harab Miliadi*, II, p. 162.

[50] Guide, III, ch. 12, tr. Friedlander, p. 268.

[51] Emunah Ramah, ed. Weil, pp. 95–98.

[52] *Op. cit.*, chs. 8, 10, 12.

[53] Gen. R. 9:2.

[54] See the discussion in Royce, *The World and the Individual*, II, p. 363, 390ff.; cf. J. Bojer, *Great Hunger*.

[55] *Ibid.*, p. 405.

[56] See Royce, *The Religious Aspect of Philosophy*, pp. 291–324.

[57] Worcester, McComb and Coriat, *Religion and Medicine*, p. 146.

[58] See the *Quimby Manuscript*, edited by Horatio W. Dresser, New York, 1921.

[59] See works of Trine, Marden and the Nautilus.

[60] *Science and Health*, p. 113; see articles on Christian Science in *Hastings' Encycl. of Religion and Ethics*, III, 576–579; Vergilius Ferm, *Encyclop. of Religion*, 160–161.

[61] *Ibid.*, p. 468, cited by Chas. W. Ferguson, *The Confusion of Tongues*, pp. 205–206.

[62] Patterson, *In the Sunshine of Health*, cited by Ferguson, *Confusion of Tongues*, p. 170.

[63] Cited *ibid.*, p. 171.

[64] *Varieties*, p. 94.

[65] Worcester, McComb and Coriat, *op. cit.*, p. 160.

[66] Tehilla Lichtenstein, art., Jewish Science, *Universal Jewish Encyclopedia*, 6, 142; Morris Lichtenstein, *Yearbook of the Central Conference of American Rabbis*, XXXVII, 1927, pp. 185–189. Rabbi Lichtenstein's writings include: *Jewish Science and Health, How to Live, Peace of Mind*, etc.

[67] Effects of Mind on Body as evidenced by Faith-Cures, American Journal of Psychology, X, 1899; cited in *Varieties*, p. 96n.; p. 112. Worcester, McComb and Coriat make a similar claim. See *Religion and Medicine*.

68 See W. F. Cobb, art., Faith-
Healing, *H.E.R.E.*, I, pp.
697–701; Ab. Zarah 55a.

69 Art. Psycho-Therapeutics,
*H.E.R.E.*, X, p. 434.

70 *Ibid.*

71 Worcester and McComb,
*Body, Mind and Spirit*, p.
xiv.

72 *Yearbook of the Central
Conference of American
Rabbis*, XXXVII, 1927, pp.
344ff.

73 *The World and the Individual*, II, p. 396.

74 *Religion and Medicine*, p.
235.

75 *Op. cit.*, 163–164.

76 *Religion and Medicine*, p.
160.

77 *Primitive Culture*, II, p. 171.

78 William Brown, Religion and
Psychology, in Needham's
*Science, Religion and Real-
ity*, pp. 319–320.

79 Shekalim 5:1.

80 See art. Medicine, *Jew. Encycl.*; Moses Perlman, *Midrash Harefuah*, 1926; C. J.
Brim, *Medicine in the Bible*,
1936; A. Cohen, *op. cit.*, pp.
253–275; H. L. Gordon, art.,
Hygiene, *Universal Jewish
Encyclopedia*, 5, 509–513;
Harry Friedenwald, *Jews

*and Medicine*, Essays, 2
Vols., 1944; H. G. Enelow.
A note on Spiritual Heal-
ing, *Yearbook, C.C.A.R.*,
XXXVII, 362–368.

81 The statement was utilized
by the rabbis. It appears in
Tanhuma, Miketz 10, Pe-
sikta Rabbati 25, Exodus R.
21, Jerushalmi Taanit 3:6,
Yalkut Job 920. See Gene-
sis R. 7 for other parallels
to this chapter.

82 *Beth Hamidrash*, I, pp. 107–
108; see also Midr. Samuel
IV, 1.

83 Sanh. 17b.

84 Ch. 192:3–4. See also Nahmanides, Torat Haadam,
Shaar Hasakanah, and p.
16f. and Comment. on Lev.
26:11.

85 Sab. 67a and Comment. of
R. Hananel. See *Kav Hay-
ashar*, ch. 28.

86 H. Akum, 11:11–12. Guide,
I:61. For Maimonides' view
on medicine see his com-
mentary on Pesahim
4:9(10). J. Pagel, Maimuni
als medizinischer Schriftstel-
ler, in *Moses ben Maimon,
sein Leben, seine Werke
und sein Einfluss*, ed. Bacher,
Brann, Simonsen and Gutt-
mann, 1908, pp. 231–247.

### Notes to Chapters IX–XII

87 See ch. IV, especially Section
83.

88 *J.Q.R.*, n.s. XI, pp. 283–284;
Apion II, 16, tr. Thackeray.

89 *The Ethical Basis of Judaism,
H.U.C. and Other Ad-
dresses*, pp. 143, 146.

90 *Judaism*, Vol. II, p. 102, n. 1.

91 On the Special Laws, On
Number Seven.

92 Yoma 8:9, cf. R. Simlai's
homily on the 613 com-
mandments in Makkot 23b–
24a.

93 Mekilta, Jetro 8, Yalkut Gen. 300.

94 Mek. Vayassa, I.

95 Orhot Tzaddikim; Introd.

96 See J. Z. Lauterbach, Ethics of the Halacha. C.C.A.R. Year Book, Vol. XXIII, pp. 249–287.

97 Tos. Shabuot 3:6.

98 Kid. 31a.

99 Sifra, Ahare Mot XIII.

100 Ber. 33b.

101 Yoma 67b.

102 See Lazarus, op. cit., pp. 111ff.

103 Gen. R. I:1. Lev. R., Behukkotai, ch. 35:1ff.; Tanhuma, Gen. I, 1.

104 Abodah Zarah 54b.

105 Science and Ethics, London, 1882, p. 430.

106 Data of Ethics, end of ch. III.

107 Newman Smyth, Christian Ethics, p. 83, n. 3.

108 J. S. Mill, Utilitarianism, ch. II.

109 The Two Sources of Morality and Religion, ch. I.

110 Sab. 39a; Sefer Haagadah IV, 20–22.

111 Abot 4:29; tr. S. Singer.

112 Peah, ch. I; Nedarim 39b.

113 B. Batra 11a.

114 Sanh. 97a–98a.

115 Ki Tisa, ed. Buber, 16; Jer. Kid. 1:9; Sanh. 10:1; 90a.

116 Sifre 32.

117 Sotah 31a; 5: 5; Zohar, I, 11b.

118 Abot 1:3; compare Letter of Aristeas, 270.

119 Apion II:30, tr. Thackeray. In the first part of his statement Josephus expresses ideas similar to those of Philo, Special Laws II:258–262.

120 Abot 4:2; see also Abot R. Nathan A 25; B 33.

121 Ab. Z. 19a.

122 Sifre 41; see also 48.

123 Sifre, Haazinu, 306.

124 Abot 4:7.

125 Pes. 50b; Naz. 23b.

126 Perek Helek, tr. Abelson, J.Q.R., o.s., XIX, p. 34; see H. Teshubah VIII–X.

127 Ikkarim IV, 29. See D. Neumark, Musar Hayahadut, Hashiloah, VI, 163ff.

128 Sefer Hasidim, ed. Wistinetzki, No. 1017. See also R. Nissim, Derashot X; Albo, op. cit., III, 31–34.

129 Abot 3:13.

130 Ibid., 3:18.

131 Mekilta, Shirata 3; Sifre, Haazinu, 306.

132 Shibbole Haleket, p. 4.

133 Seder Elijahu R., 26.

134 The saying as given in Hag. 16a reads: Whoever commits a transgression in secret, etc.

135 Commentary to Abot 4:5.

136 Sotah 10b. See also 36a. G. F. Moore confines Kiddush Hashem and Hillul Hashem to public acts, and completely overlooks their role in personal piety and morality. See Judaism, Vol. II, pp. 100–111. Cf. the words of Abot 4:5: "Whosoever profanes the name of God in secret," etc.

137 Ki Tisa, 7.

138 Israel Al Nakawa, Menorat Hamaor III, 357; cf. Deut. R. 7:4; 2:19.

[139] Yoma 86ab.

[140] Abot 4:5.

[141] Maimonides, Com. to Mishnah, *ad loc.*

[142] Sanh. 107a; Tos. Baba Kama 9:10; see also Seder Elijahu R. 26, ed. Friedmann, p. 140; Sefer Hasidim, No. 133.

[143] Kad Hakemah, 18b.

[144] Deut. R., Ekeb, 3; and in somewhat different version in Jer. B. Metz. 2:5.

[145] Jer. B. Metz. 2:5, where other examples are cited.

[146] Ed. Isny, ch. 23, p. 63b; cited in M. Guedemann's *Geschichte des Erziehungswesens*, III, p. 231.

[147] *Ibid.*, 91a, b; cited by Perles, *Beiträge*, p. 175.

[148] Kid. 40a.

[149] Abot of R. Nathan, B, ch. 32.

[150] Ahare Mot, XIII; Sanh. 74a.

[151] Sanh. 74a.

[152] Sefer Hasidim, No. 256. Tobiah b. Eliezer, Lekah Tob, Emor, p. 123; *J. E.* art., Martyrdom; Eisenstein, *Otzar Dinim Uminhagim*, pp. 157, 197–198.

[153] For a summary of Jewish teaching regarding Kiddush Hashem, see Maimonides, Maamar Kiddush Hashem, Hilchot Yesode Hatorah, ch. V; also Cecil Roth, *A History of the Marranos.*

[154] *Union Prayerbook*, Morning Service.

[155] Gen. R. 100. 1; see Sefer Hasidim, 756.

[156] Theatetus; also Phaedrus;

The Laws, Bk. IV. According to Aristoxemus "following God" forms the keynote of the Pythagorean system. See *H.E.R.E.*, X, 526.

[157] The Sibylline Books II, 23–32; Wisdom of Solomon 13:10ff.

[158] Deut. R. 1:12; cf. Hos. 9:10.

[159] Sanh. 103b; Yoma 38b; Suk. 45b; see Mek., Amalek, 3.

[160] Diwan, III, 203.

[161] *Collected Works*, Vol. I, p. 233.

[162] Cf. Ex. 20:8–11, where the Sabbath is based on the motive of *imitatio dei.*

[163] Lev. R., Behukkotai, 6.

[164] See also Is. 61:8.

[165] Sifra, Kedoshim.

[166] Mekilta, Beshalah, 3; Jer. Peah 1:1; Sab. 133b.

[167] Sifre, Ekeb, 49; see also Genesis R. 58:9.

[168] Sotah 14a. The comment is based on Gen. 3:21; 18:1; 25:2, and Deut. 34:5.

[169] Midrash Psalms 25:2. The homily is based on Gen. 3:21; 18:1; 25:2; Deut. 34:5.

[170] Ed. Friedmann, p. 135.

[171] *Aspects of Rabbinic Theology*, pp. 103–104.

[172] H. Deot, 1:4–7.

[173] Kad Hakemah, art., Emunah.

[174] Commentary to Exodus 20:2.

[175] Moral Discourses, Book I, ch. ix.

[176] Ber. 6b.

[177] Sanh. 37a; Abot R. Nathan, I, 31.

[178] Cf. Gen. 17:1 based on the Septuagint.

[179] Decalogue, X, 37–38.

[180] Yoma 85b.

[181] Yoma 8:5–7; Mekilta Ki Tisa; H. Yesode Hatorah 5:6–9.

[182] Ketubot 3a; Tosafot Yeshanim to Yoma 82a.

[183] A. Perls, Der Selbstmord nach der Halacha, Monatsschrift fuer Geschichte und Wissenschaft des Judentums, 1911, pp. 287–295. See Lamentations R. 1:17, ed. Buber, pp. 81–82; Gittin 57b; Mendelssohn, Phaedo.

[184] See Sefer Hasidim, ed. Wistinetzki, 174–175.

[185] Ber. 58a.

[186] De Vita Mosis, I, 439 (Loeb Classics).

[187] Baba Batra 60b; Ab. R. N, I, 5.

[188] Fred. C. Conybeare, Philo about the Contemplative Life, pp. 258ff.

[189] Jer. Nedarim 1:1.

[190] Jer. Kiddushim 4:12.

[191] Jer. Ned. 9:3; H. Deot 3.

[192] Taanit 22b; Tos. Taan. 2:12.

[193] Kuzari, II: 48, tr. Schechter, op. cit., p. 146; Albo, Ikkarim, III:34.

[194] Cf. Paul's view in 1 Corinthians 7:1ff.

[195] H. Ishut 14

[196] See arts. Adultery and Chastity, Jew. Enc., I, 216–18; III, 680–81.

[197] International Critical Commentary, Proverbs, p. 47; K. Kohler, Studies, Addresses and Personal Papers, p. 288.

[198] Kid. 2b.

[199] Eben Haezer 115:7, 8; Miel-ziner, Jewish Laws of Marriage and Divorce, p. 27.

[200] Sanh. 74b.

[201] Gen. R. 8:9; Yeb. 61b–64a; Eben Haezer 25.

[202] Yeb. 63b.

[203] Yoma 1:1.

[204] Gloss to Orah Hayyim 581:1.

[205] See arts. Kaddish, Memorial Service, Mourning, and Yahrzeit in Univ. Jew. Enc.; Rabbis' Manual, pp. 192ff.

[206] Kid. 30b.

[207] For a compendium of rabbinic teachings regarding the family, see Bialik and Rabnitzki, Sefer Haagadah, Bk., V, pp. 47–80; for the mutual obligations of parents and children, see Kid. 29a–33b.

[208] K. Kohler, art. Pharisees, Jew. Enc., IX, p. 662.

[209] Yoma 67b; Sifra to Lev. 20:26; Gen. R. 44:1 and notes by Theodor; Tanhuma, Shemini, 12; Maimonides, Guide, III:26.

[210] Ibid.

[211] Guide, III: 35.

[212] For a discussion of the problem, see C. G. Montefiore, Dr. Wiener on the Dietary Laws, Jewish Quarterly Review (old series), VIII, 392–413, and rejoinders by Frances A. Joseph, ibid., 642–651, and A. Hyamson, Another Word on the Dietary Laws, ibid., IX, 294–310. See also Greenstone-Kohler, arts., Dietary Laws, Jew. Enc., IV, 596–600; M.

Friedlander, *Jewish Religion*, pp. 455–466; J. Hertz, *Pentateuch*, notes to Leviticus 11; S. R. Hirsch, *Nineteen Letters of Ben Uzziel*, tr. by B. Drachman, p. 112; Morris Joseph, *Judaism as Creed and Life*, pp. 234–248; C. G. Montefiore, *Liberal Judaism*, pp. 234–48; K. Kohler, *Jewish Theology*, pp. 451ff.

213 Sifra to Lev. 19:2.

214 Sotah 9:15; Ab. Zarah 20b.

215 Guide, III: 33, tr. Friedlander.

216 Yeb. 20a; Nahmanides to Lev. 19:2.

217 C. G. Montefiore, *Florilegium Philonis*, J.Q.R., o.s., VII, p. 487; Yotzer in the morning service. See Hagigah 12b; Sab. 119b; cf. Gen. R. 3:9; 11:9; Num. R. 13:6.

218 Jer. Peah 1:1; Abot 1:10; Ab. R.N., ed. Schechter, A, 11; B, 21; B. Batra 110a.

219 Pesahim 113a; Kid. 82a; Al Nakawa, Menorat Hamaor, ed. H. G. Enelow, IV, 536–537.

220 Ab. R.N., B, 21; cf. 1:11; Midr. Hagadol, Yitro, 9, where the idea is ascribed to R. Judah Hanasi.

221 See Tanhuma, Vayetze, 13.

222 Ber. 8a.

223 Ketubot 59b.

224 Kid. 29a.

225 Ab. R.N., B, 21; A, 11.

226 Yalkut Eliezer, art., Melachah, 43; Al Nakawa, *op. cit.*, III, 299–304; IV, 536–537.

227 Abot 1:4.

228 Gittin 10b; Baba Kamma 113a; Baba Batra 54b. See Lauterbach, art., Samuel Yarhinaah, *J.E.*, XI, 31; S. Atlas, *Yearbook C.C.A.R.*, 1944, 231–232. On the whole problem see the Book of Daniel; 1 Baruch 1: 11ff.; 111 Maccabees; Antiquities XVII, 2, 4; Leviticus Rabba 23:6; Numbers R. 14:6. Cf. Matthew 22:21; 17:25–27; Luke 23:2; Romans 13:7.

229 George Adam Smith, *The Book of Isaiah*, revised ed., II, pp. 232–233.

230 Art. Righteousness, H.E.R.E., X, 781.

231 G. A. Smith, *op. cit.*, p. 236.

232 *Judaism and Its History*, p. 37.

233 Abot 1:18.

234 Jer. Taan. 4: 2; Sab. 10a; Sanh. 7a.

235 Ab. 5:12.

236 *Ibid.*, 2:17.

237 Ex. R. 22:3.

238 B.K. 113a; Tana Debe Elijahu R. 26. Cf. above on Kiddush Hashem.

239 Hullin 94a.

240 Tos. B.K. 8:3.

241 Ber. 10a.

242 Gen. R. 12:15.

243 Ahad Haam, *Selected Essays*, tr. by Leon Simon, Justice and Mercy, pp. 46ff.

244 W. R. Smith, *Religion of the Semites*, p. 274.

245 W. R. Smith, *Prophets of Israel*, pp. 162ff.; Nelson Glueck, *Das Wort Hesed im alttestamentlicher Sprachgebrauche*.

246 S. R. Driver, *A Critical and*

*Exegetical Commentary on Deuteronomy*, p. xxiv.

247 *Ibid.*, pp. 261f.

248 The Special Laws, I. 294–295, tr. by F. H. Colson, Vol. VII, pp. 269–271; Decalogue, ch. XXII, *ibid.*, pp. 61–63.

249 Against Apion, II, 28–29, tr. Thackeray, Vol. I, pp. 377–379.

250 Philo Judaeus, ed. Yonge, III, On the Virtuous Being also Free, ch. 12. See Secrets of Enoch, 50:3–4.

251 Testament of Twelve Patriarchs, Dan. 5:3; Issachar 5:1; also 7:6; Test. Zeb. 5:1–3; also 7:2; 8:1; Test Benj. 3:3; 10:3.

252 Matt. 22:37–39; Mark 12:29–31; Luke 10:27. In Luke the combination is made by a Pharisee.

253 Sifra to Lev. 19:18; Rashi, *ad loc.*; Jer. Nedar. 9:4; cf. Gen.R. 24.5; Ab. R.Nathan B, 26, p. 53. The Golden Rule in Luke 6:31 is shown by its sequel in vs. 32 to be an application of Lev. 19:18. Matt. 7:12 characterizes the Golden Rule as the sum and substance of the Law and the Prophets. See Abot 3:14; also Gen.R. 34: 6; Mid. Hagadol Lev. 19: 18; Maimonides H. Deot 6: 3; H. Abel 14:1. See art., Charity, Roman, *H.E.R.E.*, III, p. 391.

254 Abot 1:12.

255 W. A. Spooner, art., "Golden Rule," *H.E.R.E.* VI:310–312. G. B. King, the Gold-

en Rule, Journ. Rel. VIII, 268–79.

256 Tobit 4:15–21. Graetz assigns the book of Tobit to the time of Hadrian. Simpson believes that it was written about 170 B.C.E. See his introduction to the Book in Charles' A.P.E., Vol. I, 185. The Aramaic version of the Golden Rule, as given in the book, reads:

ודסנאי לך לחורני לא תעביד.

257 Kohler, in art., Didache, *Jew. Encycl.* IV:585–587. See also Harnack, art., Didache in the New Schaff-Herzog III:422.

258 Cited by Kohler, art., Didache, *ibid.* See his art. "Didascalia," *ibid.*, pp. 588–594. See also E. G. Hirsch's art. "Golden Rule," *Jew. Encycl.* VI:21–22, and Kohler's art. "Brotherly Love," *Jew. Encycl.* III:397–398.

259 Charles, *Religious Development between the Old and the New Testaments*, p. 141; Bousset, *Religion des Judentums*, 2nd ed., p. 113.

260 Schechter, *Studies in Judaism*, 2nd series, p. 117.

261 Sirach 28:2–3. This rendering by Schechter (*ibid.*, p. 94) is better than Box and Oesterley's in Charles' A.P.E.

262 T. Jos. 17:2–3; cf. T. Zeb. 8:5; T. Benj. 4:1–4; 5:4b; 8:1–2; T. Gad. 8:6–7; 5:1–5; 6:1–7; cf. T. Benj. 3:4b–5. See Charles' discussion of the Ethics of forgiveness in

Judaism and Christianity, in his Introduction to the Testaments of the Twelve Patriarchs, A.P.E., p. 293, where he misrepresents Judaism. See also Fragments of a Zadokite Work 9:50–10:6.

263 De Humanitate, 15; cited by Charles, *Rel. Development bet. the Old and New Testaments*, p. 149; cf. 2 Enoch 50:4 (a).

264 Arachin 16b.

265 Abot 1:6; 2:5.

266 Sab. 149b.

267 Yoma 8:7; 87a.

268 Megillah 28b; Sab. 151b; Yoma 87b; cf. Matthew 6:12.

269 Yoma 22a; Sab. 88b; Yalkut Shimeoni, 613.

270 Ber. 17a; *Prayer Book*, ed. Singer, p. 54.

271 B. Kamma 93a.

272 Derech Eretz, ed. M. Higger, pp. 117, 312.

273 Cited by Schechter, *Studies in Judaism*, 2nd series, p. 168.

274 Shaare Kedushah, I:5.

275 *Sefer Haberit Hashalem* by R. Phineas b. Meir of Wilna, II, ch. 13:1–12, 18; B. Metzia 62a.

276 Mesilat Yesharim, 11.

277 See Mendelssohn's *Commentary to Leviticus* 19:18.

278 Betzah 32b; Ket. 8b; Gen. R. 58:9; Schechter, *op. cit.*, pp. 215–216; 226–227.

279 B. Metz. 13b.

280 *Spirits of the Corn and of the Wild*, I, p. 234ff.; A. S. Peake, *A Commentary of the Bible*, p. 207.

281 Abot 1:2.

282 Suk. 49b; Ber. 18a; B. Batra 9a–11a.

283 Ket. 68a; Tos. Peah 4:20; Eccl. R. 7:4.

284 Sifre, Deut. 210; Sotah 9:6; 14b. See story of Nahum of Gimzo, Taanit 21a.

285 Yoreh Deah 254.

286 De Caritate, 17–18.

287 Apion II; 29.

288 Git. 61a; H. Matnot Aniyim 7:7.

289 Suk. 49b; Tos. Peah 4:19; Mid. Psalms to 118:19; cf. Mt. 25:34f.

290 Based on B. Batra 110a; Pes. 113a; cf. Sab. 118a. See Waxman, *op. cit.*, 4315.

291 Jer. Shekalim 5:6; H. Matnot Aniyim, 10.

292 Sanh. 99a.

293 H. Teshubah 8:7; 9:2; H. Melachim 12.

294 Das Gottesreich, *Juedische Schriften*, III, p. 173.

## NOTES TO CHAPTERS XIII–XV

295 Abot 1:2

296 Jer. Meg. 3:1.

297 Singer, *Prayer Book*, p. 4; Ber. 11b.

298 *Ibid.*, pp. 39–40; 131.

299 Peah 1:1; Singer, *op. cit.*, p. 5.

300 Meg. 16b.

301 Hor. 13a.

302 Mekilta, Bahodesh 2; Al Nakawa, Menorat Hamaor III, 374–375.

303 Men. 99b; see also Mid. Tehilim 1:17.

304 Hilchot Talmud Torah, 1, 8–10.
305 Taan. 30a.
306 Abot 6:7; Sab. 31a.
307 Ex. R. 25:9; Men. Ham. III, p. 216.
308 Sifre Deut. 47; Eccl. R. 1:1.
309 Kid. I:10.
310 Yeb. 109b.
311 Ab. Z. 17b.
312 Lam. R., Introd. 2; Pesikta R. Kahana, Eicha, ed. Buber, p. 216; Jer. Hag. 1:7.
313 Eccl. 12:13; Seder Elijahu Zutta 14; ed. Friedmann, p. 196.
314 Sotah 21a; Seder Elijahu Rabba 3.
315 Abot 5:25.
316 R. W. Frank, Religious Education, Nov., 1927, p. 957.
317 Prolegomena to Ethics, ch. I, par. 108, p. 111.
318 Manual for Training in Worship, 1926, p. 1; cited Rel. Ed., Nov., 1927, p. 247.
319 Abot 4:4.
320 Apion II, 16–17 (171–74).
321 Makkot 3:16.
322 Menahot 43b.
323 Sefer Hahinuch, commandment 16.
324 Tanhuma (Buber), Shemini, 12; Sifra to Lev. 20:26; Mid. Psalms to 9:2; see J. Z. Lauterbach, The Ethics of the Halachah, Yearbook, C.C.A.R., XXXIII, pp. 259ff. For a description of Jewish ceremonies see William Rosenau, Jewish Ceremonial Institutions and Customs, 1903; Abraham Z. Idelsohn, The Ceremonies

of Judaism, 1930; Louis Dembitz, Jewish Services in the Synagogue and Home, 1898.
325 Francis Thompson.
326 Louis Finkelstein, art., Ceremonial Law, Universal Jewish Encyclopedia, 3, 94–103; Mordecai Kaplan, Judaism as a Civilization (see index under Ceremonies); Israel H. Levinthal, Judaism, pp. 91–120; K. Kohler, Hebrew Union College and other Addresses, The Origin and Function of Ceremonies in Judaism, pp. 297–322; D. Philipson, The Reform Movement in Judaism (see index under Ceremonies).
327 Erubin 31a; Rosh Hashanah 28a.
328 Guide for the Perplexed, III, 27; The Eight Chapters, ed. Gorfinkle, ch. 6.
329 The Ethics of Judaism, II, pp. 270–271.
330 Menahot 43b.
331 James, Psychology, II, p. 579; Selected Papers on Philosophy, p. 83.
332 Horace Bridges, The Standard, 1932, p. 138.
333 Studies in Judaism, II, pp. 178–179.
334 See New Standard Dictionary under Crime, Vice and Sin.
335 Judah Kaufman, in his English-Hebrew Dictionary, gives for Crime the words: het, avon, pesha, zadon, ma'al resha, and mered. For Vice he gives: het, aberah,

*avon, rish'ah, hefkerut, peritzut, perikat 'ol, mum,* and *dofi.* Eliminating a few questionable words which he uses under Vice, we find all the rest also used for Sin, viz., *het, hataah, hattat, avon, pesha, zadon, shegagah, mishgeh, aberah, kalkalah, sarah, surhan, hobah.* The last four are not as common as the rest.

336 *English Synonyms,* pp. 332–33.

337 R. Otto, *The Idea of the Holy,* pp. 55–56; *Religious Essays,* p. 1; G. F. Moore, *Judaism,* I, p. 401.

338 *Greece and Babylon,* p. 152, cited in *H.E.R.E.,* XI, p. 550.

339 Cf. Is. 6:5; 1:16; Jer. 2:22; Ezek. 22:24ff.; 36:25ff.; 37:23.

340 See N. Soederblom, art., Holiness, *H.E.R.E.,* VI, p. 734.

341 *Ibid.,* XI, p. 552.

342 *Jewish Theology,* p. 242.

343 Yoma 39a.

344 Sotah 3b.

345 Sabbath 55a.

346 Baba Metzia 33b.

347 F. R. Tennant, Journal of Religion, V, p. 156. See also his *Origin and Propagation of Sin,* and his *The Sources of the Doctrine of the Fall and Original Sin.*

348 Yoma 69a.

349 Sukkah 52a.

350 Sotah 3a. See Evelyn Underhill, *Life of the Spirit,* pp. 64ff.

351 S. H. Langdon, *H.E.R.E.,* V, p. 640.

352 *Ibid.,* p. 654; see also W. R. Smith, *op. cit.,* pp. 353ff.; Ezekiel Kaufman, *op. cit.,* I, p. 546, n. 11.

353 A. B. Davidson, *Theology of the O.T.,* p. 329.

354 H. Schultz, American Journal of Theology, IV, pp. 265–266; S. R. Driver, *Book of Leviticus,* p. 78.

355 Sirach, ch. 50.

356 W. R. Smith, *Rel. Sem.,* p. 434.

357 See Ex. 34:28; Deut. 9:9; 1 Kings 19:18; Dan. 9:3; 10:2f.

358 I. Benzinger, art., Fasting, *Enc. Biblica,* II, 1506–8.

359 See also verses 3 and 14 and notes by Box and Oesterley in Charles' Apocrypha and Pseudepigrapha, I, pp. 324–326; Tobit 4:10; 12:9; cf. Deut. 29:13.

360 Also Is. 42:1–4; 49:1–7; Zech. 12:10.

361 Sotah 14a.

362 Abot of R. Nathan, B, ch. 8.

363 Berachot 15a; 26b; 32b; Taanit 2b.

364 Pesikta deRab Kahana 141a–142b; Leviticus R. 7:2.

365 Taanit 16a, ed. Malter; Jer. Pes. 6:1; cf. Sirach 34:25; Jer. Ta'anit 2:1.

366 Gittin 55a; Eduyot 7:9.

367 Abot of Rabbi Nathan, I, 7; cf. antinomian use of Hosea 6:6 in Matthew 9:13; 12:7.

368 Hagigah 27a; Menahot 97a.

369 See Prov. 21:3; Sukkah 49b.

370 Jer. Ta'anit 2:1.

371 Ber. 32b; also Ber. 17a; Sefer Hasidim, ed. Freimann-Wistinetzki, pp. 40–41.

372 Jer. Yoma 8:7.

373 Yoma 85b; Shebuot 13a; Keritot 7a; Maimonides, H. Teshubah, chs. 3–4.

374 Sifre, Deut., ed. Friedmann, 73b; see Leviticus R. 20:12; Eccl. R. 3:18.

375 G. Scholem, Major Trends in Jewish Mysticism, p. 103.

376 Hayim Vital, Etz Hayyim, Introd.; E. Vidash, Reshit Hochmah, Shaar Hateshubah, 5.

377 The Standard, 1934, Vol. XX, p. 145.

378 See note to Adler-Davis, Service of the Synagogue, Day of Atonement, part 1, p. 79.

379 Sab. 32a; Yoma 36b; Torat Haadam, Shaar Hasof; Singer, Prayer Book, p. 317, and Abrahams' Historical and Explanatory Notes; Rabbis' Manual, pp. 57–60.

380 Likkute Muharan 4a.

381 Varieties, p. 126; Spinoza, Tract on God, Man and Happiness, Bk. II, 10. In his Theologico-Political Tractate, ch. 14, he includes forgiveness and repentance among the principles of universal faith.

382 Abodah Zarah 55a.

383 Jewish Theology, p. 246.

384 Pes. 54a; Ned. 39b; Midr. Psalms to Ps. 74.

385 Yoma 86ab.

386 Ber. 34b.

387 Tanhuma, ad loc., and Yalkut to Leviticus, No. 480.

388 The Truth of Religion, pp. 496–497.

389 For the First Day. See S. Baer, Abodat Yisrael, p. 134.

390 The Truth of Religion, p. 497.

391 Tamid 31a. Cf. Mt. 10:39; 16:25; Lk. 9:24.

392 Art., Fasting, Jew. Enc., V, 347–349; H. Taaniyot; Shulhan Aruch, Orah Hayyim, 549–580; for fasting on the ten days of penitence, see L. Ginzberg's Ginze Schechter, II, 541–542, 564–566; Sefer Rabiah, ed. Optovitzer, II, 246–247.

393 Sifre, Deut. 11:13; Taan. 2a.

394 Ber. 26b; 32b.

395 Sotah 38b.

396 Horodetzki, Torat R. Nahman, Tephillah.

397 H.E.R.E., X, p. 191.

398 Golden Sequence, p. 157.

399 The Religious Sentiment, p. 118.

400 Religion within the Limits of Pure Reason; cited by Heiler, Prayer, pp. 93–94.

401 Union Prayerbook Version.

402 Singer, Authorized Daily Prayer Book, p. 69.

403 See Josephus, Ant. IV. 212; also Is. 43:7ff.; Ps. 30; 1 Chron. 29:10–19.

404 Lev. R. 9:7.

405 Self-Reliance.

406 In Israel Abrahams' Ethical Wills, I, p. 147; see also Kuzari, III, 17–18; Lewin, Otzar Geonim, Rosh Hashanah, p. 83. Citation of

Saadia's statement regarding the seven reasons for the rejection of man's prayers; Emunot Vedeot V:6.

[407] Ex. R. 22:3.
[408] B. Batra 10a; Num. R. 2:11; Megillah 17b; see also Sanh. 6b; Sefer Hasidim, 1023, p. 257.
[409] See Psalms 78, 105, 111, etc.
[410] Pss. 15, 24, 25, etc.
[411] Seder Rab Amram Hashalem I, p. 40.
[412] S. S. Cohon, art., Kavvanah, *Univ. Jew. Enc.*, 6, 346–348.
[413] *Function of Religion*, p. 99.
[414] Tos. Ber. 7:5; Hobot Halebabot, Heshbon Hanefesh, 3.
[415] *Op. cit.*, pp. 36–37; Shulhan Aruch, Orah Hayyim 98.
[416] Apion, II; 197.
[417] Deut. R., Nitzabim 8:1.
[418] Sermon, What Would You Have Us Do? p. 17.
[419] *The Religious Sentiment*, p. 131.
[420] Mekilta, Beshalah, 3; B. Batra 123a; Tanhuma, Beshalah, 3.
[421] *Reality in Worship*, p. 230.
[422] Guide, III: 51, tr. Friedlander, pp. 386–387.

[423] Cited by Evelyn Underhill, *The Golden Sequence*, p. 10.
[424] Pauline.
[425] Winfield, Masnavi, p. 192, cited by Soederblom, *The Living God*, p. 31.
[426] Frank Granger, *The Soul of a Christian*, p. 202, cited *ibid.*
[427] J. F. Astie, *Pensees de Pascal*, cited *ibid.*
[428] Ber. 1:4; 5:5; Tos. Ber. 1:4ff.; Jer. Ber. 1:8.
[429] Abot 2:4; cf. Ber. 29b–30a.
[430] Ber. 8a.
[431] Ber. 6a, 8a.
[432] F. Heiler, *Prayer*, p. 67.
[433] Ueber Juden und Judentum, p. 8.
[434] Abot 2:18.
[435] Sanh. 106b.
[436] Ber. 30b.
[437] Ber. 13a, 33a; Sotah 33a–33.
[438] Sefer Hasidim, ed. Wistinetzki, par. 1590, p. 389.
[439] A. Kahana, *Sefer Hahasidut*, p. 344.
[440] Sefer Hamiddot, Tephillah.
[441] *The Life of Prayer*, p. 53.
[442] *Reality in Worship*, pp. 312–313.
[443] L. Ginzberg, Adoration, Forms of, *Jew. Encycl.*, I, 208–211.
[444] Arachin 11a.
[445] Ber. 28b.

# GLOSSARY

AB, fifth month of the Hebrew calendar.

ABODAH, *worship;* the first in the final group of benedictions in the 'Amidah; the service of the High Priest as restated in the Musaph of Yom Kippur.

ABODAH ZARAH, *foreign worship;* idolatry; name of a tractate of the Talmud.

ABOT, *fathers;* a tractate of the Mishnah, known also as Pirke Abot, "Chapters of the Fathers" or "Sayings of the Fathers."

ABOT OF RABBI NATHAN, a supplementary treatise to Abot, ascribed to R. Nathan.

AHAD HAAM, *one of the people;* pen name of Asher Ginzberg (1856–1927).

AL HET, *for the sin;* opening words of confession in the Yom Kippur liturgy.

ALENU, opening word of the Adoration, "It is our duty to praise the Lord." See Malchuyot.

'AMIDAH, *standing;* applied to the Eighteen Benedictions because they are recited standing.

ASHAMNU, *we are guilty;* opening word of a confession of sin.

ASHKENAZI, *German;* based on Gen. 10:3; applied to Jews of Central European origin and to their liturgy.

'AZAZEL, *scapegoat.* See Lev. 16.

BERACHOT (sing., *berachah*), *benedictions;* tractate of the Talmud.

BET HAKENESET, *house of assembly;* Bet Hamidrash, *house of study;* Bet Hatephillah, *house of prayer;* names for synagogue, expressive of its functions.

BIRCHAT HAGOMEL, benediction of thanksgiving for deliverance from peril.

BIRCHAT HAMAZON, benediction after meals.

BORCHU, *praise ye;* opening word of call to public worship.

CABBALAH, *tradition;* mystic Jewish lore; Cabbalist, an adherent of the Cabbalah.

382

CODES, Rabbinic compilations of the legal contents of the Talmud in systematic form.

DERECH ERETZ, *way of the land;* decency; moral behavior; ethics.

DERECH ERETZ RABBA, an extra Talmudic tractate dealing with moral conduct. The shorter tractate is known as Derech Eretz Zutta.

'EIN YAACOB, *Fountain of Jacob;* a compilation of the Haggadic material contained in the Babylonian Talmud by R. Jacob Ibn Habib (1480–1545).

EMUNOT VEDEOT, *Religious Principles and Opinions;* a theological treatise by R. Saadia Gaon, 933.

ESSENES, an ascetic Jewish sect, which appeared in Maccabean times, and continued until the fall of Jerusalem in 70 C.E. It was dedicated to saintliness, celibacy and communal ownership of property.

GEMARA (Aramaic), *completion;* supplement; study; applied to the discussions of the Mishnah in the schools of Palestine and Babylonia. Hence Palestinian Gemara and Babylonian Gemara. See Talmud.

GITTIN (sing., *get*), *bills of divorce;* tractate of the Talmud.

GRACE, God's abounding love dispensed to man without regard to his merits.

HABDALAH, *separation;* benediction recited over a beverage as part of the ceremony marking the conclusion of the Sabbath and the festivals to distinguish between the sacred (kodesh) and the ordinary (hol) day.

HAGGADAH, *narrative;* the non-legal parts of the Midrashim and the Talmud. Haggadah shel pesah, ritual for the home service for the Passover built around the narrative of the Exodus; known also as Seder Haggadah.

HAGIOGRAPHA (Greek), *sacred writings;* the third part of the Hebrew canon.

HALACHAH, *going;* way or rule of conduct; practice; Rabbinical law; the legal portions of the Midrashim and the Talmud.

HALLEL, *praise;* Psalms of praise sung on Rosh Hodesh, the festivals and Hanukkah, viz., 113–118; the great Hallel, Ps. 136.

HANUKKAH, *dedication;* Feast of Lights, commemorating the Maccabean victory in 165 B.C.E., observed from the 25th of Kislev to the 2nd of Tebet.

HAPHTARAH, *conclusion;* prophetic lesson recited after the reading of the Pentateuchal lesson on the Sabbath and the Holy Days.

HASIDIM (sing., *Hasid*), *pious* (often referred to as Hasideans); men of piety in pre-Christian centuries, who emphasized the rule of hesed or love toward God and man as well as the study and practice of the Law.

HASIDISM, mystical movement in modern Judaism, founded by R. Israel Baal Shem Tob in the 18th century.

HESHVAN, eighth month of the Hebrew calendar.

HILCHOT DEOT, *principles of Moral Opinions;* the second part of Maimonides' Code dealing with ethics.

HILLUL HASHEM, *profanation of God's name;* a public disgrace.

HOBOT HALEBABOT, *duties of the heart;* a theological and ethical treatise by Bahia Ibn Pakkudah (11th cent.).

HOSHANA RABBA, name of the seventh day of Sukkot.

HUKKIM, *statutes;* transcending the requirements of reason.

IYAR, second month of the Hebrew calendar.

KADDISH (Aramaic), *holy;* doxology based on Daniel 2:20. The opening words are adapted from Ezekiel 38:23. It is inserted in certain parts of the service, and is recited by mourners (Kaddish yatom, orphan's kaddish) in memory of the dead.

KAPPAROT, *atonements;* a ceremony performed on the eve of the Day of Atonement in which men take roosters and women chickens and, circling them around their heads, recite Biblical verses and a formula transferring their personal sins upon the fowls. After this ceremony the fowls are slaughtered and their meat or the value thereof is given to the poor. Money may be used in place of a fowl. This reversion to the old "scapegoat" procedure evoked the protests of leading Rabbinical authorities, and has been abandoned by both Reform and Conservative Jews.

KASHER, *fit;* applied to food which is ritually proper from the standpoint of traditional Judaism.

KASHRUT, *fitness;* applied to objects and persons, and principally to food, which meet the requirements of traditional Judaism.

KAVVANAH, *intention;* devotion; attuning the mind; applied also to special meditations before performing certain religious acts.

KEDUSHAH, *holiness;* a sanctification of God inserted between the second and third benedictions during the public recitation of the 'Amidah in the Shaharit, Musaph, and Minhah services. Its nucleus consists of Isaiah 6:3, Ezekiel 3:12 and Psalm 146:10.

KETUBIM, *writings;* Hagiographa, the third part of the Biblical canon.

KETUBOT, *marriage contracts;* a tractate of the Talmud dealing with dower and marriage settlements.

KIDDUSH, *sanctification* of the Sabbath and festivals, spoken over a beverage or bread.

KIDDUSH HAHAYYIM, investing life with sanctity; way of consecrated living.

KIDDUSH HASHEM, *sanctifying the name* of God by one's conduct; applied also to martyrdom, the supreme testimony to faith.

KIDDUSHIN, *consecration;* setting apart as holy or inviolable; marriage ceremony; name of Talmudic treatise.

KIPPUR (pl., Kippurim), Atonement.

KITZUR SHULHAN ARUCH, Abridged Code of Jewish Law by R. Solomon Ganzfried (1804–1886).

LISHMAH, *for its name;* doing a thing for its own sake rather than with an ulterior motive.

MAAMADOT, *posts;* groups of lay representatives from the outlying communities sent to the Temple in Jerusalem to stand by the divisions of priests and Levites (mishmarot— guards) during the services. The name is also used for special readings from the Bible and Rabbinic literature supplementary to the morning service.

MAARIB, evening service.

MAHARSHA, abbreviation of the name of R. Solomon Edels, Talmudic commentator (1555–1631).

MALCHUYOT, *Kingship;* the first of the intermediary benedictions of the Musaph 'Amidah for Rosh Hashanah on the theme of God's sovereignty. It opens with the 'Alenu and contains ten verses from the Pentateuch, Psalms and Prophets, which proclaim God as King.

MEGILLAH, *scroll;* applied to the Song of Songs, Ruth, Lamentations, and Ecclesiastes, and especially to Esther; name of Talmudic treatise.

MENAHOT (sing., minhah), *meal offerings;* name of a Talmudic treatise.

MENORAT HAMAOR, *Lamp of Illumination;* title of a work by Israel Al Nakawa (14th cent.) and also by Isaac Aboab (15th cent.).

MEZUZAH, *door-post;* applied to the roll of parchment inscribed with Deut. 6:4–9 and 11:13–20 and fastened in a wood or metal container to the upper right-hand post of the entrance of a Jewish home.

MIDRASH, *exposition* of Scripture with the view to deducing haggadic or halachic teaching.

MINHAG, *custom;* rite; minhag ashkenaz, German rite; minhag sepharad, Spanish rite.

MISHNAH, *repetition;* teaching; collection of legal teachings by R. Jehudah Hanasi (about 220 C.E.) which forms the basis of the Talmud. It is divided into six orders, and subdivided into tractates, chapters and paragraphs, which are referred to likewise as Mishnahs.

MITZVAH, *commandment;* also an obligation; a good deed.

MUSAPH, *additional offering* for the Sabbath and the festivals (Num. 28–29) and applied to the additional services of the synagogue on these days in substitution for the sacrifices.

MUSAR, *chastisement;* moral discipline; correction; ethics.

NEBIIM, *Prophets;* the second part of the Biblical canon.

NEILAH, *closing* of the Temple gates; closing service of the Day of Atonement.

NEZIKIN, *damages;* an order of the Mishnah devoted to civil law.

NOMISM, from the Greek, nomos, law. Emphasis on religion as law and strict adherence thereto.

NUMINOUS, coined by Rudolf Otto from the Latin, numen, divine, to express the unique category of religious value transcending ethics and reason; the mysterious object of religious apprehension.

ORAL LAW, Torah shebeal peh, known also as Tradition. By the side of the Written Law or Torah shebiktab, in the belief of the rabbis, God revealed to Israel at Sinai a body of oral interpretations and teachings supplementary to it. It has developed through the centuries and was embodied into the Midrashim and the Talmud.

ORHOT TZADDIKIM, *Paths of the Righteous;* a 14th century work on moral conduct.

OSIRIS, Egyptian god of the Nile, the underworld and the sky.

PARASHA, *section;* one of the 54 parts into which the Pentateuch is divided.

PARUSH (pl., Perushim), *separated;* used for Pharisee and also for ascetic. See Pharisees.

PERISHUT, *separateness;* asceticism.

PESAH, *Passover;* observed in memory of the liberation of the Israelites from Egyptian slavery, from the 15th through the 21st of Nisan. Orthodox Jews observe an eighth day.

PHARISEES, adherents of the party which appeared after the Maccabean revolt and became the dominant force in Judaism. They sought to raise all Jews to the religious level of the priests, emphasizing ceremonial purity and strict regard for all the requirements of the Written Torah as interpreted by them in the light of their Oral Tradition. They kept themselves apart not only from the gentiles but also from fellow Jews who refused to follow their interpretations of the requirements of the Law.

PIYYUT (pl., Piyyutim), from the Greek, poetry; refers to medieval liturgic poetry.

PRIESTLY CODE, the stratum of the Pentateuch dealing with genealogies, chronologies, sacrificial cult, the tabernacle, priesthood, the Sabbath, circumcision, the Passover, the Day of Atonement, etc., contained in scattered passages in Genesis and Exodus, principally Ex. 25-31; 35-40; Lev. 1-16; most of Num.; Deut. 31-34 and some sections in Joshua. The Holiness Code, Lev. 17-26, is incorporated in the Priestly Code.

PURIM, *Feast of Lots;* the 14th of Adar. Shushan Purim, the 15th of Adar. See Esther 9:21-28.

RAB, *teacher, master.*

RABBI, *my teacher, my master.*

RASHI, initials of Rabbi Solomon, son of Isaac of Troyes (1040-1105). Commentator of the Bible and Talmud.

RESHIT HOCHMAH, *Beginning of Wisdom;* a Cabbalistic work by R. Elijah de Vidas (16th cent.).

ROSH HASHANAH, New Year, the first of Tishri, ushers in the ten days of repentance which end with Yom Kippur. Orthodox Jews observe two days of Rosh Hashanah. Name of tractate of the Talmud.

ROSH HODESH, the first of the month. In months containing 30 days, the 30th is considered as the first day of Rosh Hodesh.

SABBATH, the seventh day of the week ordained as a day of rest from physical labor and of sanctification. Gen. 2:1-3; Ex. 20:8-11; Dt. 5:12-15.

SACRAMENT, in Christianity an outward sign or channel of divine grace. It has no exact parallel in Judaism.

SADDUCEES, from the Hebrew Tzedukim or B'nai Zadok. A Jewish party dominated by the priestly aristocracy, which descended from Zadok, the head priest under David and Solomon. Opposed the Pharisaic emphasis on the Oral Law as equally binding as the Written Law.

SANHEDRIN, Greek Synedrion; the supreme court and the high council of the Jewish state. A tractate of the Talmud.

SEDER (pl., sedarim), *order;* applied also to the home service for the eve of Passover. See Haggadah.

SEFER HASIDIM, *Book of the Pious;* an ethical work by Jehudah Hasid (12th cent.).

SELIHOT, Propitiatory prayers and poems for penitential days.

SHAARE KEDUSHAH, *Gates of Holiness;* a Cabbalistic work on ethics by R. Hayyim Vital (1543-1620).

SHABUOT, Feast of Weeks, Pentecost, observed on the 6th of Sivan. Orthodoxy requires the observance of an additional day.

SHAHARIT, morning service.

SHECHINAH, *dwelling;* Divine Presence.

SHEHITA, ritual slaughter of animals and birds.

SHEMA, *hear;* opening word of the Jewish confession of faith, consisting of three passages. Deut. 6:4–9; 11:13–21 and Num. 15:37–41.

SHEMONEH ESREH, *Eighteen Benedictions.* See 'Amidah.

SHEMONEH PERAKIM, *Eight Chapters;* introduction to the commentary on Abot by Maimonides (1135–1204), devoted to psychology and ethics.

SHOFAR, *ram's horn* used in the service for the New Year.

SHOFAROT, third intermediary benediction in the Musaph 'Amidah for Rosh Hashanah, consisting of an introduction and ten verses from the Pentateuch, Psalms and Prophets, recalling the blasts of the Shofar during the revelation at Sinai and referring to the sounds of the Shofar that shall herald the Messianic redemption in the future.

SHUL (Yiddish), synagogue.

SHULHAN ARUCH, *Arranged Table;* Rabbinical code compiled by Joseph Caro (1488–1575).

SHUTAPH, *associate;* co-worker; Shutaph lehakadosh boruch hu, *co-worker with God.*

SIDDUR, prayer book.

SIFRA, SIPHRA, *the book;* a halachic Midrash on Leviticus.

SIFRE, SIPHRE, *the book of;* a halachic Midrash on Numbers and Deuteronomy.

SUKKAH, *booth; Tabernacle;* name of a tractate of the Talmud.

SUKKOT, feast of Tabernacles, from 15th to the 21st of Tishri, followed by Shemini Atzeret, the *Eighth Day of Assembly,* and Simhat Torah, *Rejoicing in the Law.*

SYNAGOGUE, Greek, assembly; building or place of meeting for Jewish worship, religious instruction and social work. A Jewish religious community. See Bet Hakeneset.

TA'ANIT, *fast;* name of Talmudic tractate.

TAHANUN, *supplication for favor;* penitential prayers added to the traditional week-day, morning and afternoon services after the 'Amidah. A longer form of the Tahanun is added to the morning service on Monday and on Thursday.

TALLIT, prayer-shawl worn by adult males in traditional morning services.

TALMID HACHAM, *a disciple of the wise;* a scholar.

TALMUD, *Study* of the Law, combines Mishnah and Gemara. Palestinian Talmud (Jerushalmi) compiled about the end of the 4th century; the Babylonian Talmud (Babli), end of the fifth century.

TALMUD TORAH, *study of Torah;* applied also to a community Hebrew school.

TARGUM, Aramaic version of the Pentateuch or the Bible.

TASHLICH, *thou shalt cast;* opening word of Micah 7:19 which gives the name to the ceremony of casting away sin into flowing waters on the afternoon of the first day of Rosh Hashanah. The ceremony is disregarded by both Reform and Conservative Judaism.

TEHINNAH (pl., Tehinnot), private devotion.

TEPHILLAH, *prayer;* also the central prayer of the liturgy, the 'Amidah. Tephillah belahash, silent prayer; Tephillah betzibbur, public prayer.

TEPHILLIN, *phylacteries;* parchments inscribed with four texts (Exodus 13:1-10; 11-16; Deut. 6:4-9 and 11:13-20) encased in two leather cubicles. These are attached by means of leather straps to the left arm and to the head and worn during morning service on week-days.

TEREPHA, *torn* by wild beasts; applied to all food which is regarded unfit from the standpoint of traditional Judaism.

TESHUBAH, *repentance;* Asseret Yeme Teshubah, the ten days of repentance.

THERAPEUTAE, a body of Jewish ascetics near Alexandria in Egypt, in the first century B.C.E. It included both men and women. See Philo's essay on The Contemplative Life.

TIKKUN, order of readings from the Bible and Rabbinic literature for the nights of the Seventh Day Pesah, Shabuot, and Hoshana Rabba.

TIKKUN MIDDOT HANEPHESH, *Improvement of the Qualities of the Soul;* an ethical treatise by Solomon ibn Gabirol (1021-1058).

TISH'A BEAB, Ninth of Ab, fast in commemoration of the fall of Jerusalem.

TISHRI, seventh month of the Hebrew calendar.

TOMER DEBORAH, *Palm of Deborah;* a Cabbalistic work on ethics by R. Moses Cordovera (16th cent.).

TORAH, *Religious teaching;* revelation, inadequately represented by "Law"; the Pentateuch; also the entire body of Jewish religious knowledge.

TOSEPHTA, *addition* or supplement to the Mishnah; composed of related teachings and divided into the same orders, tractates and chapters.

TUR YOREH DEAH, the second section of R. Jacob ben Asher's Code ("The Four Rows") dealing with ritual law (14th cent.).

TZEDAKAH, *righteousness;* charity.

TZITZIT, *fringes* attached to the four corners of the tallit, in accordance with Num. 15:37ff.

V'HAKOHANIM, *and the priests;* the opening word of a section of Mishnah Yoma 6:2 used in the 'Abodah of Yom Kippur.

VIDDUY, *confession.*

YAHRZEIT (Yiddish), anniversary of the day of death of parents or other relatives, etc.

YEBAMOT, *sisters-in-law;* a tractate of the Talmud dealing in large part with levirate marriage, based on Deut. 25:5–10.

YESHIBAH, Talmudical high school, academy.

YETZER, *inclination* for good (yetzer tob); inclination for evil (yetzer hara).

YIREAH, *fear;* solemn awe, reverence; yireat shamayim, fear of Heaven; reverence for God; religion; Yireat Hakabod, *fear of the Glory,* i.e., of God.

YOM KIPPUR, Day of Atonement, the 10th of Tishri.

YOMA, Talmudic tractate devoted to the Day of Atonement.

YOTZER, *creator;* first benediction before the Shema in the morning service referring to God as creator.

ZECHUT, *merit;* Zechut abot, merit of the fathers.

ZICHRONOT, *remembrance;* the second of the intermediary benedictions of the 'Amidah in the Musaph for Rosh Hashanah, consisting of an introduction and ten verses from the Pentateuch, Psalms and Prophets, expressing God's omniscient providence.

# BIBLIOGRAPHY

### Religion in Life and Life of Faith

#### 1. General

Alexander, Franz, and Thomas French, *Psychoanalytic Therapy, Principles and Application*, 1946.

Brill, A. A., *Lectures on Psychoanalytic Psychiatry*, 1947.

Brown, William, *Mind, Medicine and Metaphysics*, 1936.

Deutsch, Albert, *The Mentally Ill in America: A History of Their Care and Treatment from Colonial Times*, 1937.

Ferguson, Charles, *The Confusion of Tongues*, 1929.

Freud, *General Introduction to Psychoanalysis*, 1920.

*Hastings' Encyclopedia of Religion and Ethics*, arts., Disease and Medicine, Faith-Healing, Psycho-Therapeutics.

James, William, *The Varieties of Religious Experience*, 1922.

King, Irving, The Religious Significance of the Psycho-Therapeutic Movement, *American Journal of Theology*, XV, pp. 533–551.

Stolz, Karl R., *The Psychology of Religious Living*, 1937.

Wise, Caroll A., *Religion in Illness and Health*, 1942.

Worcester, McComb and Coriat, *Religion and Medicine*, 1905.

Worcester and McComb, *Body, Mind and Spirit*, 1931.

#### 2. Jewish

Brim, C. J., *Medicine in the Bible*, 1936.

Friedenwald, Harry, *Jews in Medicine*, 2 Vols., 1944.

*Jewish Encyclopedia*, arts., Amulets, Medicine, Optimism and Pessimism.

Katzenelson, I. L., *Hatalmud Vehachmat Harefuah*, 1928.

Perlman, M., *Midrash Harefuah*, 2 Parts, 1926–1929.

Preuss, Julius, *Biblisch-Talmudische Medizin*, 1911.

*Universal Jewish Encyclopedia*, arts., Eugenics, Hygiene, Medicine.

*Yearbook of the Central Conference of American Rabbis*, Vol. XXII, pp. 300–318, Maurice Lefkowitz, The Attitude of Judaism toward Christian Science; Vol. XXXVIII, pp. 165–193, Report by Louis Witt and Discussion on the Relation of the Synagogue to Healing, and papers by Dr. Bernard Glueck, Clifton Harby Levy, and H. G. Enelow, *ibid.*, pp. 344–368.

### THE ETHICAL LIFE: JEWISH

ABELSON, J., *Hastings' Encyclopedia of Religion and Ethics*, X, art., Righteousness (Jewish), pp. 807–810.

ABRAHAMS, ISRAEL, *Hebrew Ethical Wills*, 2 Vols., 1926.

——, *Studies in Pharisees and the Gospels*, II, pp. 138–182, 1924.

AHAD HAAM, *Al Parashat Derachim*, II, pp. 79–90 (Hamusar Haleumi); IV, pp. 38–58 (Al Shete Haseippim), 1899, 1910.

BAECK, BERNFELD, ELBOGEN, etc., *Die Lehren des Judentums*, 5 Parts, 1922–1929. (The first part translated into English by Koller, *The Foundation of Jewish Ethics*.)

BAECK, LEO, *Essence of Judaism*, 1936.

BAECK, S., Die Sittenlehre vom 13 bis 18 Jahrhundert, in Winter und Wuensche, *Die Juedische Literatur*, III, 627–51.

BIALIK, H. N., and I. H. RABNITZKI, *Sefer Haagadah*, Vols. II–III, 1934.

BLOCH, M., *Die Ethik der Halacha*, 1886.

BUBER, MARTIN, Nachahmung Gottes, in *Kampf um Israel*, 1933.

BUNIN, H. I., *Limmude Hayahadut: Hamishpaha, Hatzedek, Haahaba*, 1917.

COHEN, A., *Everyman's Talmud*, chaps. III, V–VII, 1934.

COHEN, HERMANN, *Juedische Schriften*, 3 Vols., 1924.

——, *Religion der Vernunft*, chaps. XVIII–XXII, 1919.

COHON, SAMUEL S., Love, Human and Divine, *Yearbook C.C.A.R.*, XXVII, pp. 244–300, 1917.

——, *Why Do the Heathen Rage*, 1939.

DUFF, A., *The Theology and Ethics of the Hebrews*, 1902.

EHRENFELD, ALEXANDER, *Der Pflichtbegriff in der Ethik d. Judentums*, 1932.

FASSEL, *Tzedek u-Mishpat: Die mosaisch-rabbinische Tugend und Rechtslehre*, 2nd ed., 1862.

FEDERBUSH, SIMON, *Hamusar Vehamishpat Beyisrael*, 1944.

FRANKEL, Z., Zur Ethik des Jüedischen Alexandrinischen Philosophie Philo, in *Monatsschrift d. Geschichte u. Wissenschaft d. Judentums*, pp. 241–252, 1867.

FRIEDLANDER, G., *Rabbinic Philosophy and Ethics*, 1912.

GLUECK, NELSON, *Hesed*, 1927.

GRAY, G. B., *The Divine Discipline of Israel, An Address and Three Lectures on the Growth of Ideas in the O.T.*, 1900.

GRUENEBAUM, E., *Die Sittenlehre des Judentums*, 1878.

GUEDEMANN, M., *Nächstenliebe*, 1890.

——, Juedische u. Christliche Nächstenliebe, *Monatsschrift*, pp. 153–164, 1893.

GUTTMAN, M., *Das Judentum und seine Umwelt*, 1927.

HAMBURGER, J., *Real-Encyclopedie d. Judentums*, Vol. I, art., Sittenlehre; Supplementary Vols. 1–2, art., Ethik, Philosophische.

HERFORD, R. T., *Talmud and Apocrypha, A Comparative Study of the Jewish Ethical Teaching in the Rabbinical and Non-Rabbinical Sources in the Early Centuries*, 1933.

HIRSCH, E. G., K. KOHLER and I. BRODIE, *Jewish Encyl.*, art., Ethics, Vol. V, pp. 245–258; Right and Righteousness, Vol. X, pp. 420–424.

HUGHS, H. M., *The Ethics of Jewish Apocryphal Literature*, 1909.

HUSIK, I., *A History of Medieval Jewish Philosophy* (Index, under Ethics), 1910.

JOSEPH, M., *Zur Sittenlehre d. Judentums*, 1902.

JOSEPH, MORRIS, *Judaism as Creed and Life*, Bk. III, Moral Duties, pp. 319–512, 1919.

KAYSERLING, M., *Das Moralgesetz des Judentums in Beziehung auf Familie, Staat und Gesellschaft*, 1882.

KENNETT, ADAM, and GWATKIN, *Early Ideas of Righteousness —Hebrew, Greek and Roman*, 1910.

KLAUSNER, J., *Torat Hamidot Hakedumah Beyisrael*, 1918.

KOHLER, K., *Jewish Theology* (chaps. XXXVIII–XLII, XLVI– XLVII, LIX), 1918.

———, Three Discourses on Jewish Ethics, 1901, in *Studies, Addresses and Personal Papers*, pp. 236–50.

———, Human Brotherhood, 1893, *ibid.*, pp. 266–274.

———, The Harmonization of the Jewish and Civil Laws of Marriage and Divorce, *ibid.*, pp. 215–315.

———, The Ethical Basis of Judaism, 1886, in *H.U.C. and Other Addresses*, pp. 143–160.

LAUTERBACH, J. Z., The Ethics of the Halacha, *C.C.A.R. Yearbook*, XXIII, pp. 249–287, 1913.

———, The Attitude of the Jew toward the Non-Jew, *ibid.*, XXXI, pp. 186–233, 1921.

LAZARUS, M., *Die Ethik des Judentums*, Vol. I, 1898 (tr. into English in 2 Parts, 1901–02); Vol. II, 1911.

MARMORSTEIN, A., Die Nachahmung Gottes in der Aggada, *Wohlgemuth's Festschrift*, pp. 141–159, 1928.

MIELZINER, M., Outlines of Talmudical Ethics, *Introduction to the Talmud*, pp. 267–280, 1894.

MONTEFIORE, C. G., and H. LOEWE, *A Rabbinic Anthology*, 1938.

OWEN, JOHN, Optimism and Pessimism in Jewish Philosophy, *Jewish Quarterly Review*, old series, III, pp. 182–207.

PERLES, F., Zur Wuerdigung der Sittenlehre des Talmuds, in *Juedische Skizzen*, pp. 114–124 (Kiddush Hashem, Love of Truth), 1912.

——, Soziale Gerechtigkeit im alten Israel, *ibid.*, pp. 145–162.

POOL, D. DE SOLA, *Capital Punishment among the Jews*, 1916.

ROSIN, D., The Ethics of Solomon Ibn Gabirol, *J.Q.R.* (O.S.), III, pp. 159–181.

——, *Die Ethik des Maimonides*, 1876.

ROTH, LEON, *The Imitation of God and the Idea of the Holy*, Ahad Haam Memorial Lecture (Hebrew), Jerusalem, 1931.

SCHECHTER, S., *Studies in Judaism*, Vol. III, Jewish Saints in Medieval Germany, pp. 1–24, 1924.

——, *Aspects of Rabbinic Theology*, chaps. XIII–XVIII.

SCHEFTELOWITZ, J., Grundlagen einer juedischen Ethik, *Monatsschrift*, pp. 129–146; 359–378; 478–495 (Love of the Neighbor; Enemy; Child; Protection of Animals), 1912.

SCHULMAN, SAMUEL, *Jewish Ethics*, Jewish Tracts, No. 4, Union of American Hebrew Congregations.

SILVER, ABBA H., *The Democratic Impulse in Jewish History*, 1928.

SILVER, MAXWELL, *Justice and Judaism in the Light of To-day*, 1928.

SMITH, J. M. P., *The Moral Life of the Hebrews*, 1923.

WASSERZUG, D., *The Messianic Idea and Its Influence on Jewish Ethics*, 1913.

WAXMAN, M., *A History of Jewish Literature*, I, pp. 359–375; II, pp. 288–300; IV, pp. 907–927.

WIENER, MAX, *Universal Jewish Encyclopedia*, 4, art., Ethics, pp. 174–181.

ZIEGLER, J., *Die Sittliche Welt des Judentums*, 2 Vols., 1924–1928.

Zunz, L., Sittenlehrer (1845), in *Gesammelte Schriften*, I, pp. 60–85; also edited by I. Elbogen, 1921.

## Religious Practice

### A. STUDY OF TORAH

Abrahams, I., *Jewish Life in the Middle Ages*, chaps. xix–xx, 1896.

Assaf, S., *Mekorot Letoledot Hahinuch Beyisrael*, 4 Vols., 1925, 1930, 1936 and 1943.

Cohen, A., *Everyman's Talmud*, chap. iv, 1934.

Gamoran, E., *Changing Conceptions in Jewish Education*, 1924.

Ginzberg, Louis, *Students, Scholars and Saints*, pp. 1–87, 1928.

Isaacs, Nathan, Study as a Mode of Worship, in Leo Jung's *Jewish Library*, 2nd ed., I, pp. 51–70, 1943.

### B. SELF-RENEWAL

#### 1. General

H.E.R.E., arts., Expiation and Atonement, Vol. V, pp. 635–671; Sacrifice, Vol. XI, pp. 1–39; Sin, Vol. XI, pp. 528–571 (representing the viewpoints of primitive and advanced religions on these subjects).

Morgenstern, J., *The Doctrine of Sin in the Babylonian Religion*, 1905.

Smith, W. R., *Religion of the Semites*, ed. by S. A. Cook, Lecture XI and notes by Editor, pp. 645–654.

Tennant, F. R., *The Origin and Propagation of Sin*, 1902.

——, *The Sources of the Doctrines of the Fall and Original Sin*, 1903.

#### 2. Jewish

Abelson, J., *The Immanence of God*, chap. xxiii, 1912.

Buechler, A., *Studies in Sin and Atonement*, 1927.

398 BIBLIOGRAPHY

COHEN, HERMANN, *Juedische Schriften*, I, pp. 125–144, 1924.

——, *Religion der Vernunft*, chaps. XI–XII, 1919.

DAVIDSON, A. B., *The Theology of the Old Testament*, chaps. VII, X, 1928.

EISENSTEIN, J. D., art., Sin in *Jewish Encyclopedia*, XI, pp. 376–79.

HEHN, JOHANNES, *Suende und Erlaesung nach biblischer und babylonischer Anschauung*, 1903.

KOEBERLE, J., *Suende und Gnade im religiösen Leben des Volkes Israel bis auf Christentum*, 1905.

KOHLER, K., *J.E.*, Atonement, II, pp. 275–284; Repentance, X, pp. 377–379, 1918.

——, *Jewish Theology*, chaps. XXXVIII–XXXIX, pp. 238–255.

MOORE, G. F., *Encyclopedia Biblica*, IV, art., Sacrifice, pp. 4183–4226.

——, *Judaism*, I, Part II, pp. 445–552.

OESTERLEY, W. O. E., *The Jewish Doctrine of Mediation*, 1910.

OESTERLEY and BOX, *The Religion and Worship of the Synagogue*, 1911.

SCHECHTER, S., *Aspects of Rabbinic Theology*, chaps. XIV, XVII, XVIII, 1909.

SCHULTZ, HERMANN, The Significance of Sacrifice in the Old Testament, *American Journal of Theology*, IV, pp. 257–313.

TOY, C. H., *Judaism and Christianity*, chap. IV, 1891.

C. WORSHIP

*1. General*

BROWN, WILLIAM ADAMS, *The Life of Prayer in a World of Science*, 1928.

*Hastings' Encyclopedia of Religion and Ethics*, arts., Prayer, X, pp. 154–214; Worship, XII, pp. 752–812.

HEILER, FRIEDRICH, *Prayer, A Study in the History and Psychology of Religion*, translated from the German, 1932.

HUEGEL, FRIEDRICH VON, *The Life of Prayer*, 1929.

PATERSON, W. P., and D. RUSSEL, *The Power of Prayer* (22 essays by various authors and bibliography), 1920.

PUGLISI, MARIO, *Prayer*, tr. from the Italian, with bibliographical appendix, 1929.

SPERRY, WILLARD L., *Reality in Worship*, 1927.

STREETER, H., *Concerning Prayer, Its Nature, Its Difficulties and Its Value* (14 essays by various authors), 1916.

UNDERHILL, EVELYN, *Worship*, 1937.

VOGT, VON OGDEN, *Art and Religion*, 1921.

———, *Modern Worship*, 1917.

### 2. Jewish: Historical and Theological

ABELSON, J., *The Immanence of God*, chap. XXIV, 1912.

ABRAHAMS, I., *Historical and Explanatory Notes to the Authorized Daily Prayer Book*, 1914.

———, Some Rabbinic Ideas on Prayer, *J.Q.R.*, o.s., XX, pp. 272–293, 1908.

COHON, S. S., Theology of the Union Prayer Book, *C.C.A.R. Yearbook*, 1928.

DEMBITZ, LEWIS N., *Services in Synagogue and Home*, 1898.

ELBOGEN, ISMAR, *Der juedische Gottesdienst in seiner geschichtlichen Entwicklung*, 1913.

ENELOW, H. G., Kawwana: The Struggle for Inwardness, in Kohler's *Festschrift*, pp. 82–107, 1923.

FREEHOF, BETTAN, COHON, and J. B. WISE, The Union Prayer Book—A Symposium, *C.C.A.R. Yearbook*, 1930.

FREEHOF, S. B., *The Small Sanctuary*, 1942.

FRIEDLANDER, M., *The Jewish Religion*, Divine Worship, pp. 413–455, 1891.

GEIGER, A., Der Hamburger Tempelstreit, eine Zeitfrage (1842), in *Nachgelassene Schriften* I, pp. 113–196.

——, Notwendigkeit und Maass einer Reform des juedischen Gottesdienstes, *ibid.*, pp. 203–229, 1891.

GUEDEMANN, M., Die Liebe, die Grundlage des hebraischen Gebetes, *Monatsschrift*, pp. 145–155, 1915.

HELLER, BERNHARD, Gott wuenscht das Herz, *H. U. C. Annual*, IV, pp. 365–403, 1927.

HIRSCH, S. R., *Horeb*, Part VI, Gottesdienst, pp. 631–750, 1837.

IDELSOHN, A. Z., *Jewish Liturgy*, 1931.

——, *Jewish Music*, 1929.

*Jewish Encyclopedia*, arts., Devotional Literature (Eisenstein) IV, pp. 550–552; Liturgy (Blau) VIII, pp. 132–140; Prayerbook (Eisenstein) X, pp. 164–180. See Bibliographies at the end of the articles.

JOEL, M., *Zur Orientierung in der Cultusfrage*, 1869.

KOHLER, K., *Jewish Theology*, pp. 261–277, 1918.

——, *The Origins of the Synagogue and the Church*, Part I, 1929.

LOEW, R., Die Reform des rabbinischen Ritus auf rabbinischen Standpunkt (1839), in *Gesammelte Schriften*, I, pp. 15–19.

MOORE, G. F., *Judaism*, II, Part VI, Piety, pp. 201–275, 1927.

OESTERLEY and BOX, *Religion and Worship of the Synagogue*, 1907.

PERLES, F., art., Prayer, Jewish, *H.E.R.E.*, X, pp. 191–196; Gebet im Judentum (1904) in *Jüdische Skizzen*, 1912.

PHILIPPSON, LUDWIG, *Die israelitische Religionslehre*, 1861.

PHILIPSON, DAVID, *The Reform Movement in Judaism*, 1907; 2nd ed. 1931, Index under Prayerbook.

——, The Reform Prayer Book, in D. Neumark's *Journal of Jewish Lore and Philosophy*, pp. 69–82, 210–223, 1919.

ZUNZ, L., *Die gottesdienstlichen Vortraege der Juden,* 1832; 2nd ed., pp. 379–407, 1892.

——— , *Literaturgeschichte d. Synagogalen Poesie,* 1865.

——— , *Ritus des synagogalen Gottesdienstes geschichtlich entwickelt,* 1859.

——— , *Synagogale Poesie d. Mittelalters,* 2nd ed., 1920.

# QUESTIONS FOR DISCUSSION

## Questions for Chapters I–IV

1. What justifies our speaking of Judaism as an art of life?
2. Can we dispense with form in spiritual religion?
3. Is Reform Judaism opposed to authority?
4. What role does symbolism play in Judaism?
5. Is religion primarily the product of personal or of social experience?
6. Is organization essential to religion?
7. On what grounds did early Reform identify piety with morality?
8. Is piety limited to old-fashioned Orthodoxy?
9. Can spirituality be acquired?

## Questions for Chapters V–VII

10. Does religion affect personal life?
11. Is fear always an evil?
12. How does religion deal with the problem of evil?
13. What is the ground for Jewish optimism?
14. How does Maimonides explain evil?

## Questions for Chapter VIII

15. What are the grounds for faith-cures?
16. What is the attitude of Judaism to medicine?

## Questions for Chapter IX

17. In what way are ethics and religion related to one another?
18. What makes ethics Jewish? Is it racial experience or religion?

## Questions for Chapters X, XI

19. What is meant by Kiddush Hashem? Hillul Hashem?
20. Compare Christian and Jewish views of Imitatio Dei.
21. What are the implications of the belief in the sacredness of human life for moral behavior?
22. How can man cooperate with God?
23. Discuss the attitude of Judaism toward labor.
24. How are the individual and society interrelated?

25. What do we mean by the good?
26. What is conscience? How does it emerge and function?

## QUESTIONS FOR CHAPTER XII

27. What is righteousness?
28. How did the word Tzaddik come to mean "pious"?
29. What does Judaism teach regarding non-resistance of evil?
30. Does the end justify the means?
31. How is mercy related to justice?
32. Compare the positive and the negative form of the Golden Rule.
33. Does Judaism teach hatred toward the enemy? How did the misrepresentation of this idea find its way into the Sermon on the Mount?
34. What provisions does the Torah make for the poor?
35. What is the rabbinic attitude toward the non-Jewish poor?
36. What is the ultimate goal of charity?

## QUESTIONS FOR CHAPTER XIII

37. How does one acquire religion? What are the Jewish ways?
38. What is the role of Torah in Jewish life?
39. How does the study of Torah affect character?
40. Discuss the chief character-building agencies.

## QUESTIONS FOR CHAPTER XIV

41. Has sin lost its meaning in modern life?
42. What did the prophets understand by sin?
43. What does rabbinic Judaism mean by sin?
44. Is sin an inherited infection in man?
45. What is the significance of repentance for the religious life?
46. How did the fall of the Temple affect the Jewish idea of atonement?
47. Contrast the idea of vicarious atonement in Christianity and in Judaism.

QUESTIONS FOR CHAPTER XV

48. Why is worship central in religion?
49. What are the main types of prayer? Which seems most significant to you?
50. What is the logic of prayer?
51. Of what value are ancient forms in modern worship? Use of Hebrew? Distinctive music? Ceremonies?
52. Is public worship on festive days enough?

# INDEX OF NAMES, SUBJECTS, AND HEBREW TERMS

## A

# M